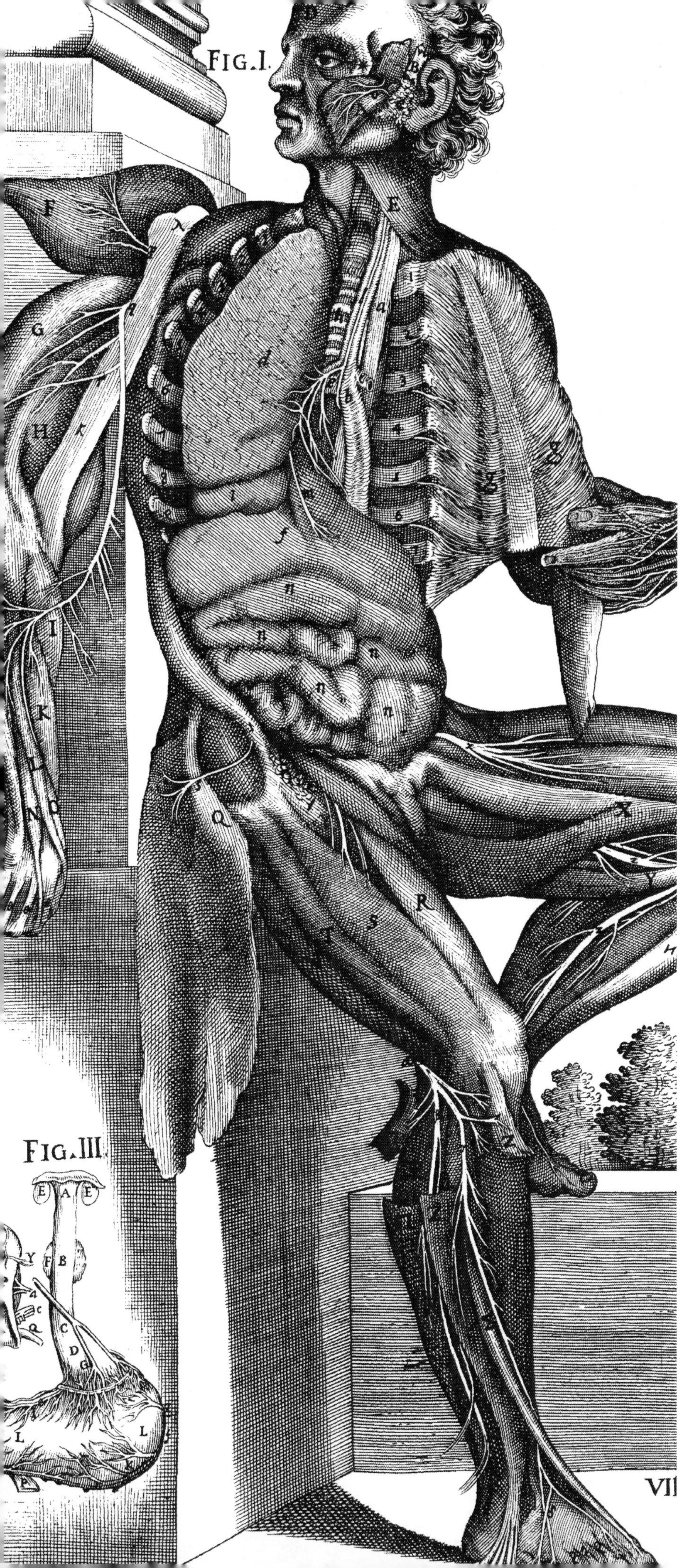

MORBID ANATOMY

AN IMAGE ARCHIVE FOR
ARTISTS *And* DESIGNERS

INTRODUCTION

Step into the shadowy corridors of history with *Morbid Anatomy: An Image Archive for Artists and Designers*. This unique publication from Vault Editions offers a meticulously curated collection of the most grotesque and eerily fascinating anatomical illustrations from the 16th to the 18th centuries. Created by master artists and engravers of their time, these images delve deep into the human form, exposing the intricate workings of the body in vivid detail. From flayed figures and detailed dissections to skeletal forms and nervous systems, this book not only showcases historical artistry but also serves as an invaluable tool for contemporary artists and designers looking to infuse their work with a touch of the macabre.

We extend our deepest gratitude to the master artists and engravers whose exceptional work forms the foundation of *Morbid Anatomy*. The meticulous detail in each image reflects a profound understanding of human anatomy, rendered with an artistry that transcends time. These illustrations, crafted initially between the 16th and 18th centuries, continue to inspire awe and appreciation for their historical and artistic significance. We are honoured to present their work and thank them posthumously for their indispensable contributions to art and science. Their legacy endures through the pages of this archive.

vaulteditions.com

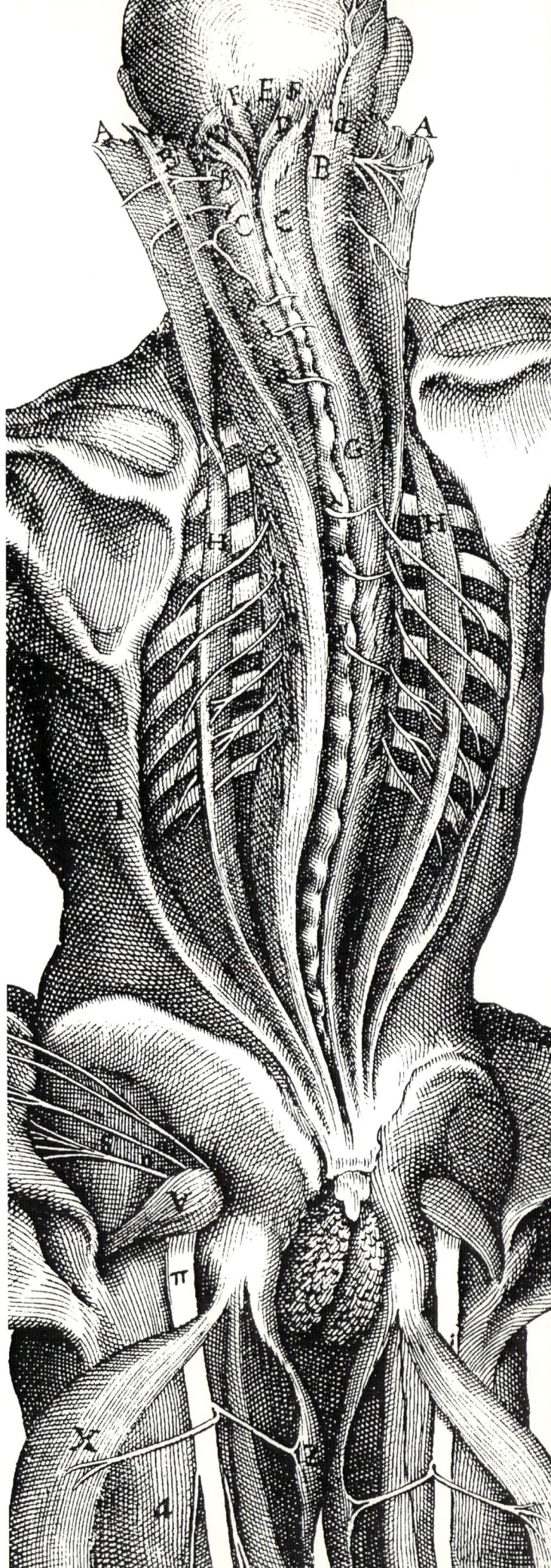

VOLUME.01   A PICTORIAL ARCHIVE

TABLE OF CONTENTS

Exploring the Human Body with Ecorché Figures	01-40
Skull & Skeleton	41-58
Head & Neck	59-72
Thorax	73-92
Upper Extremity	93-100
Abdomen	101-112
Lower Extremity	113-122

DOWNLOAD YOUR FILES

Downloading your files is simple. To access your digital files, please go to the last page of this book and follow the instructions.

For technical assistance, please email:
info@vaulteditions.com

Copyright
Copyright © Vault Editions Ltd 2024.

Bibliographical Note

This book is a new work created by Vault Editions Ltd.

ISBN: 978-1-922966-38-4

MORBID ANATOMY

VAULT EDITIONS

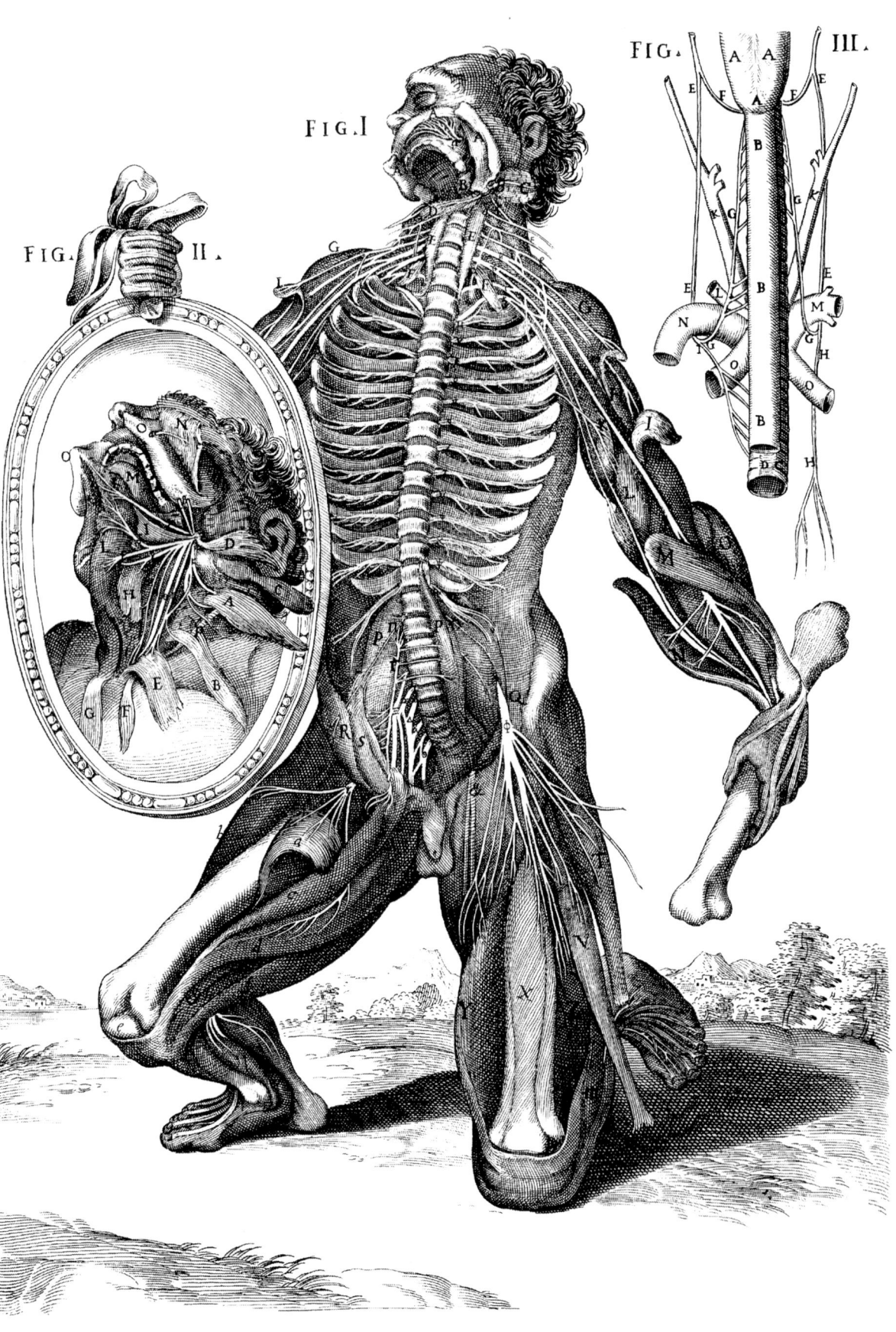

01. Ecorché figure kneeling, anterior view,
looking left, holding a bone by Pietro da Cortona.
(1597–1669) 1741

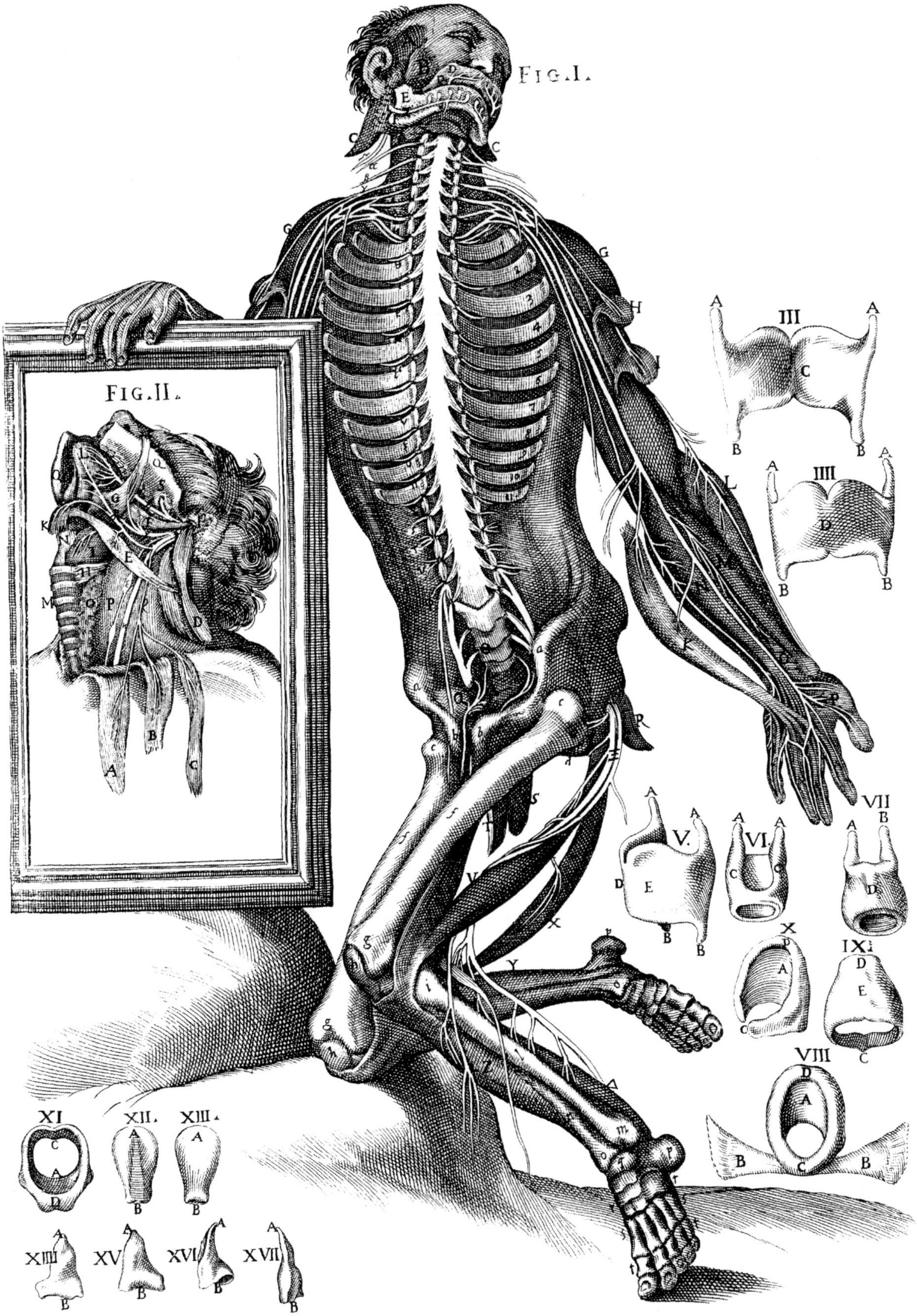

02. Ecorché figure kneeling, anterior view,
looking left, by Pietro da Cortona, (1597–1669)
1741

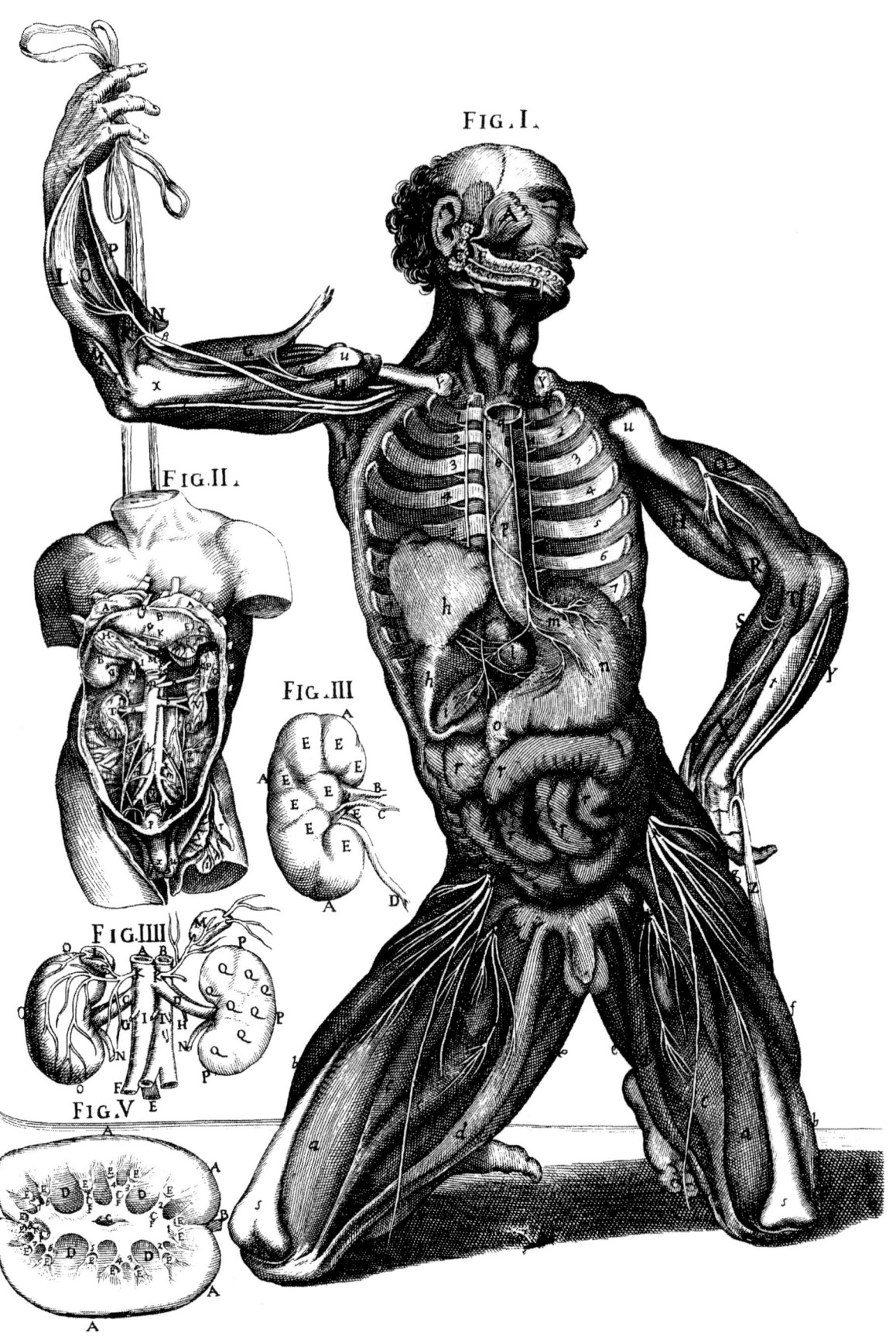

03. Ecorché figure kneeling, anterior view, looking left displaying internal organs and male torso by Pietro da Cortona, (1597–1669) 1741

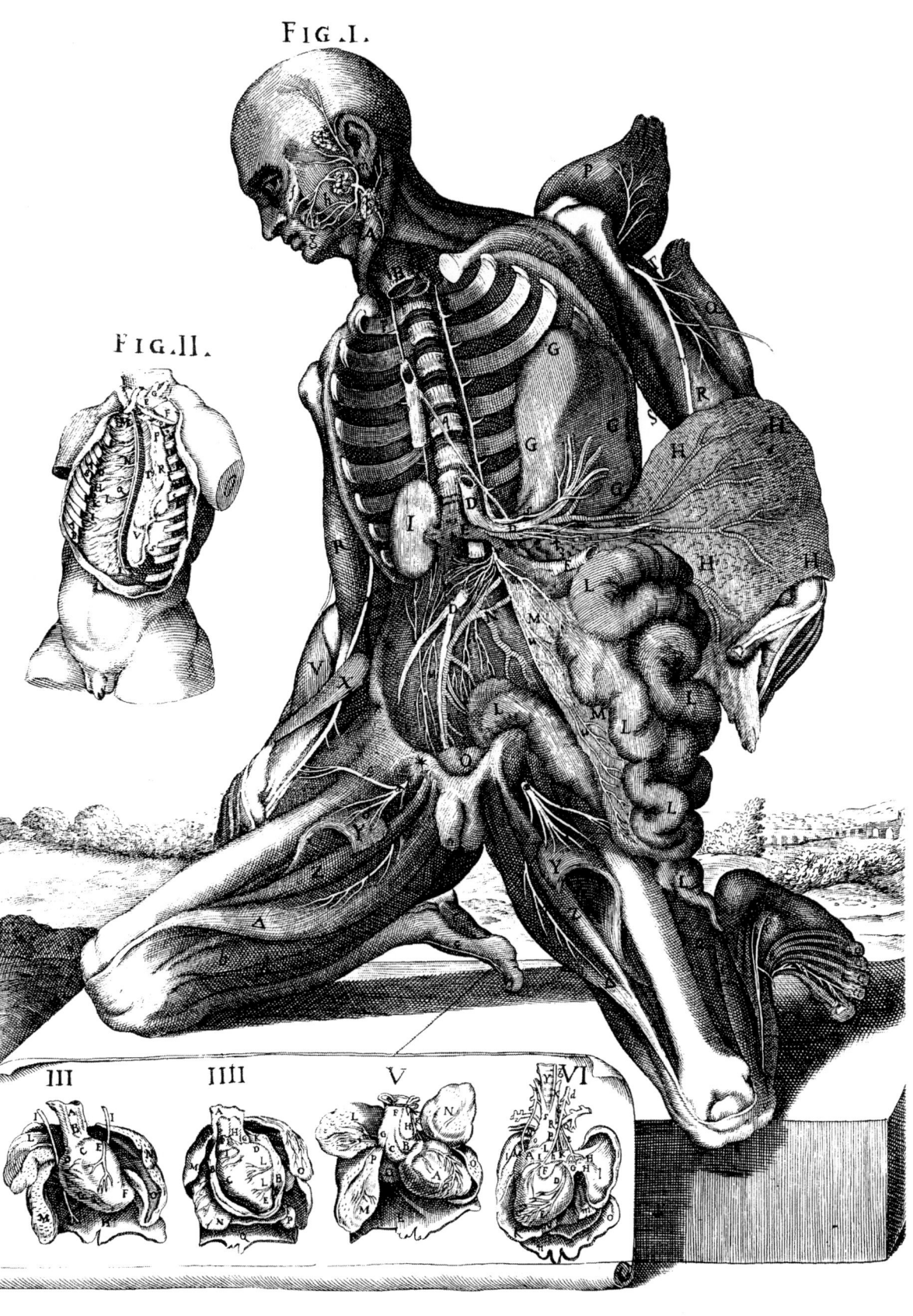

04. Ecorché figure kneeling, anterior view, looking left with internal organs and male torso by Pietro da Cortona, (1597–1669) 1741

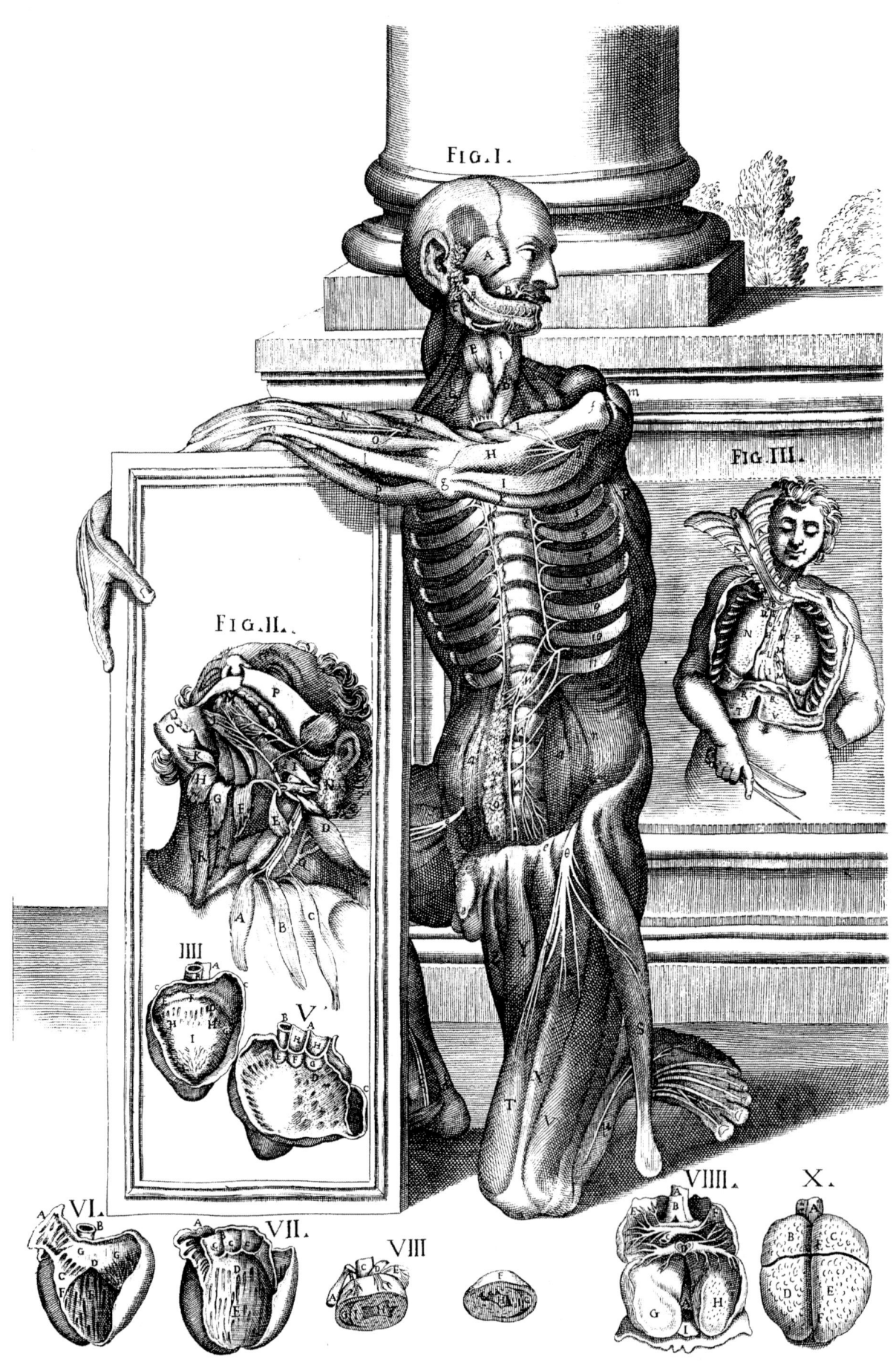

05. Ecorché figure kneeling, anterior view, looking right with internal organs, by Pietro da Cortona, (1597–1669) 1741

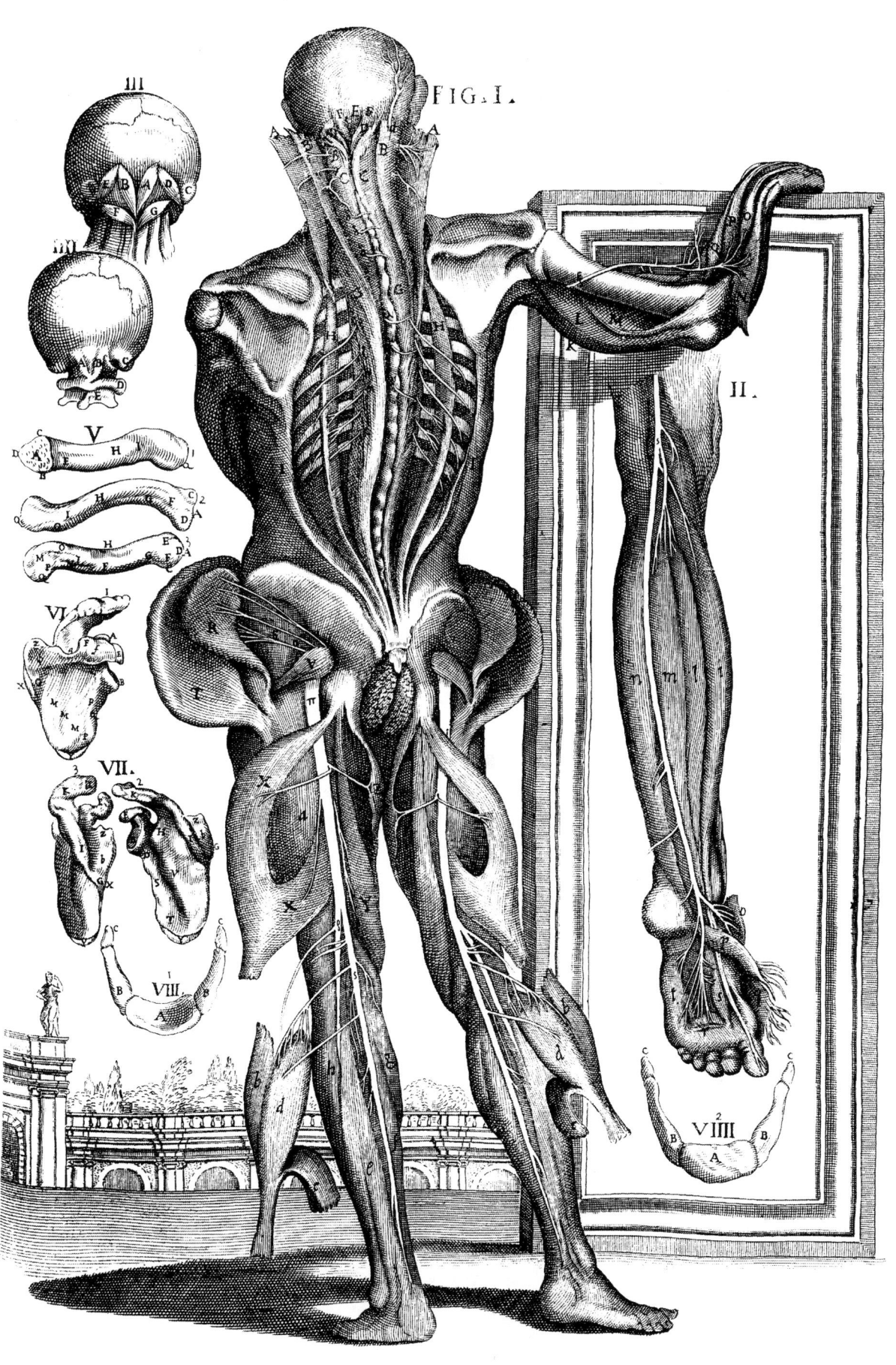

06. Ecorché figure posterior view with images of the head and leg by Pietro da Cortona, (1597–1669) 1741

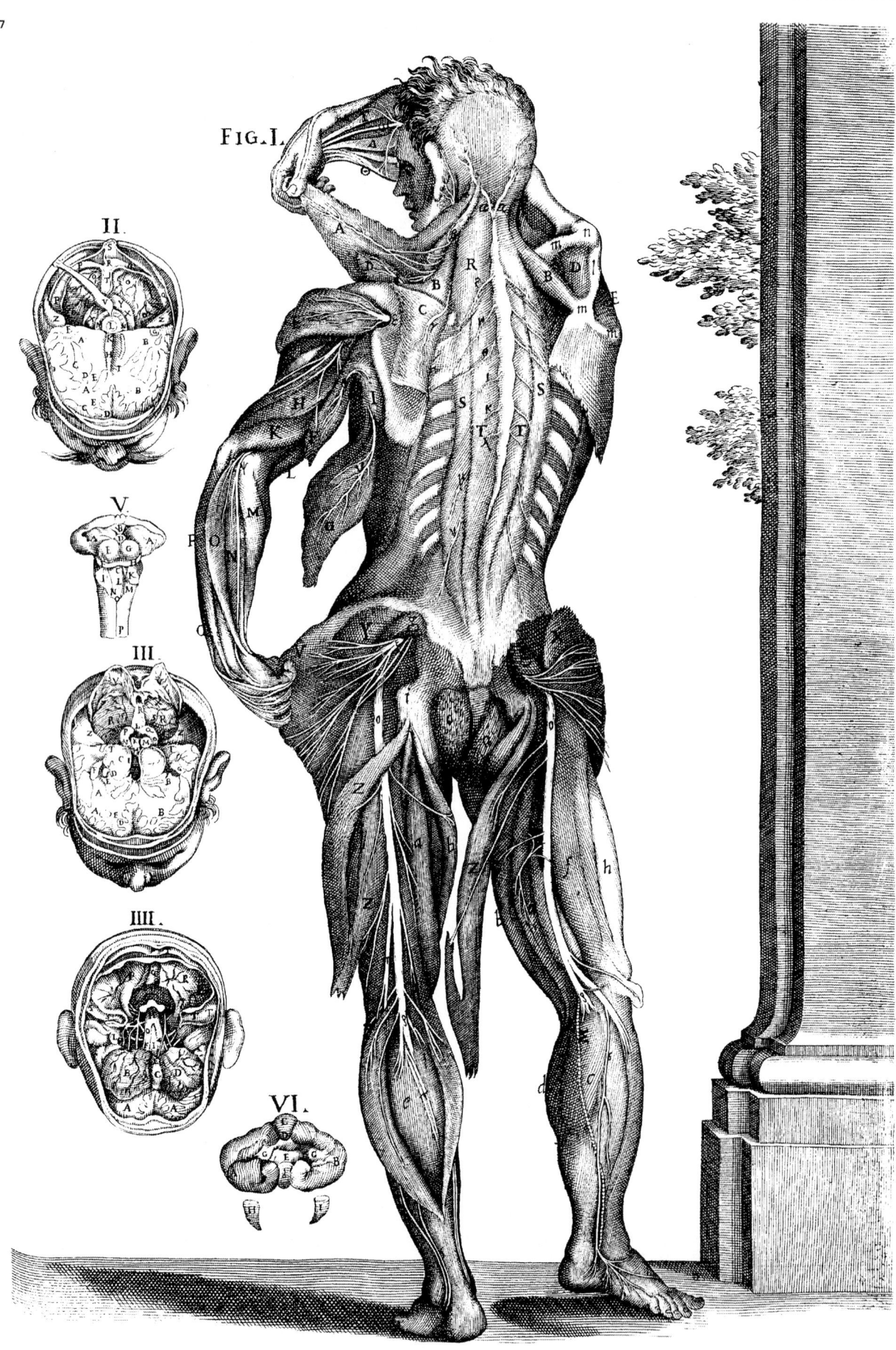

07. Ecorché figure posterior view, arms raised, surrounded by images of the brain by Pietro da Cortona. (1597–1669) 1741

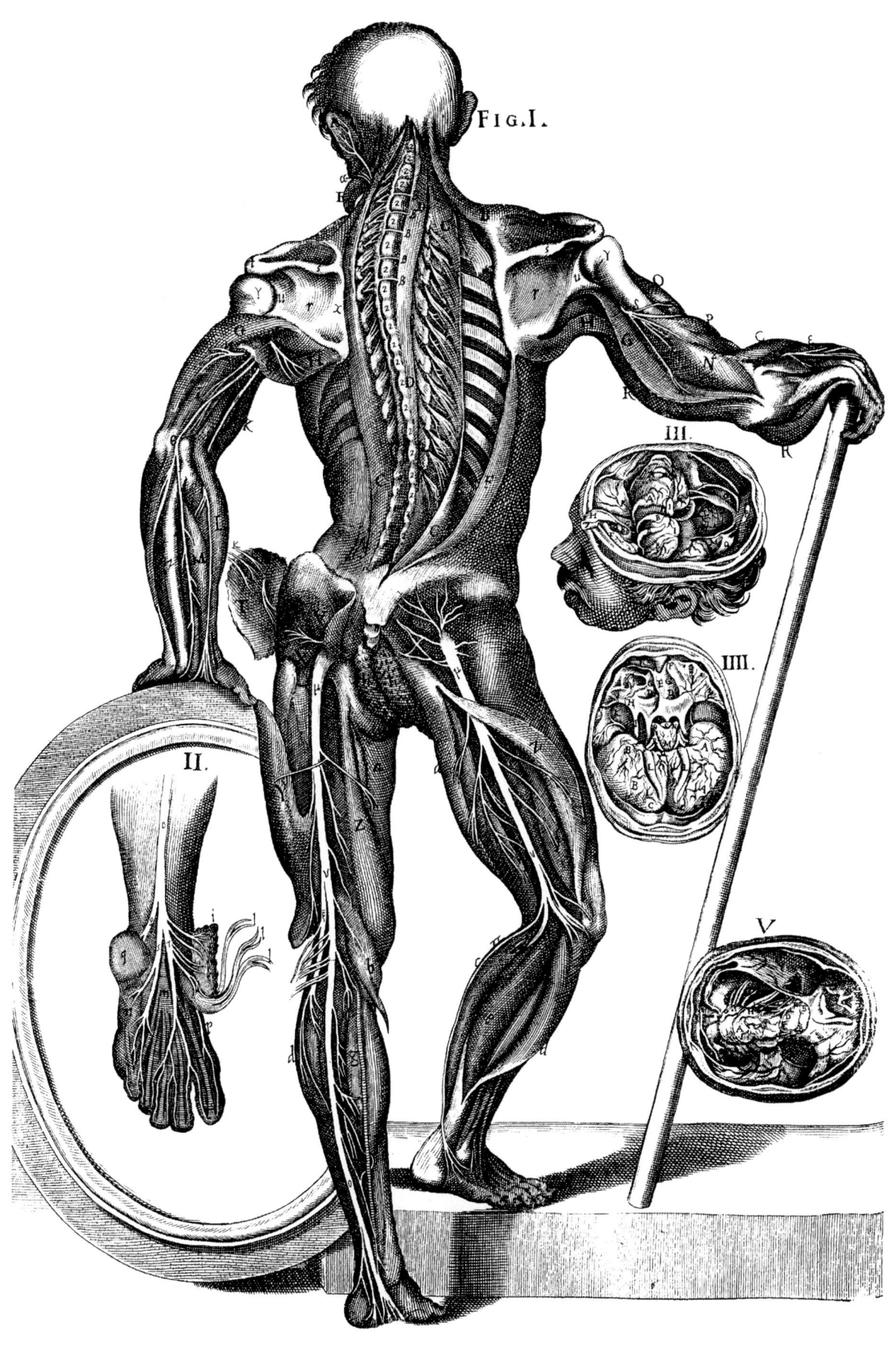

08. Ecorché figure posterior view, leaning on a cane, with images of the brain and foot, by Pietro da Cortona, (1597–1669) 1741

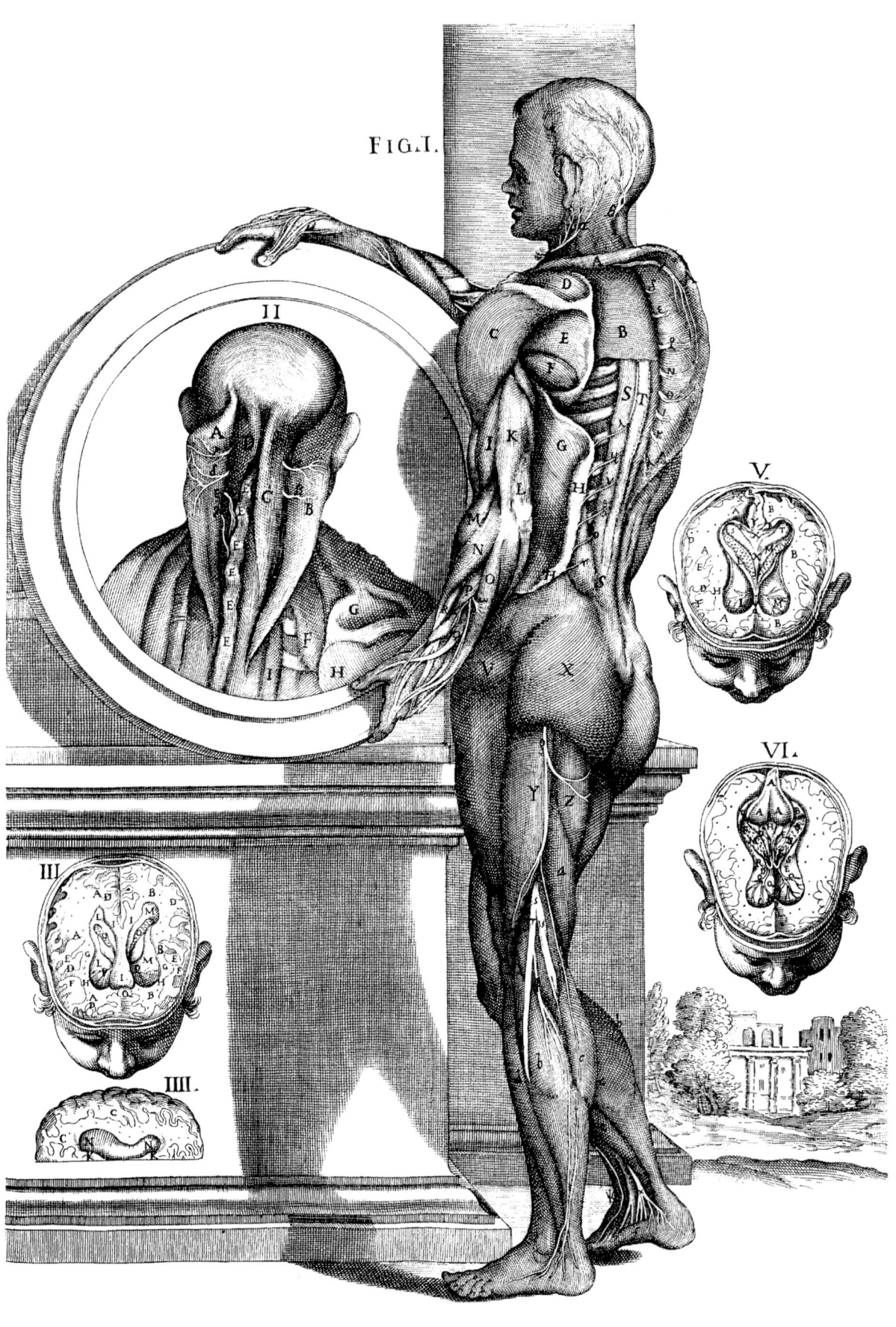

09. Ecorché figure side view, facing left surrounded by images of the brain by Pietro da Cortona, (1597–1669) 1741

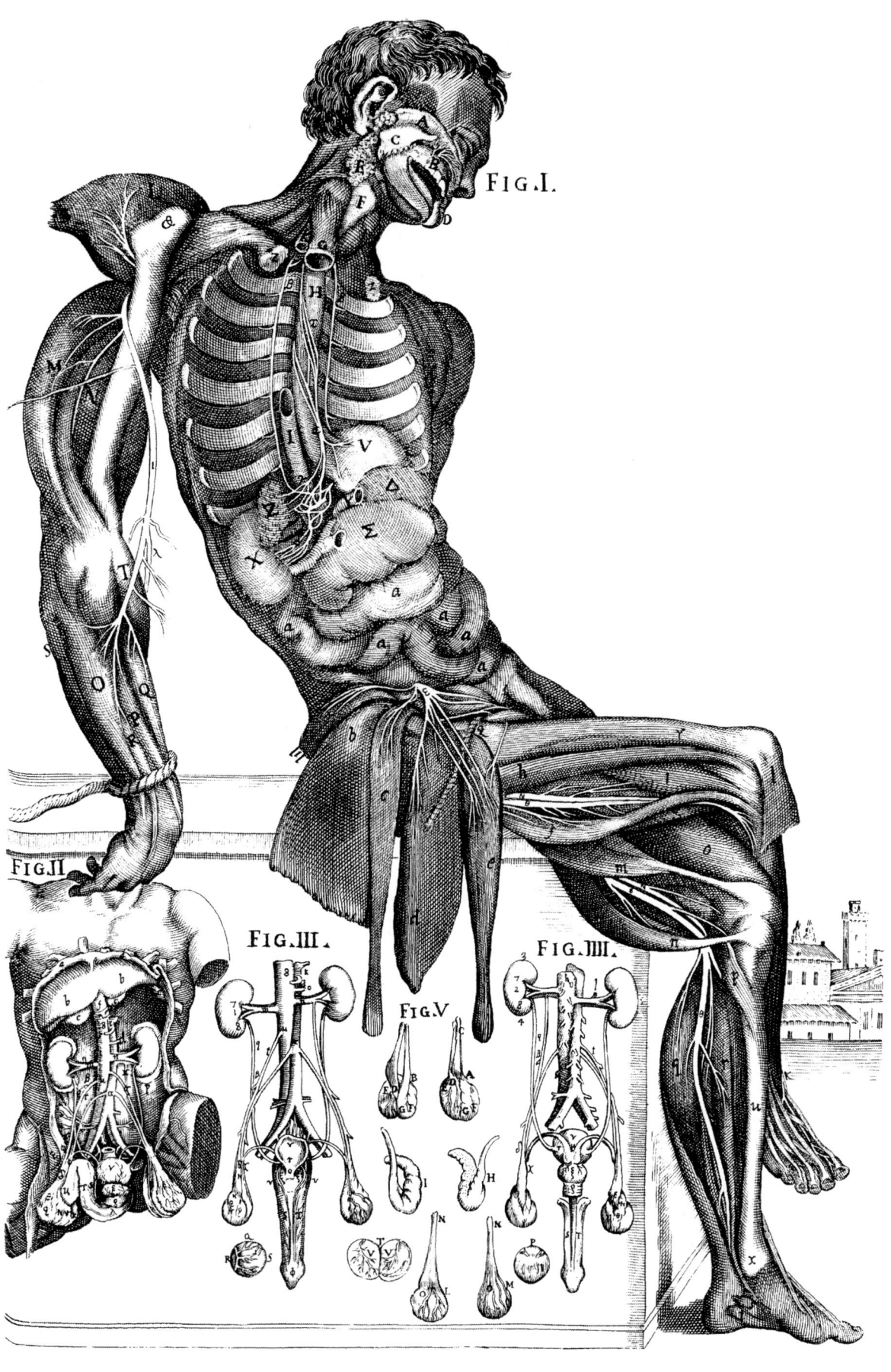

10. Ecorché figure sitting cross legged, anterior view, looking right with internal organs by Pietro da Cortona, (1597–1669) 1741

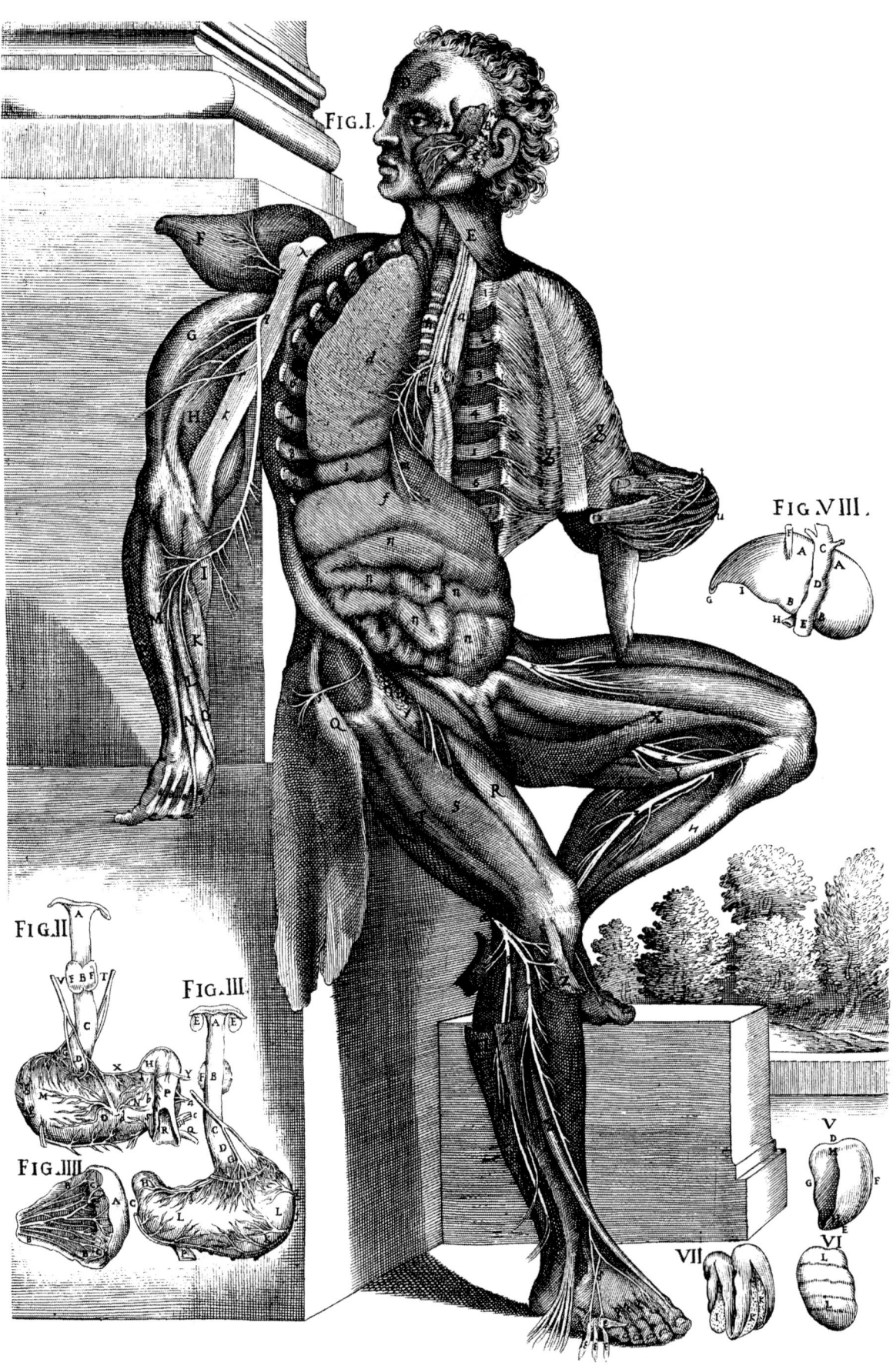

11. Ecorché figure, anterior view, looking left with internal organs by Pietro da Cortona, (1597–1669) 1741

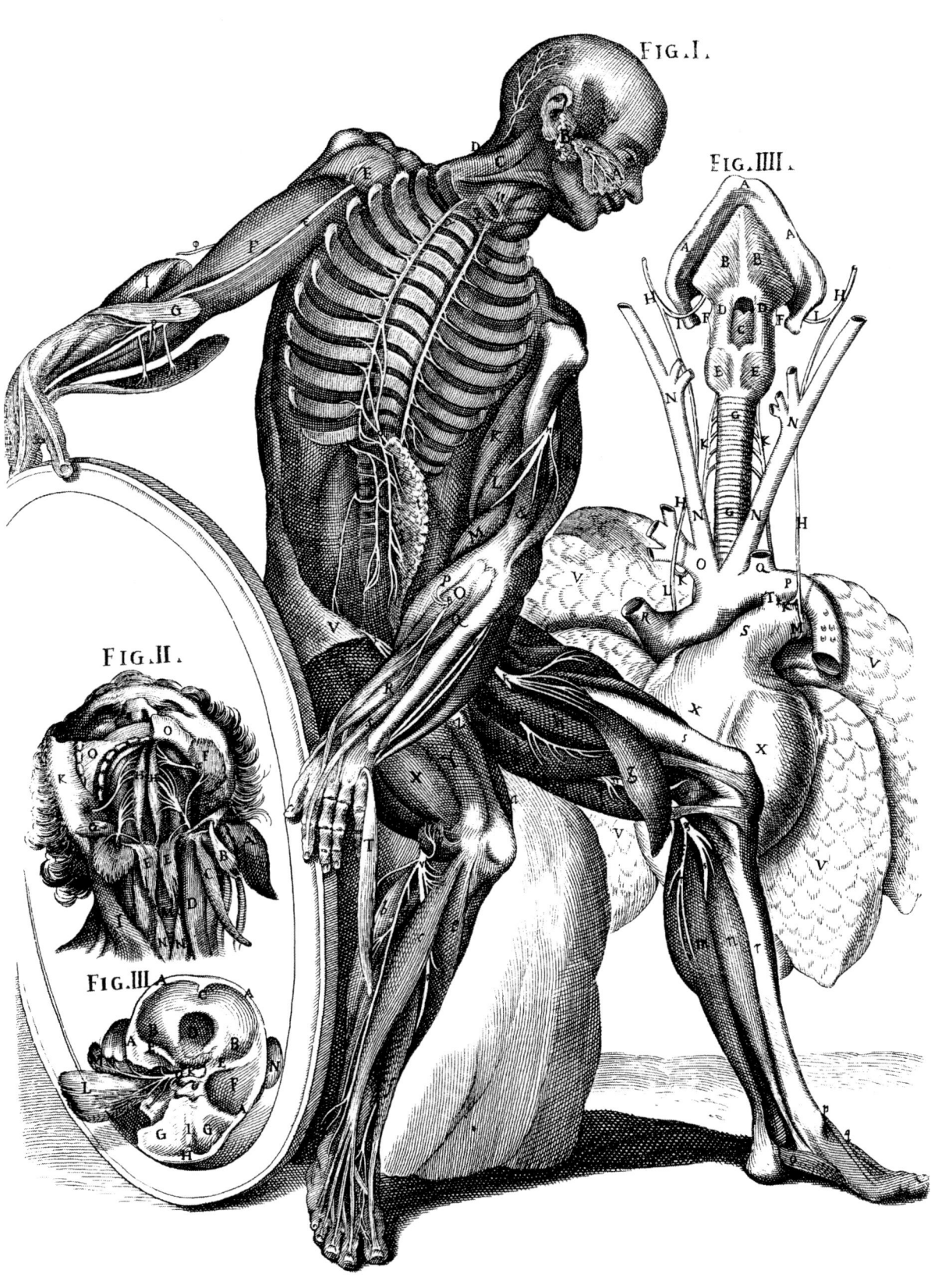

12. Ecorché figure sitting, anterior view, looking right with internal organs and head by Pietro da Cortona, (1597–1669) 1741

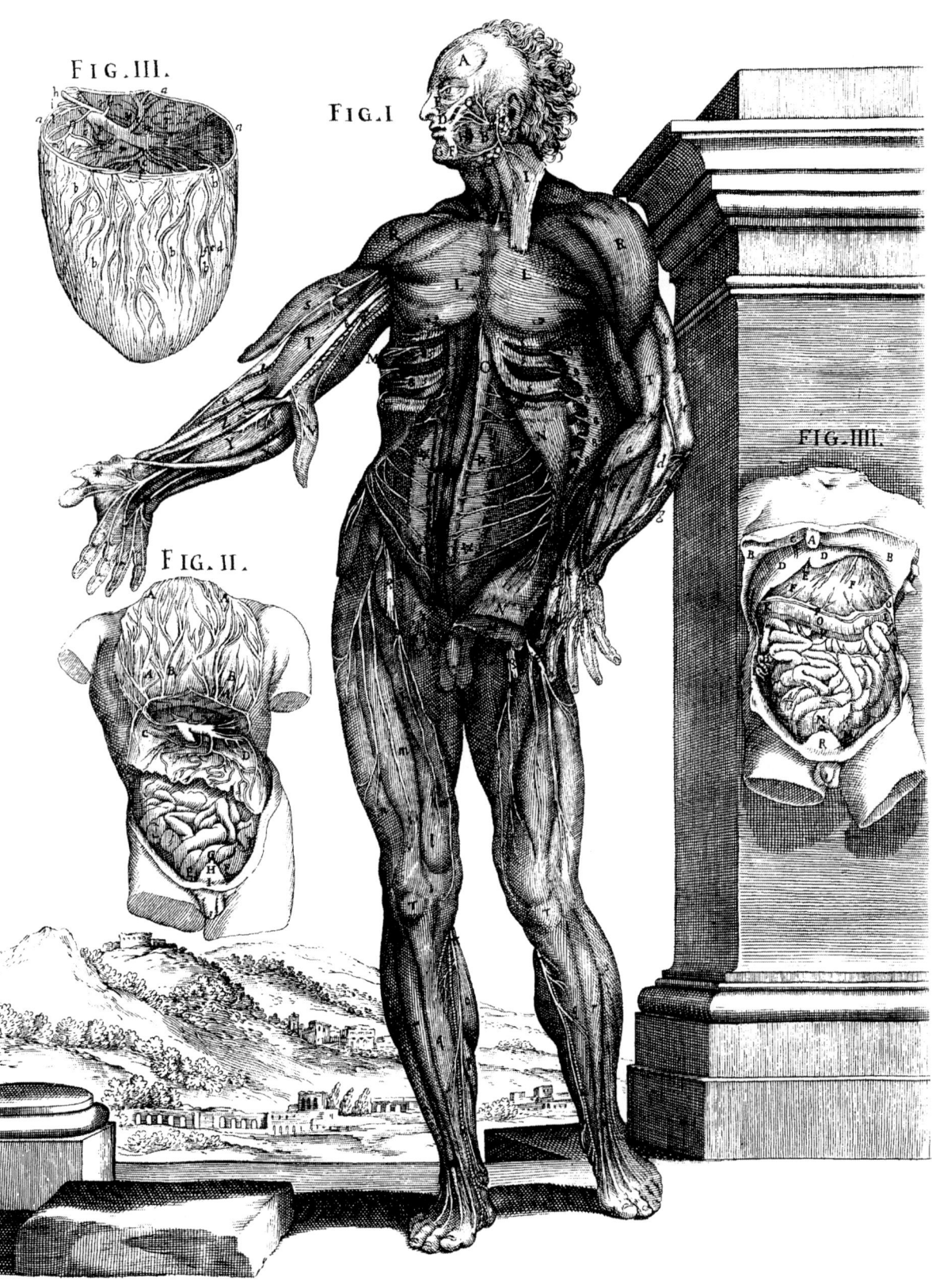

13. Ecorché figure, anterior view, looking left flanked by two male torsos, by Pietro da Cortona, (1597–1669) 1741

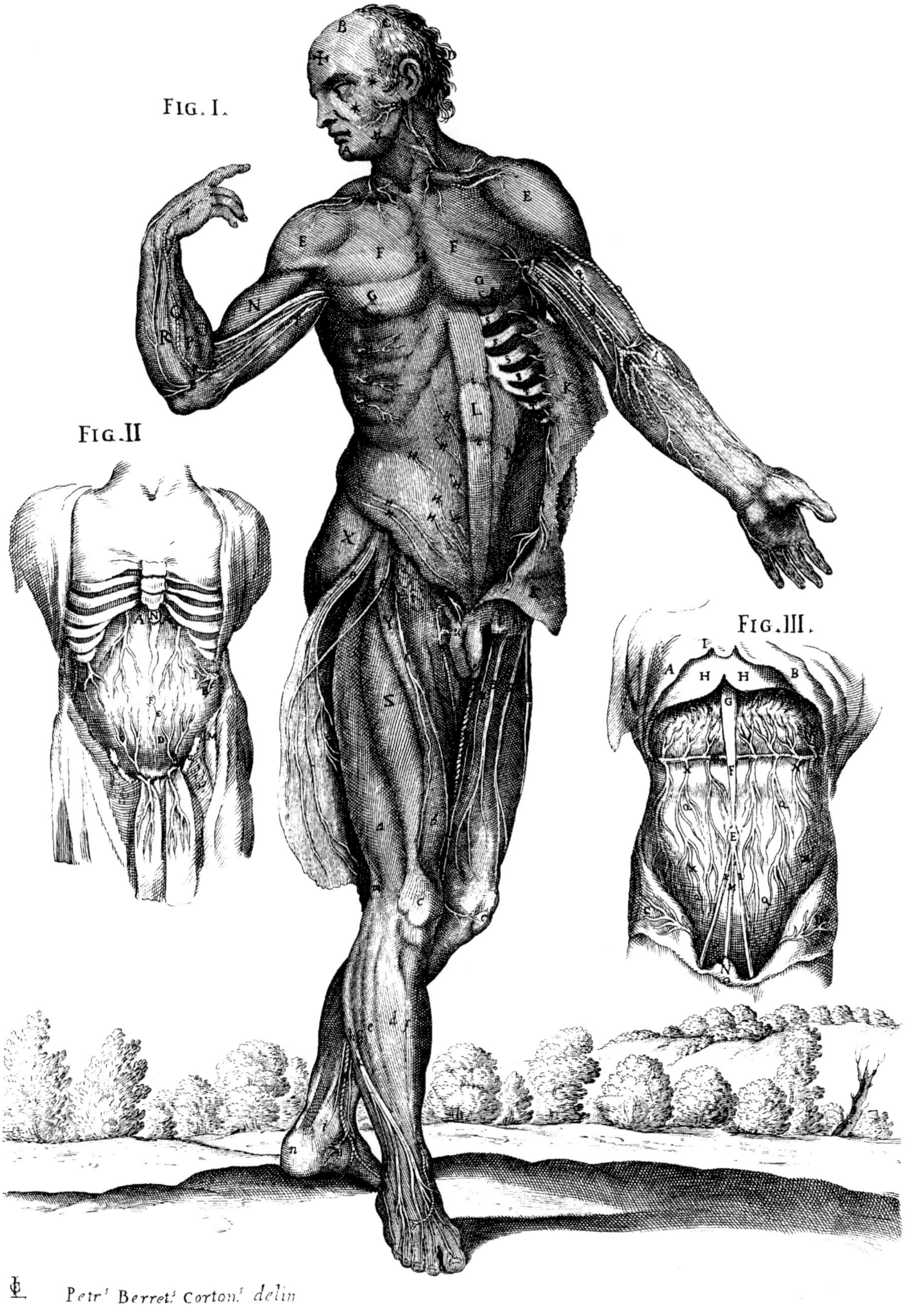

14. Ecorché figure, anterior view, looking left by Pietro da Cortona, (1597–1669) 1741

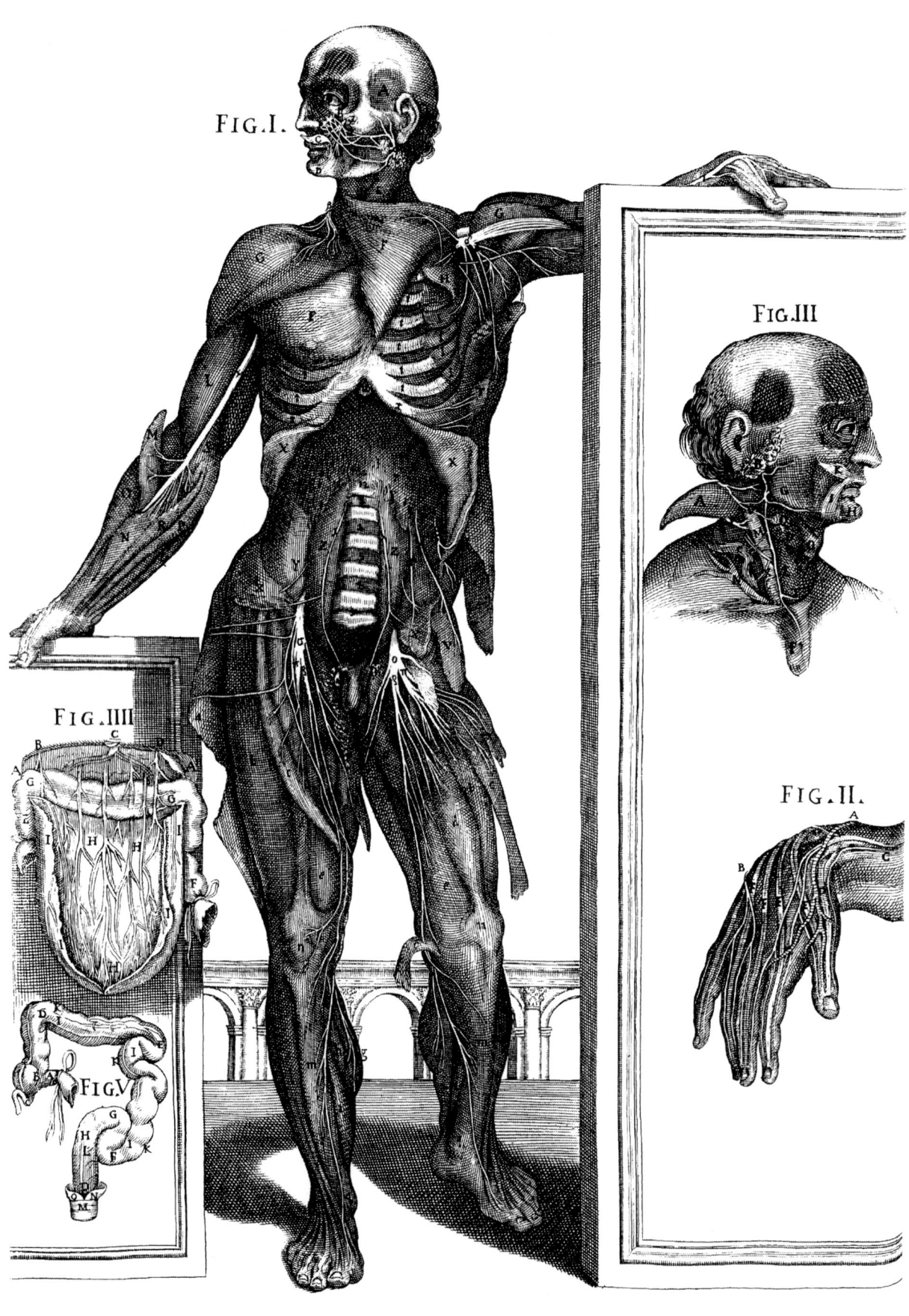

15. Ecorché figure, anterior view, looking left with internal organs, head and neck of a man and a hand, by Pietro da Cortona, (1597–1669) 1741

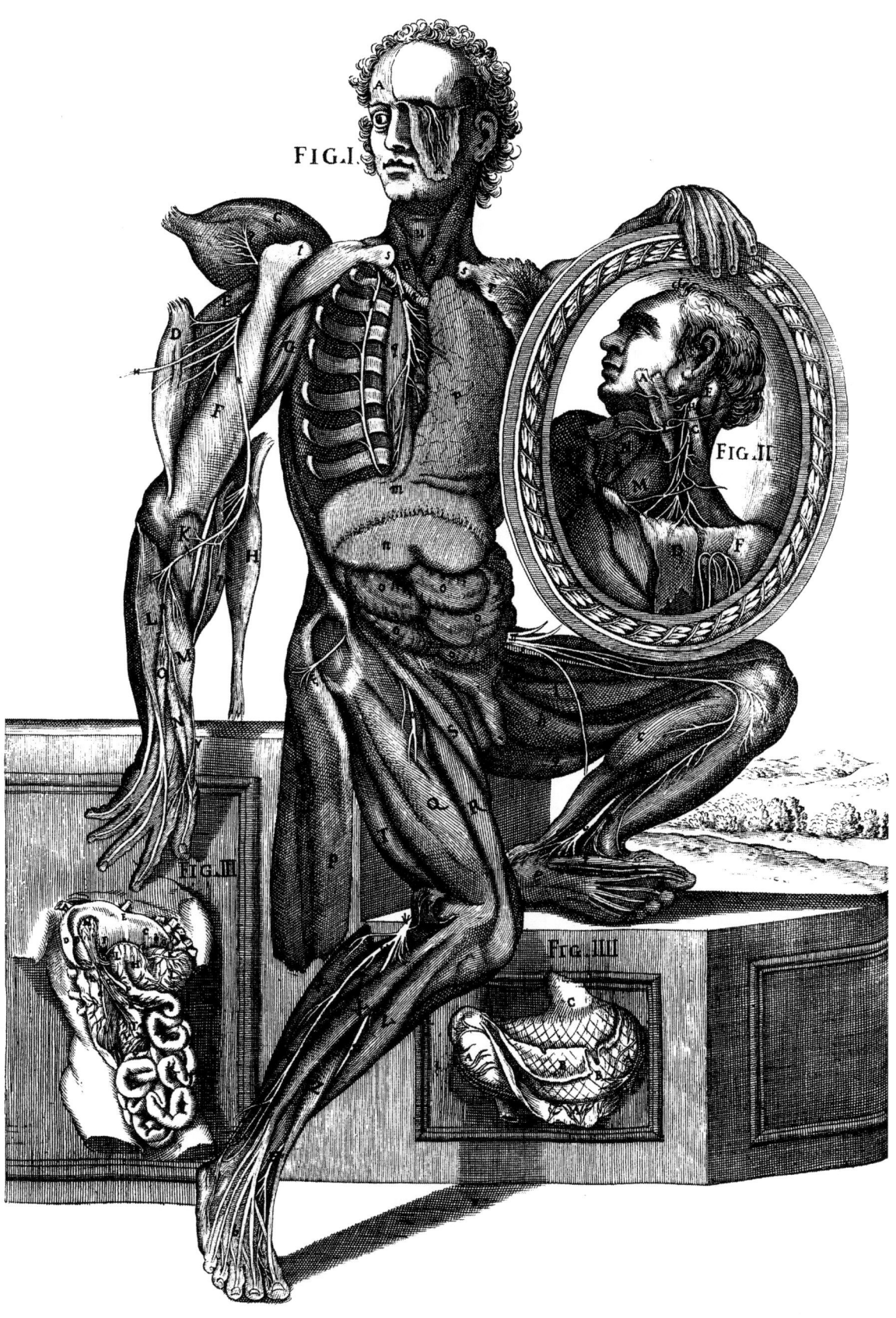

16. Ecorché figure, anterior view, looking left with portrait by Pietro da Cortona, (1597–1669) 1741

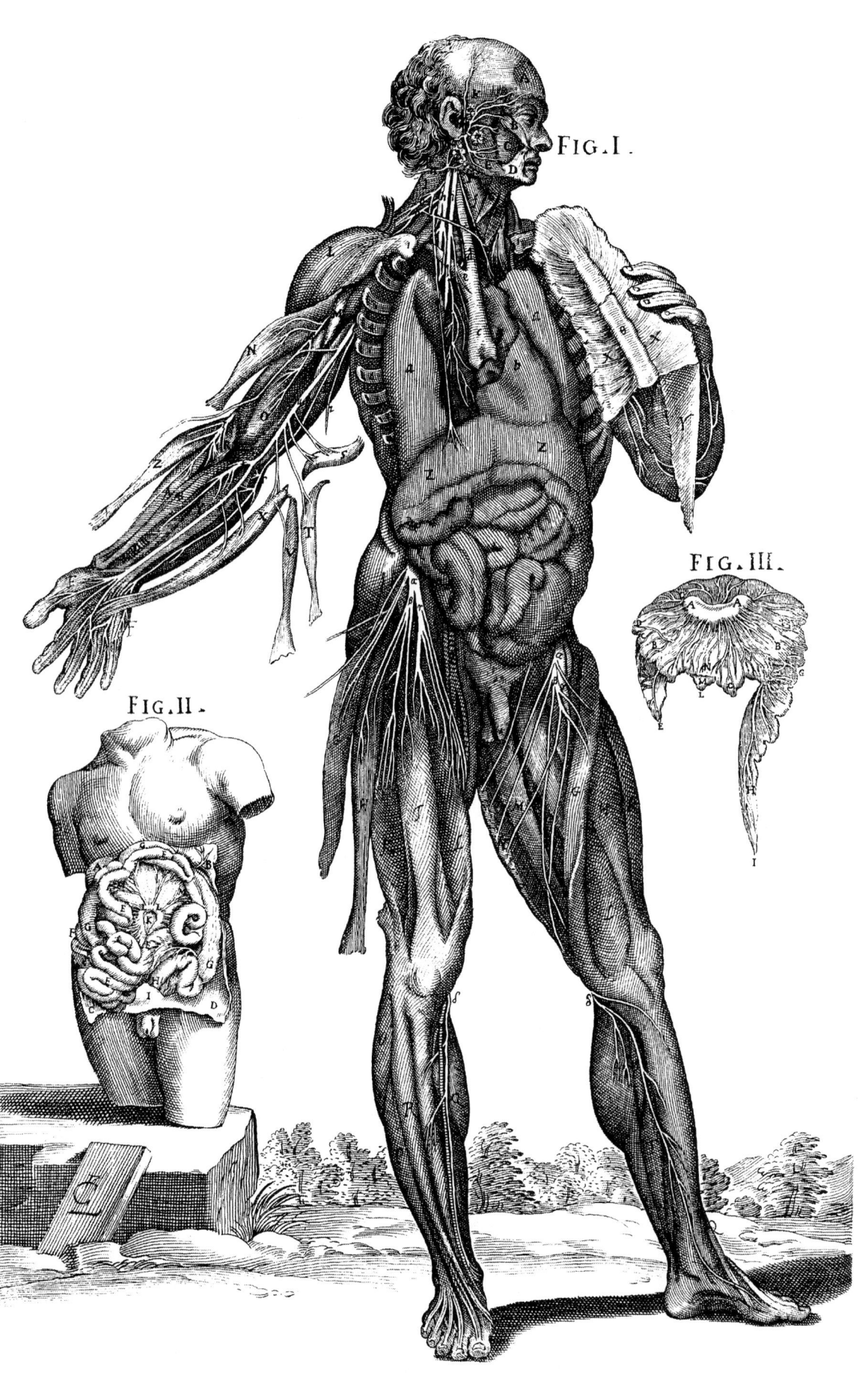

17. Ecorché figure, anterior view, looking right with arm outstretched, by Pietro da Cortona, (1597–1669) 1741

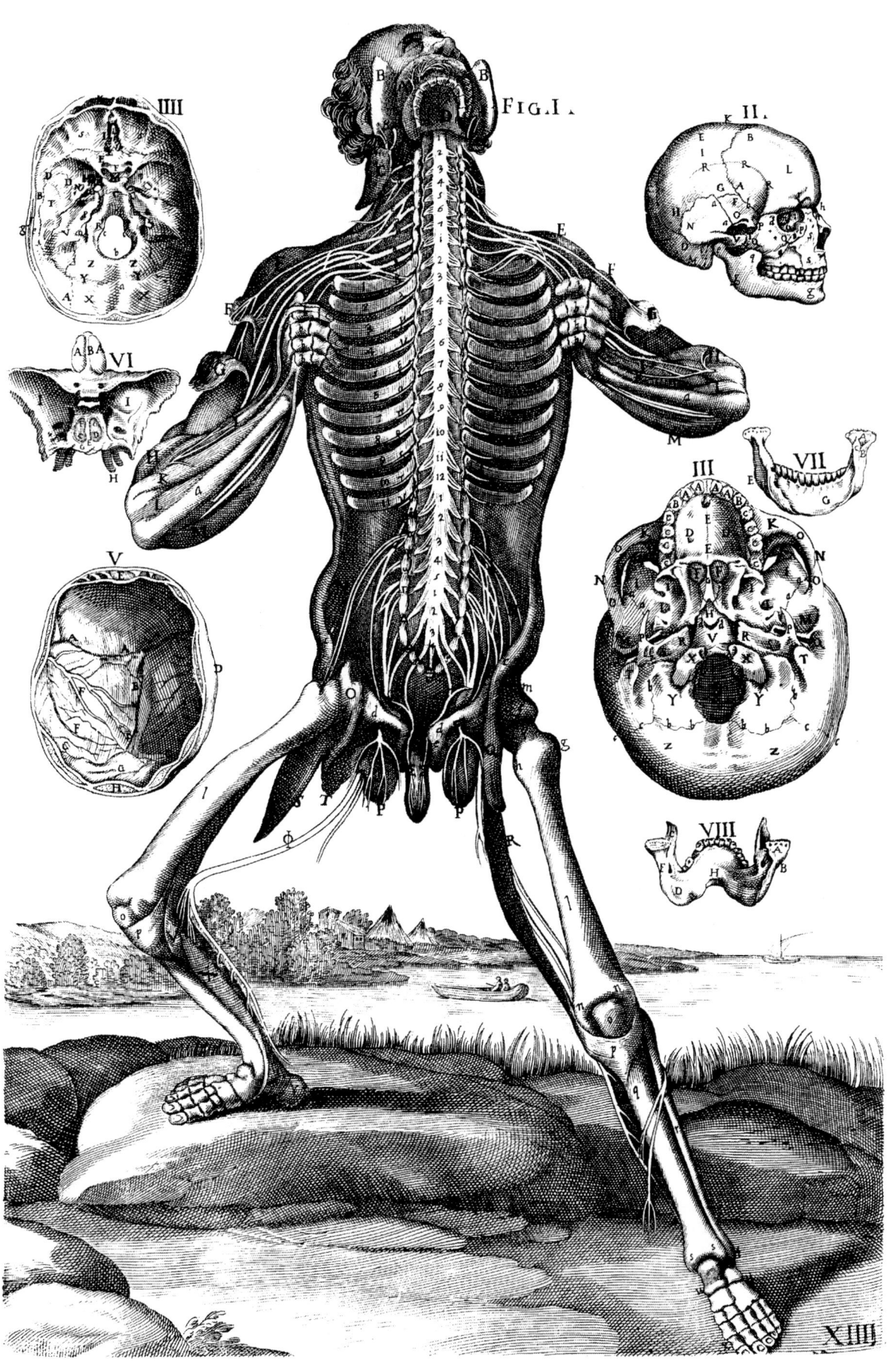

18. Ecorché figure facing forward surrounded by skulls by Pietro da Cortona, (1597–1669) 1741

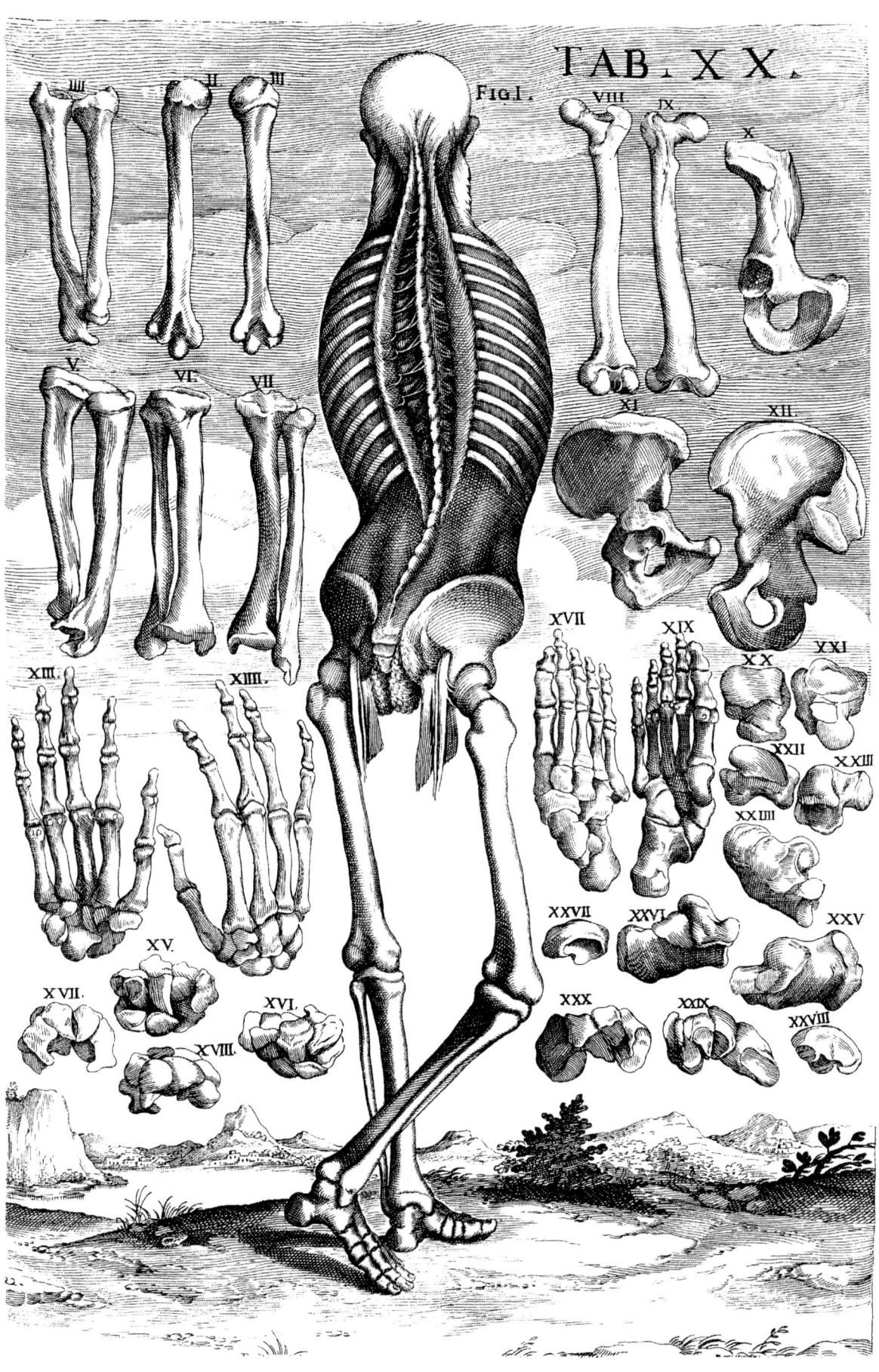

19. Ecorché figure posterior view, surrounded by bones by Pietro da Cortona, (1597–1669) 1741

20. Ecorché figure posterior view surrounded by images of the brain by Pietro da Cortona, (1597–1669) 1741

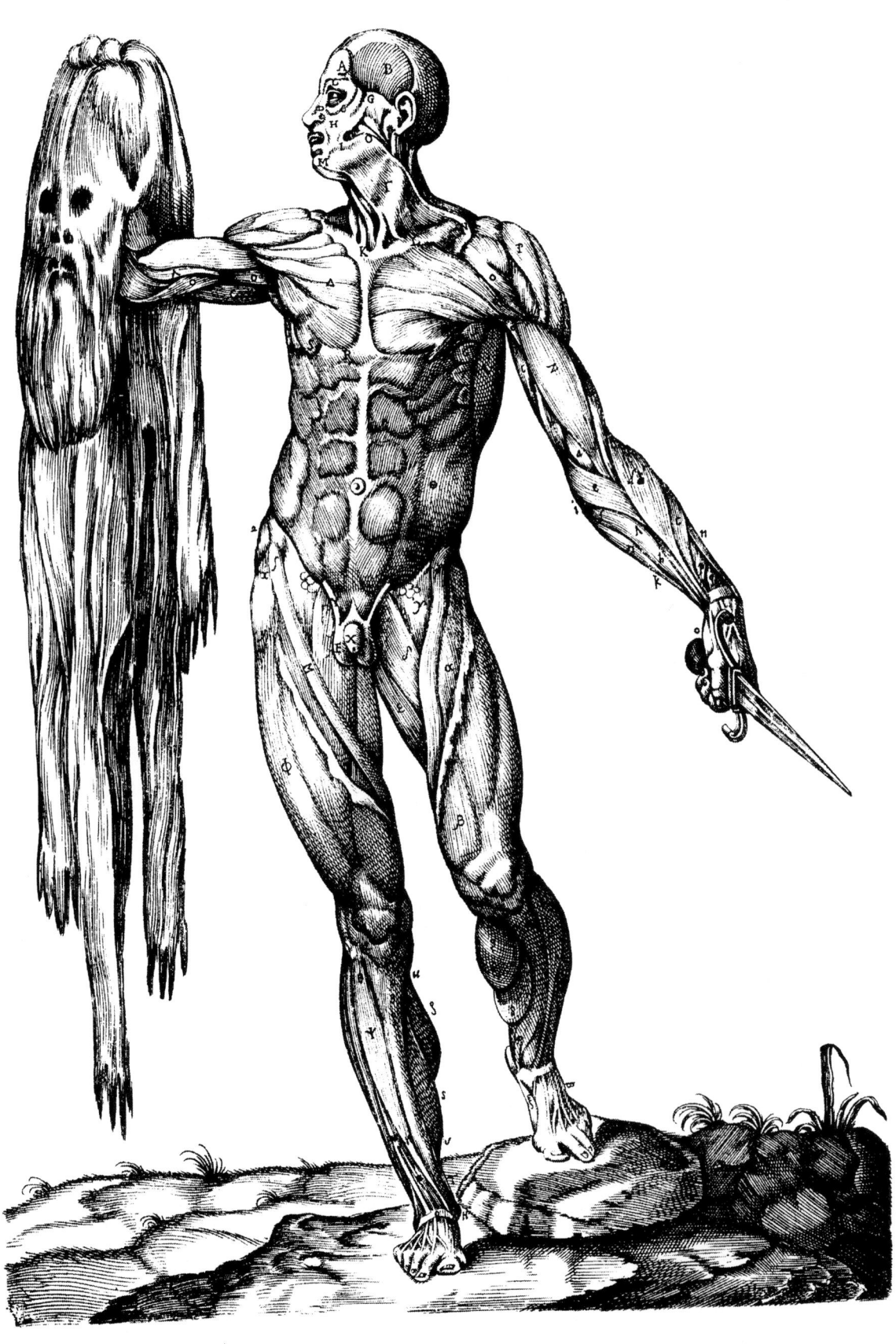

21. Muscles, superficial dissection, by Juan Valverde de Amusco, ca.1525–ca.1588

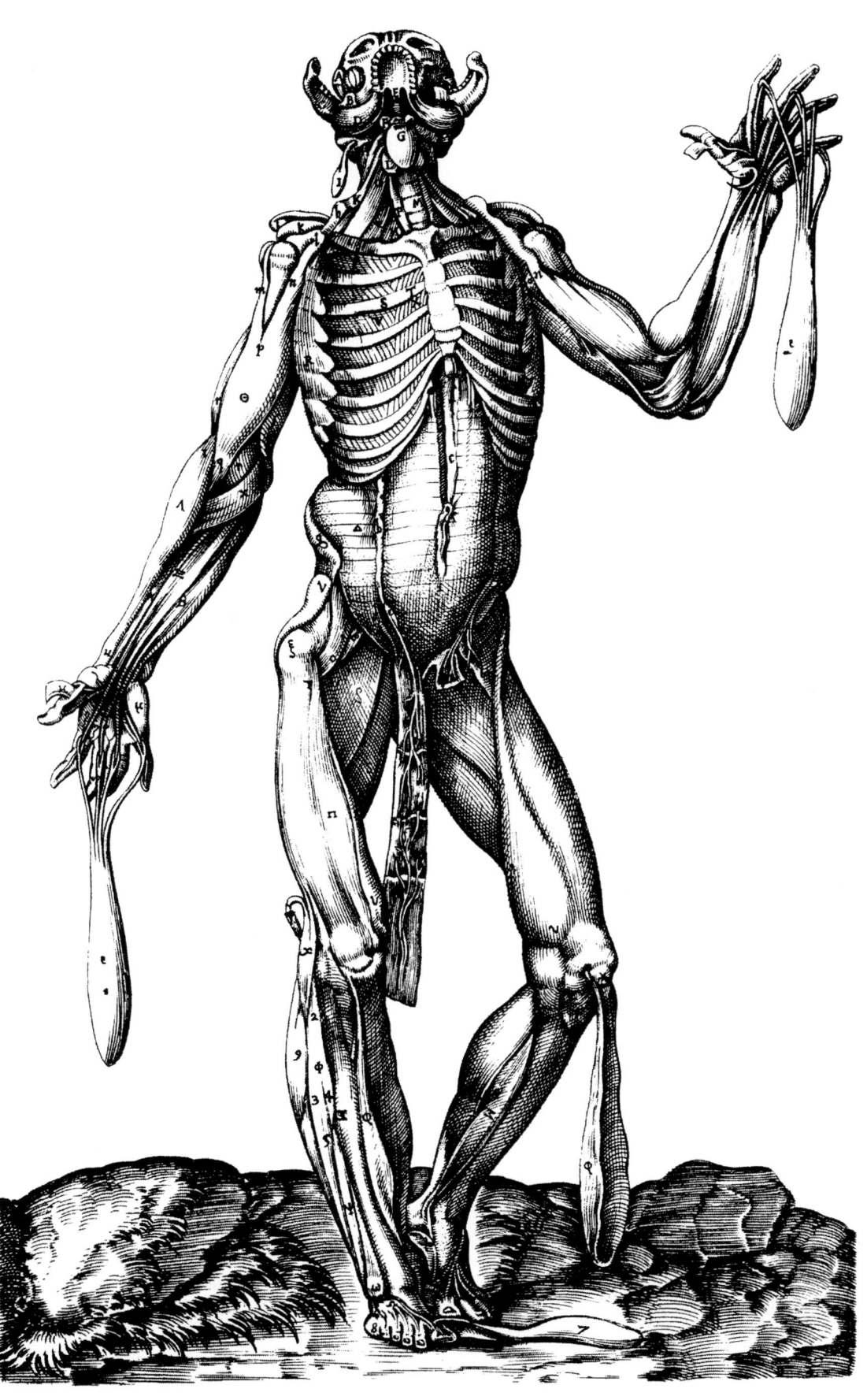

22. Muscles, deep dissection. Dissection of the mouth, by Juan Valverde de'Amusco, ca.1525–ca.1588

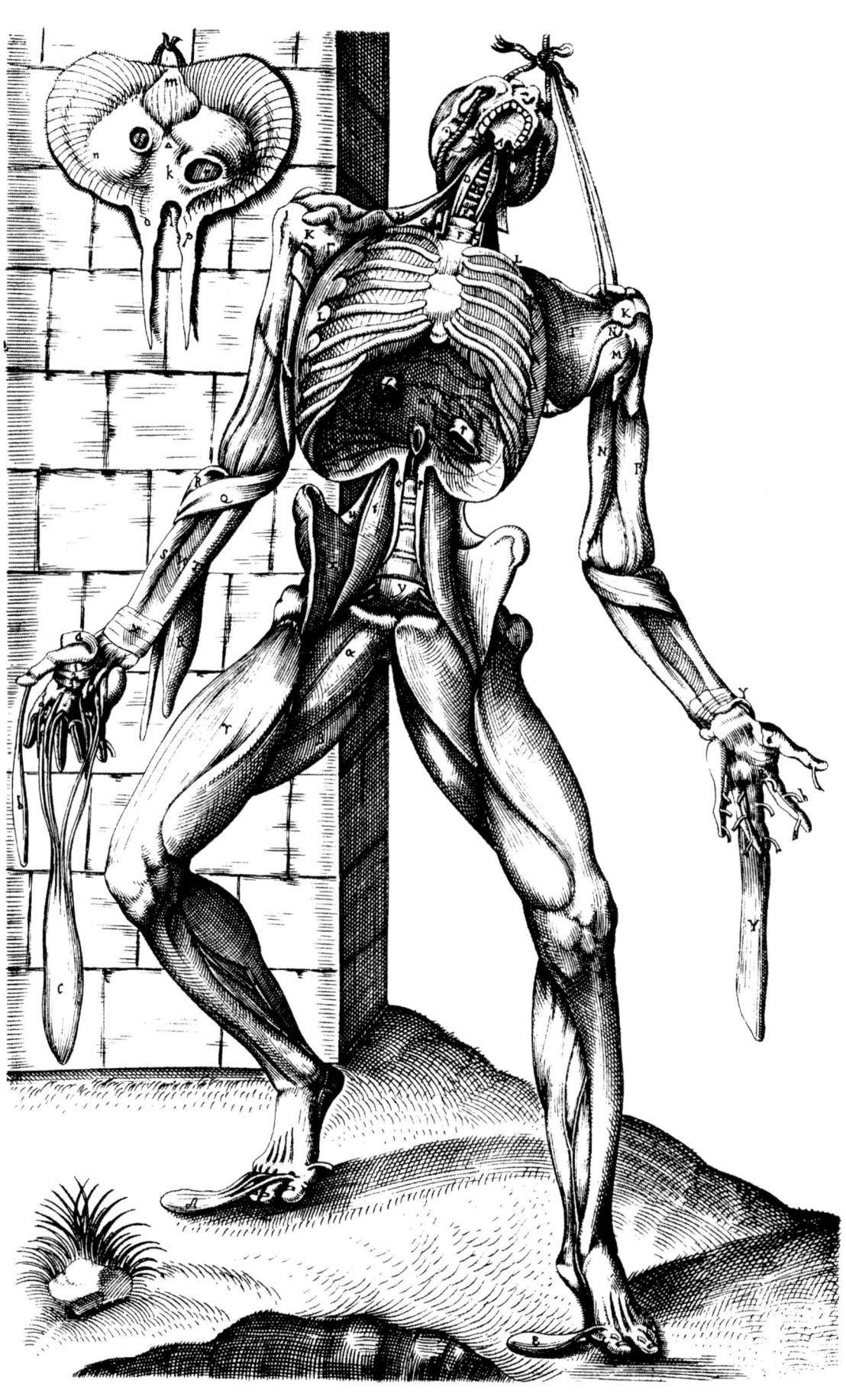

23. Muscles, including muscles of respiration by
Juan Valverde de Amusco, ca.1525–ca.1588

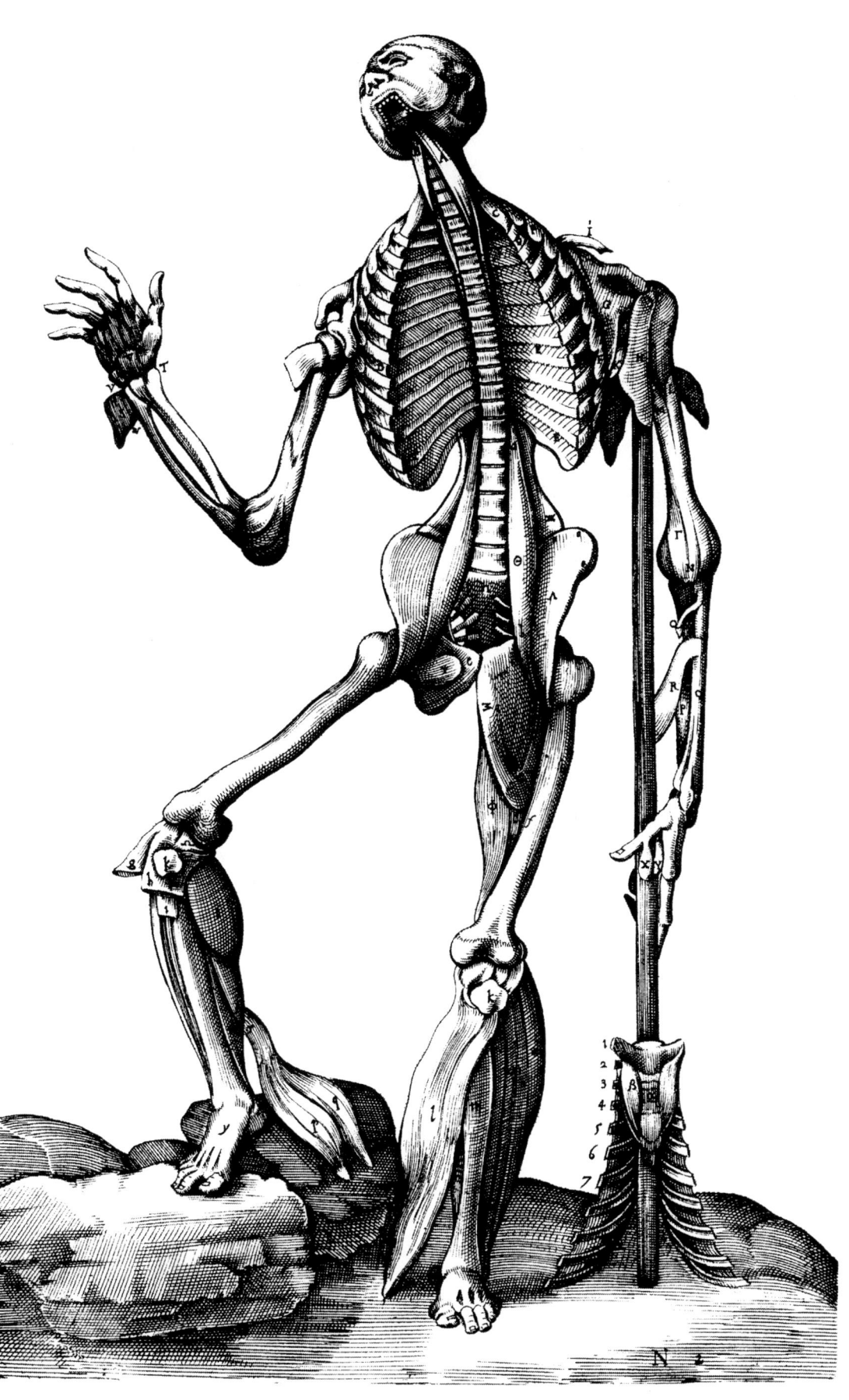

24. Skeleton and muscles by Juan Valverde de Amusco, ca.1525–ca.1588

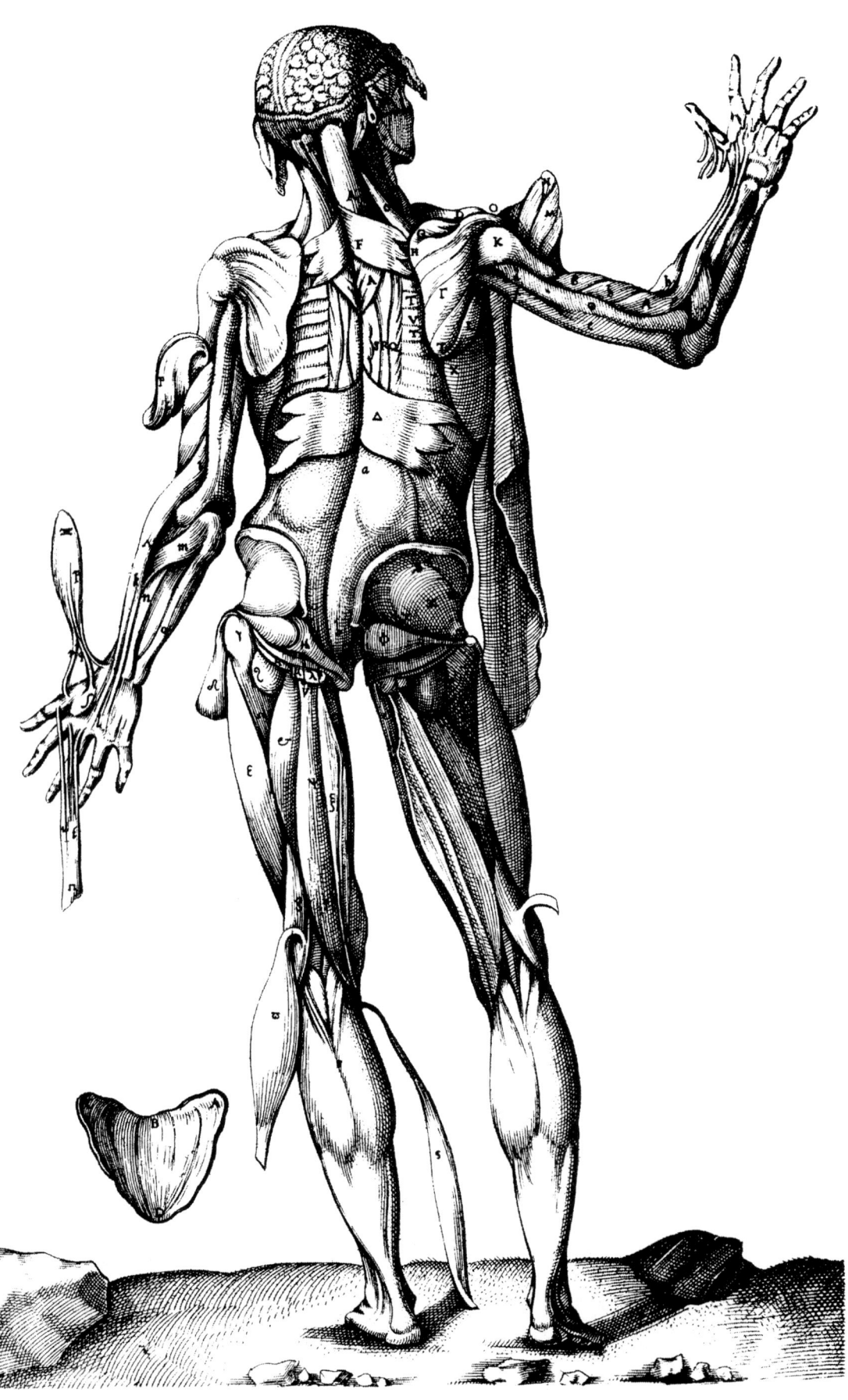

25. Back muscles, deep dissection. Inset of deltoid muscle. Male figure, by Juan Valverde de Amusco, ca.1525–ca.1588

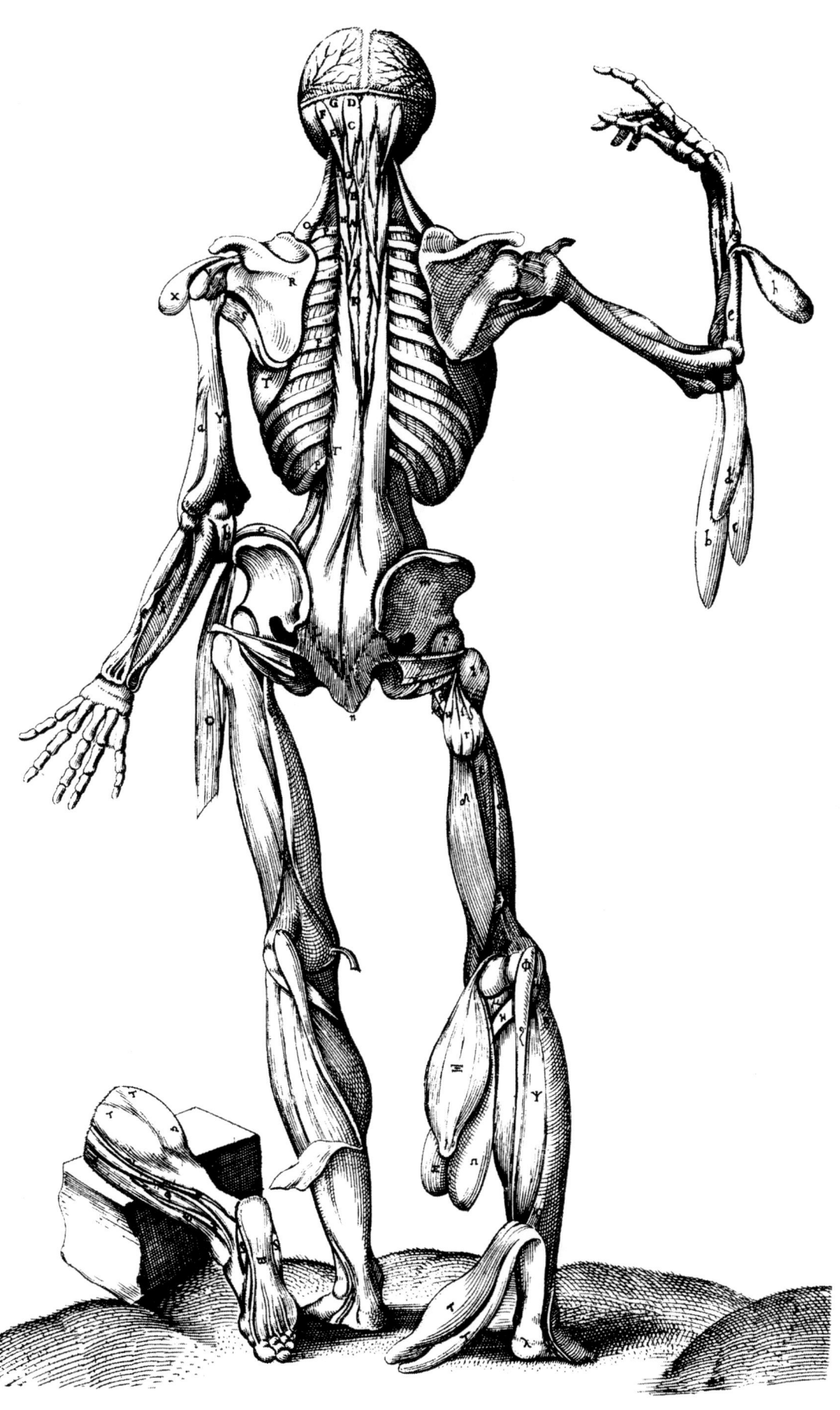

26. Deep muscles of the body, and their attachments to the skeleton, by Juan Valverde de Amusco, ca.1525–ca.1588

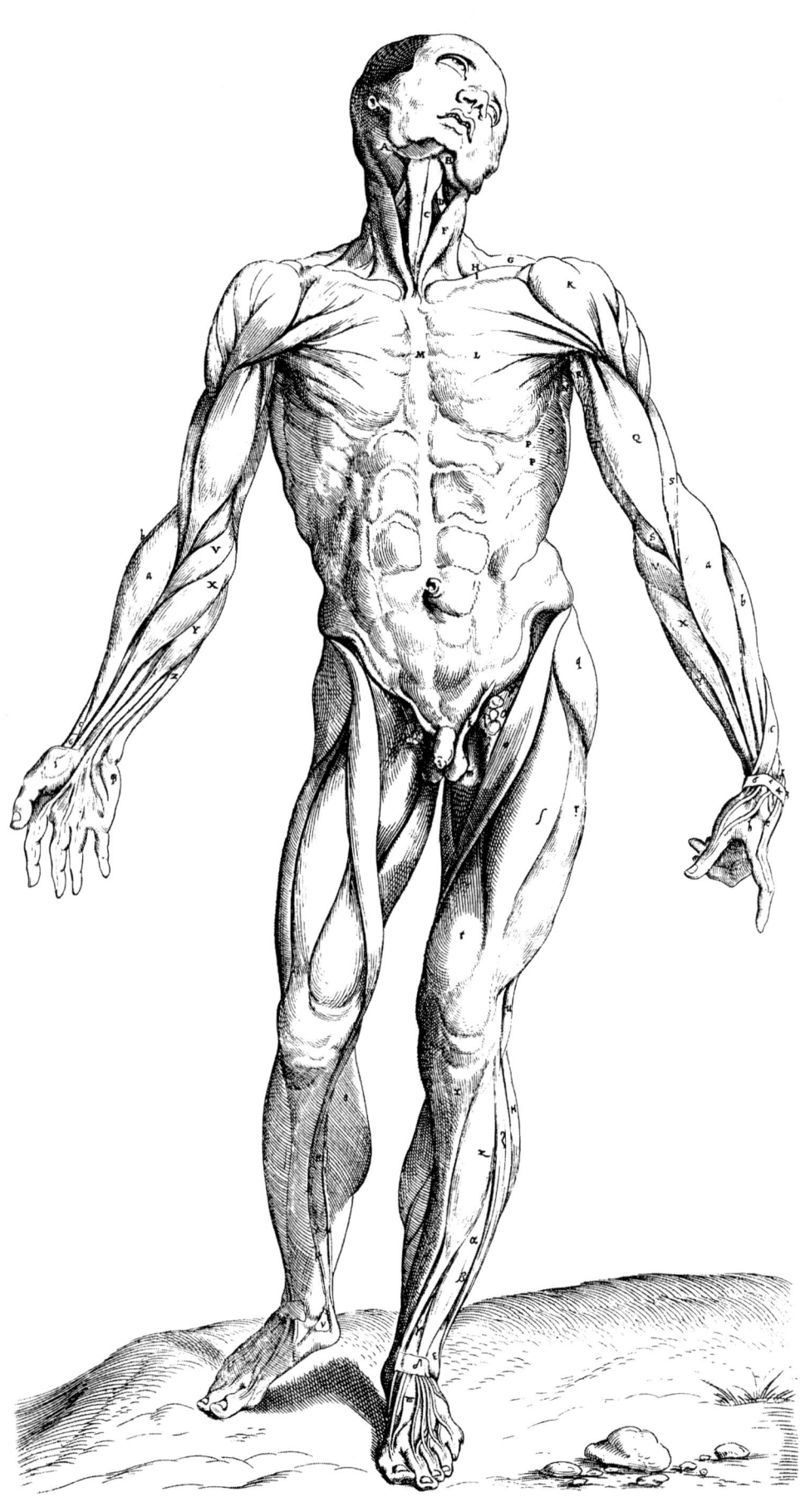

27. Muscles, superficial. Male figure, in vivo, anterior view, by Thomas Geminus, d.1562

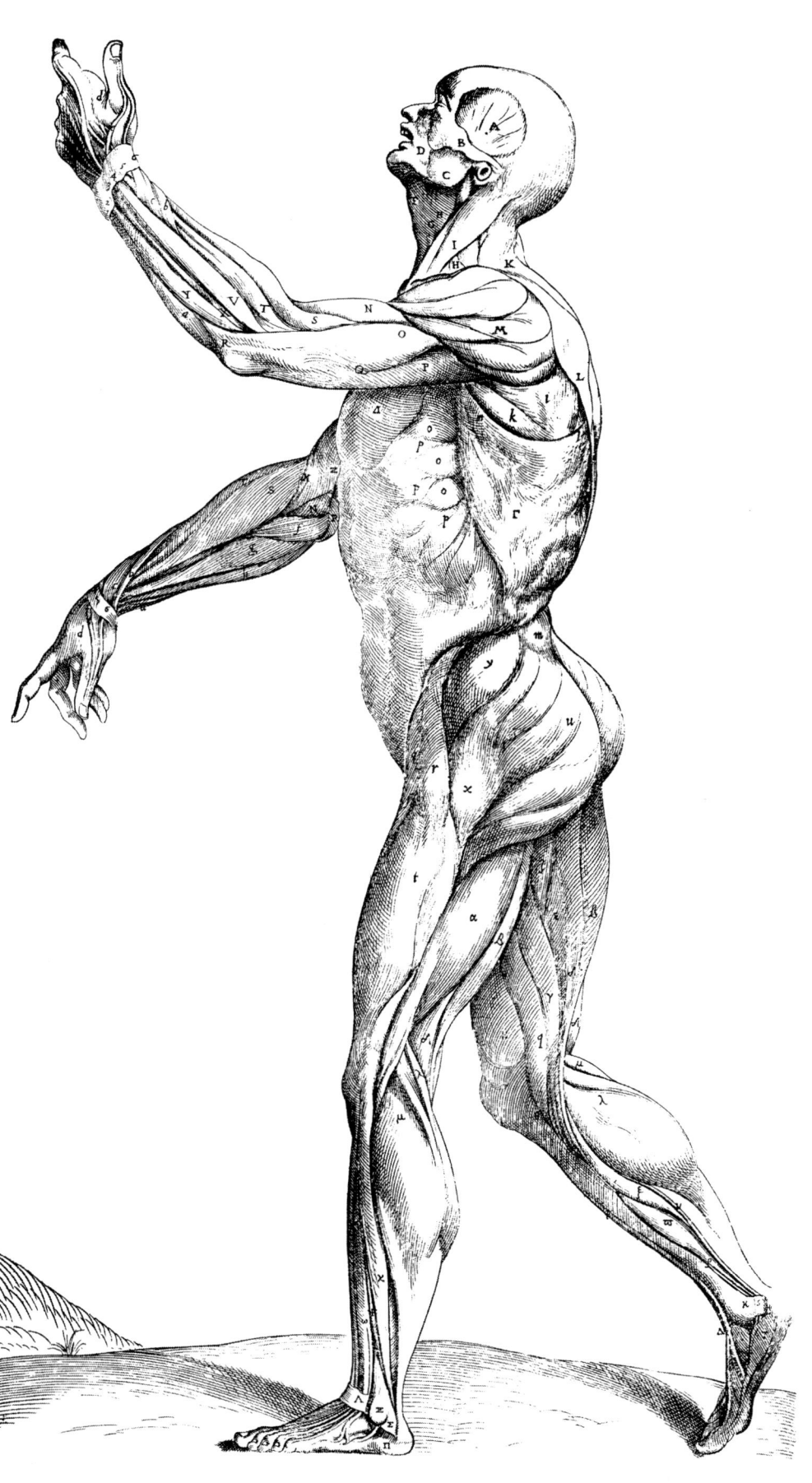

28. Muscles, superficial. Male figure, in vivo, lateral view, by Thomas Geminus, d.1562

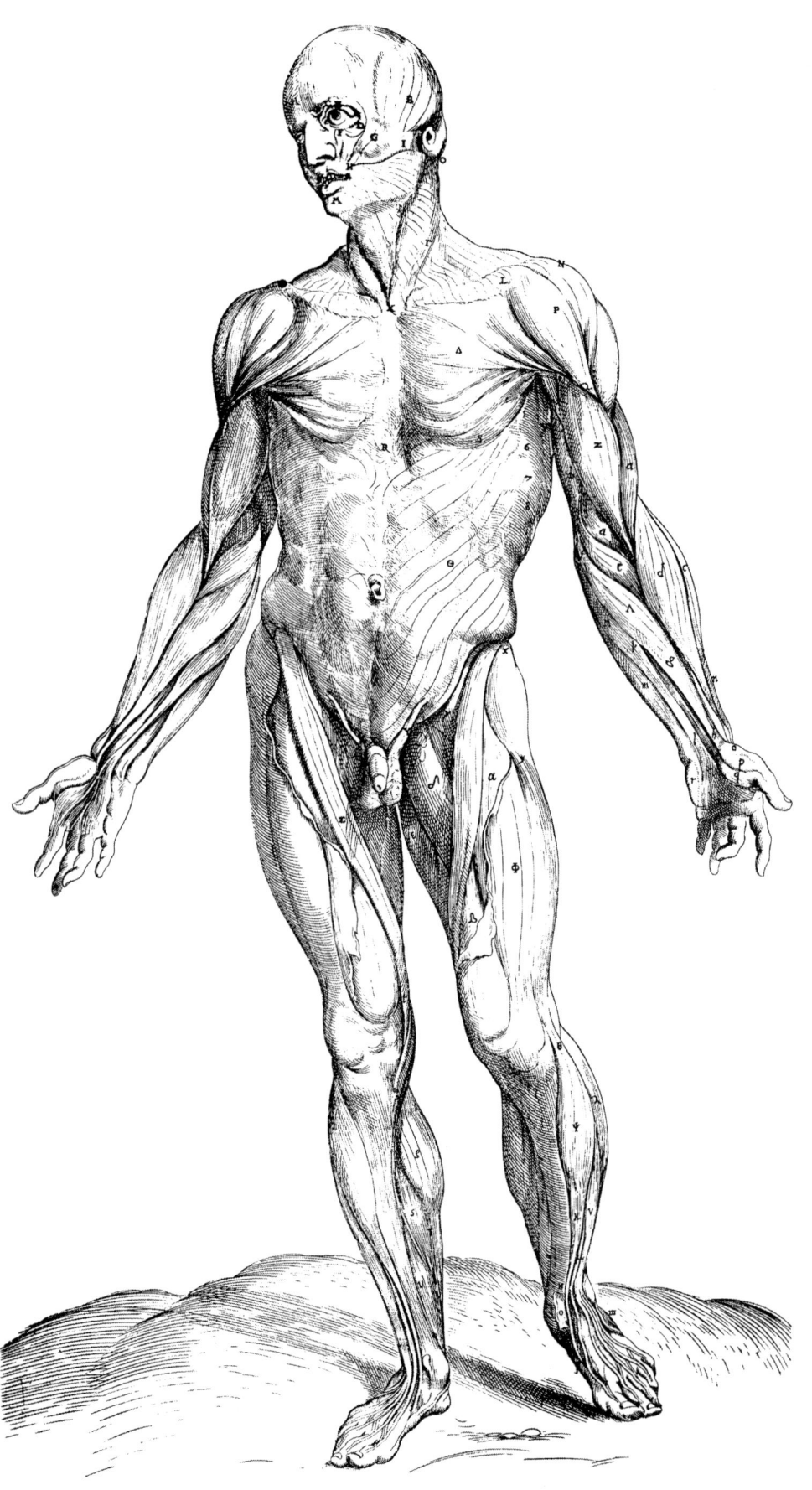

29. Muscles, superficial dissection. Male figure, in vivo, anterior view by Thomas Geminus, d.1562

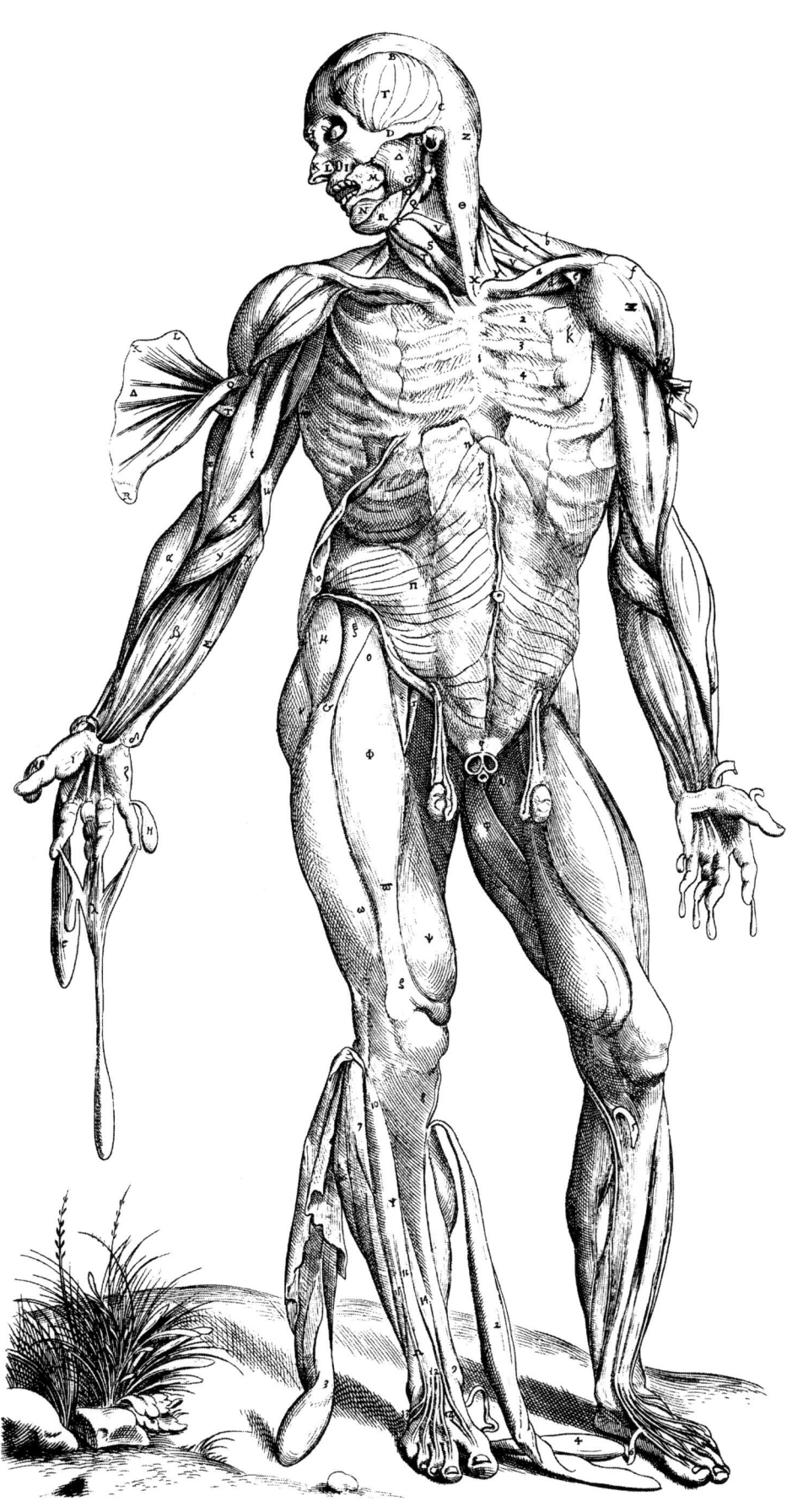

30. Muscles, deep dissection. Penis removed, testis dissected free from the scrotum, by Thomas Geminus, d.1562

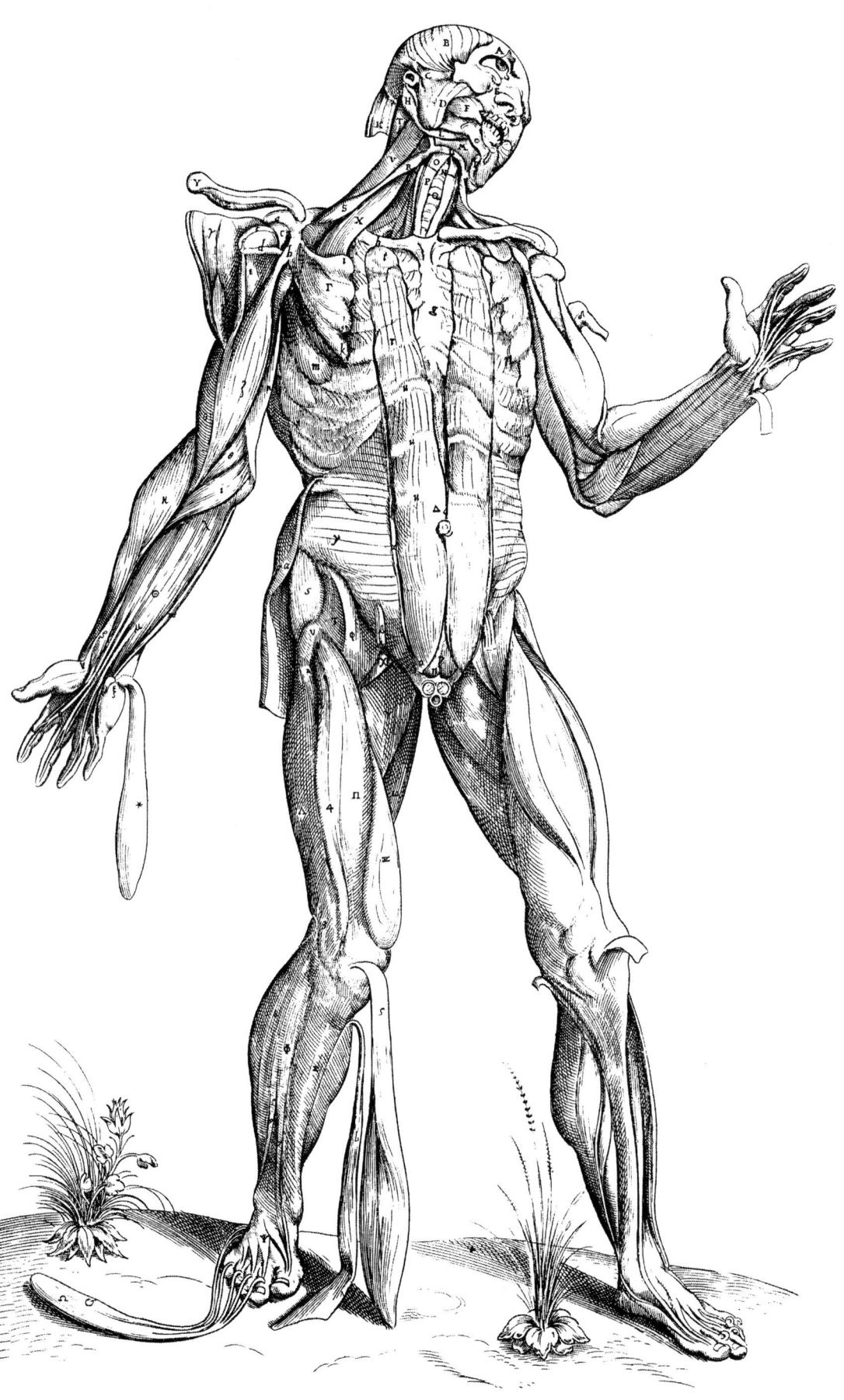

31. Muscles, deep dissection. Genitalia removed.
Male figure, in vivo, anterior view, by Thomas
Geminus, d.1562

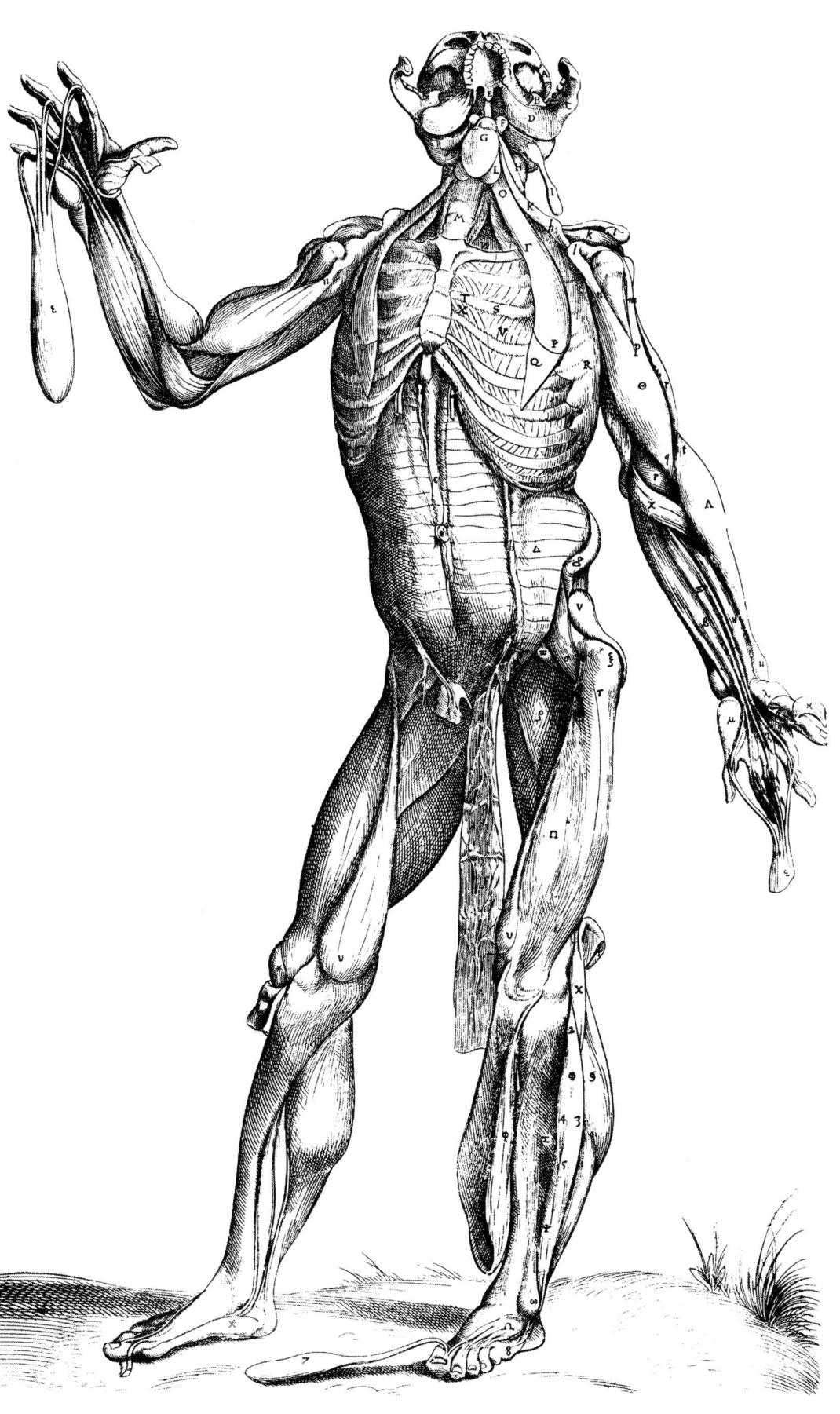

32. Muscles, deep dissection. Dissection of the mouth, mandible divided and reflected to show palate and tongue, by Thomas Geminus, d.1562

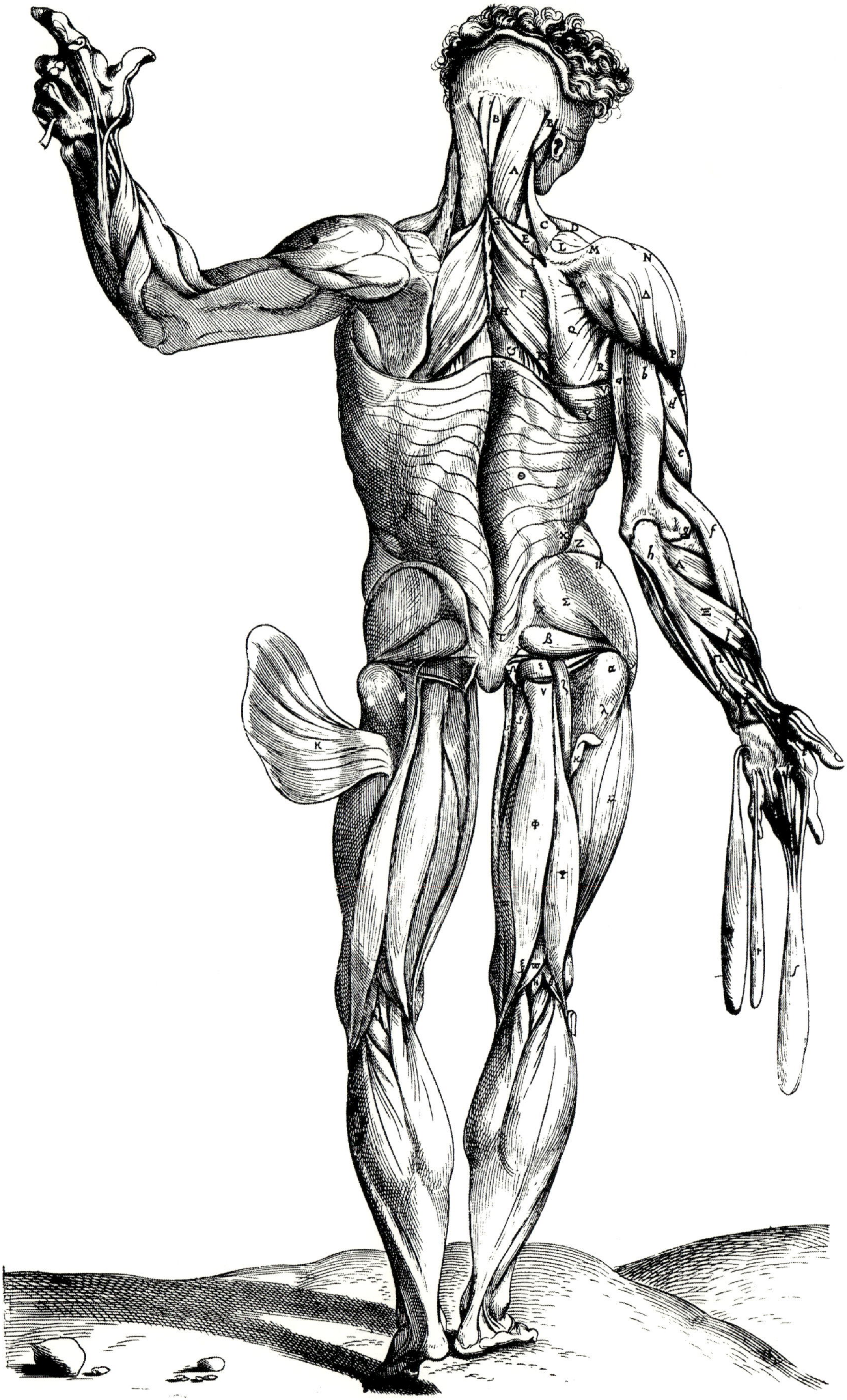

33. Muscles, deep dissection. Male figure, in vivo, posterior view., by Thomas Geminus, d.1562

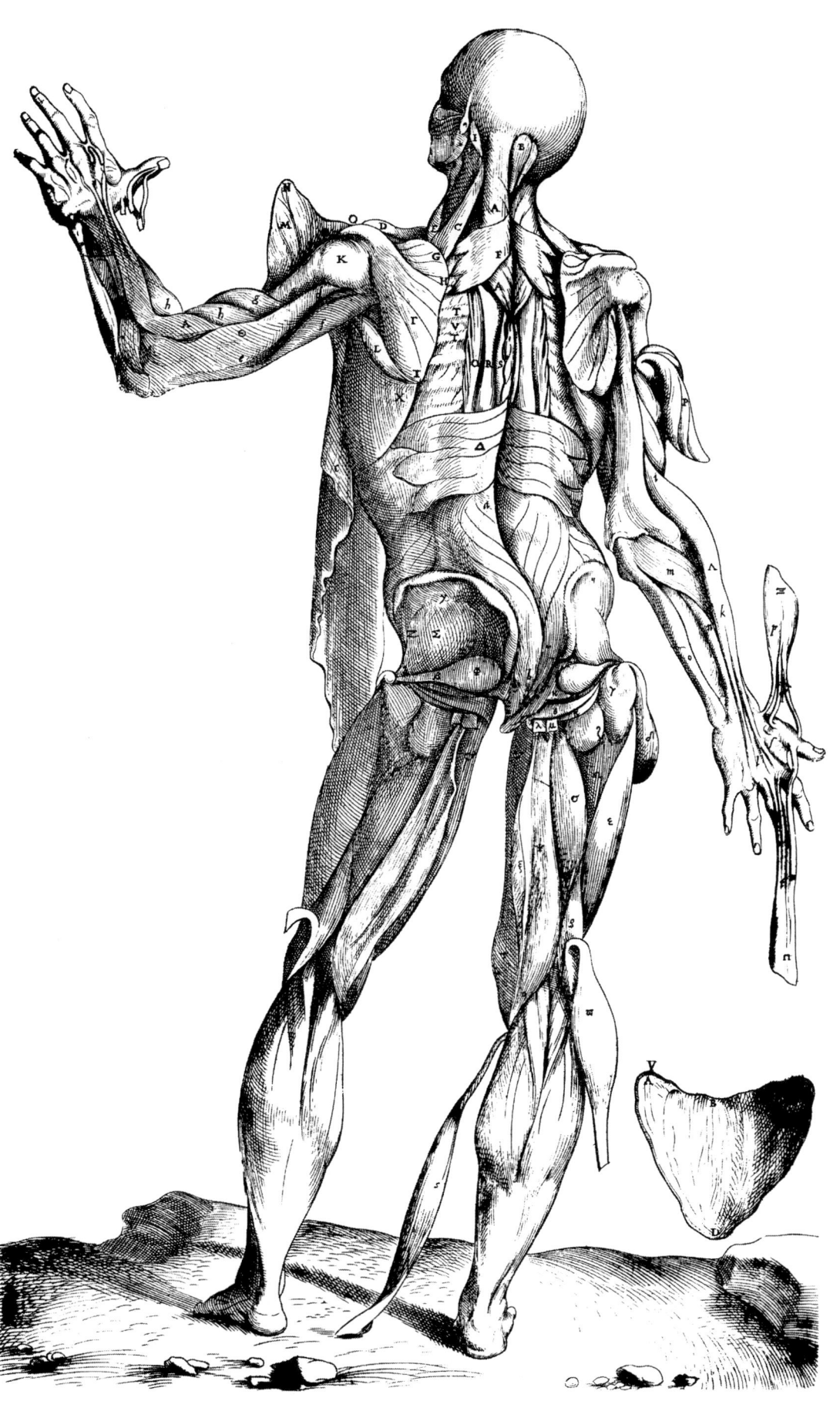

34. Back muscles, deep dissection. Inset of deltoid muscle. Male figure, in vivo, posterior view, by Thomas Geminus, d.1562

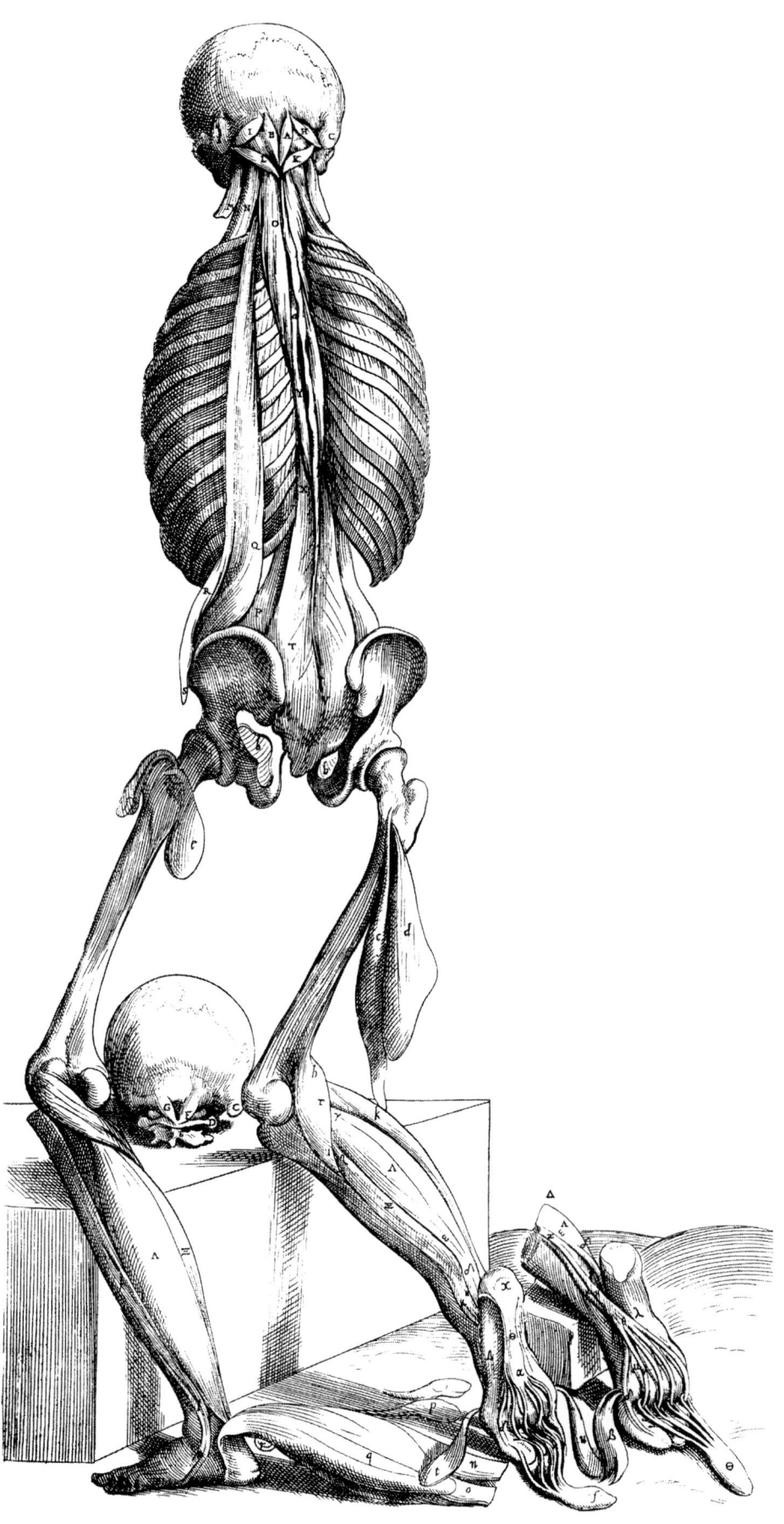

35. Deep muscles of the body, and their attachments to the skeleton, by Thomas Geminus, d.1562

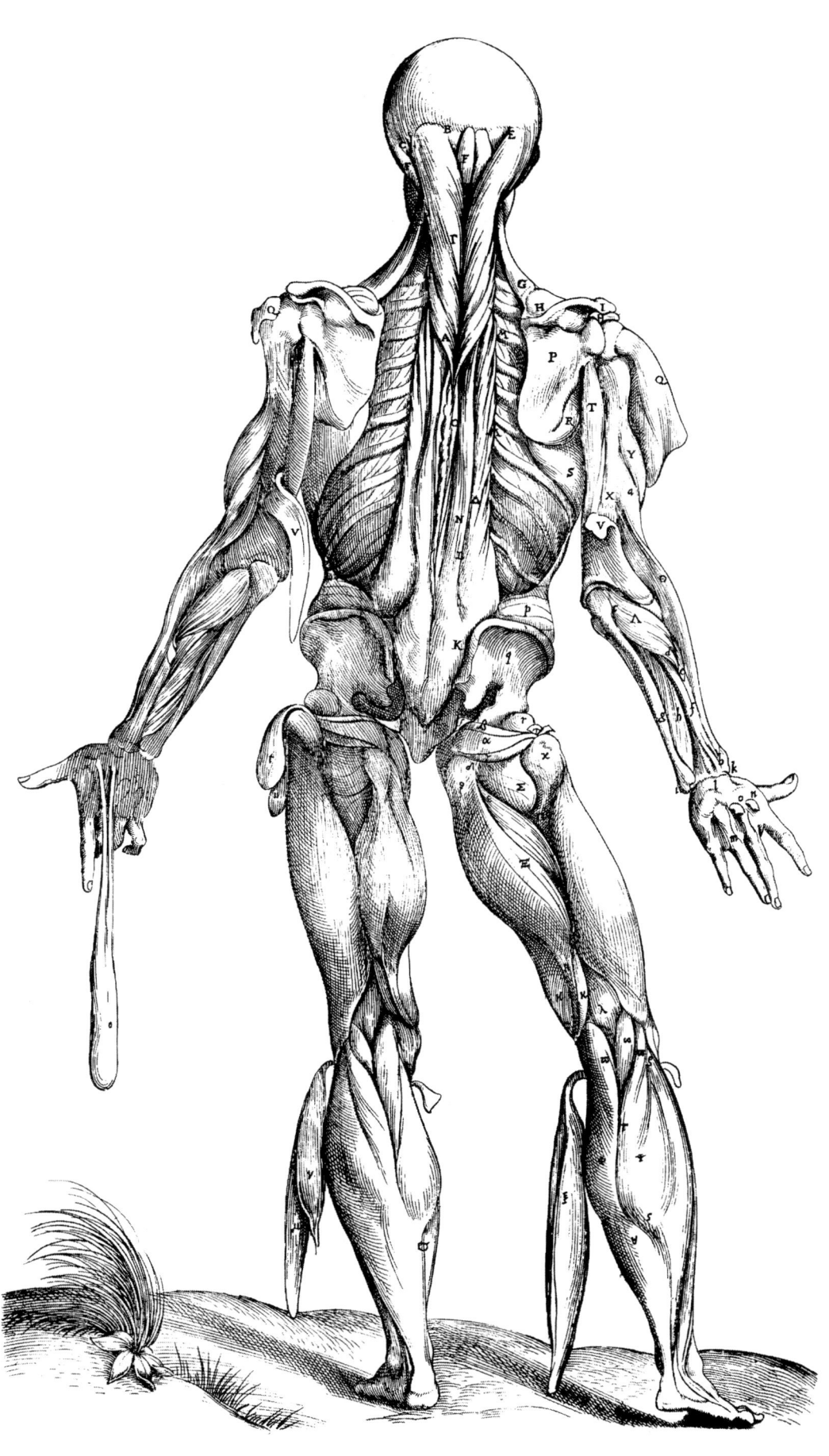

36. Back muscles, deep dissection. Pelvic bones visible. Male figure, in vivo, posterior view, by Thomas Geminus, d.1562

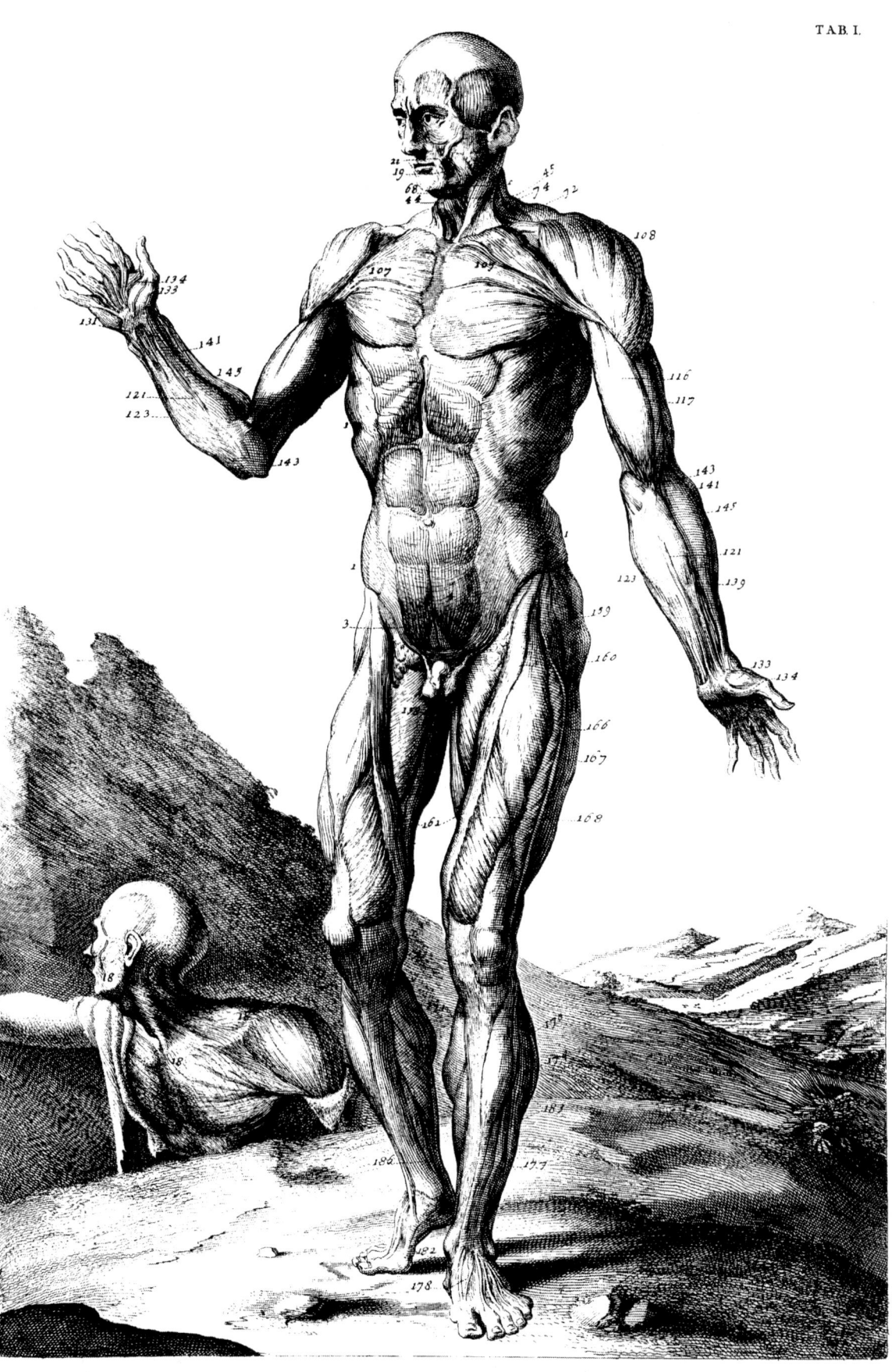

37. Muscles of the body, superficial dissection.
Male figure, anterior view, by William Cowper
1666–1709

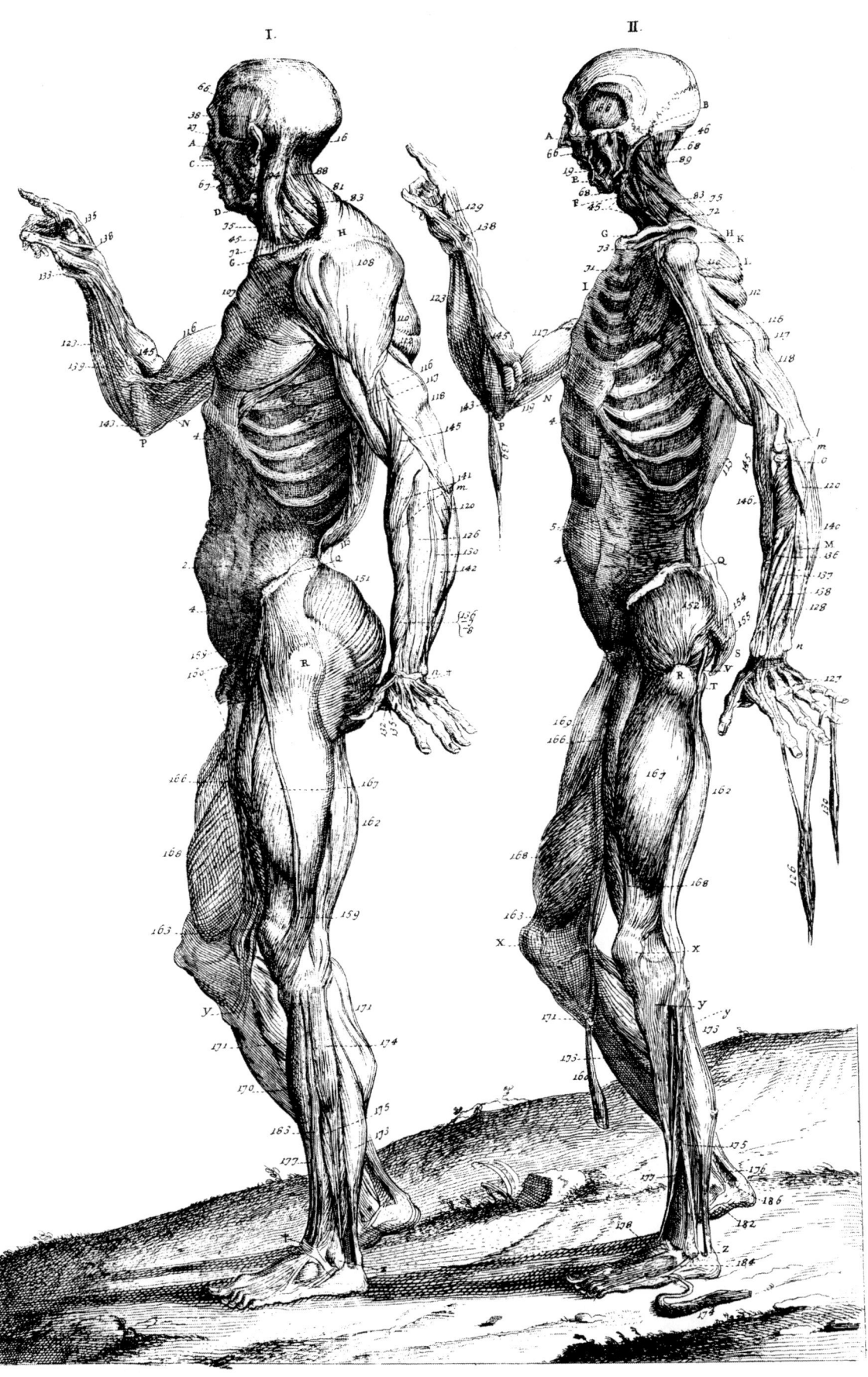

38. Muscles, deep dissection. 2 male figures, in vivo, lateral views, by William Cowper 1666–1709

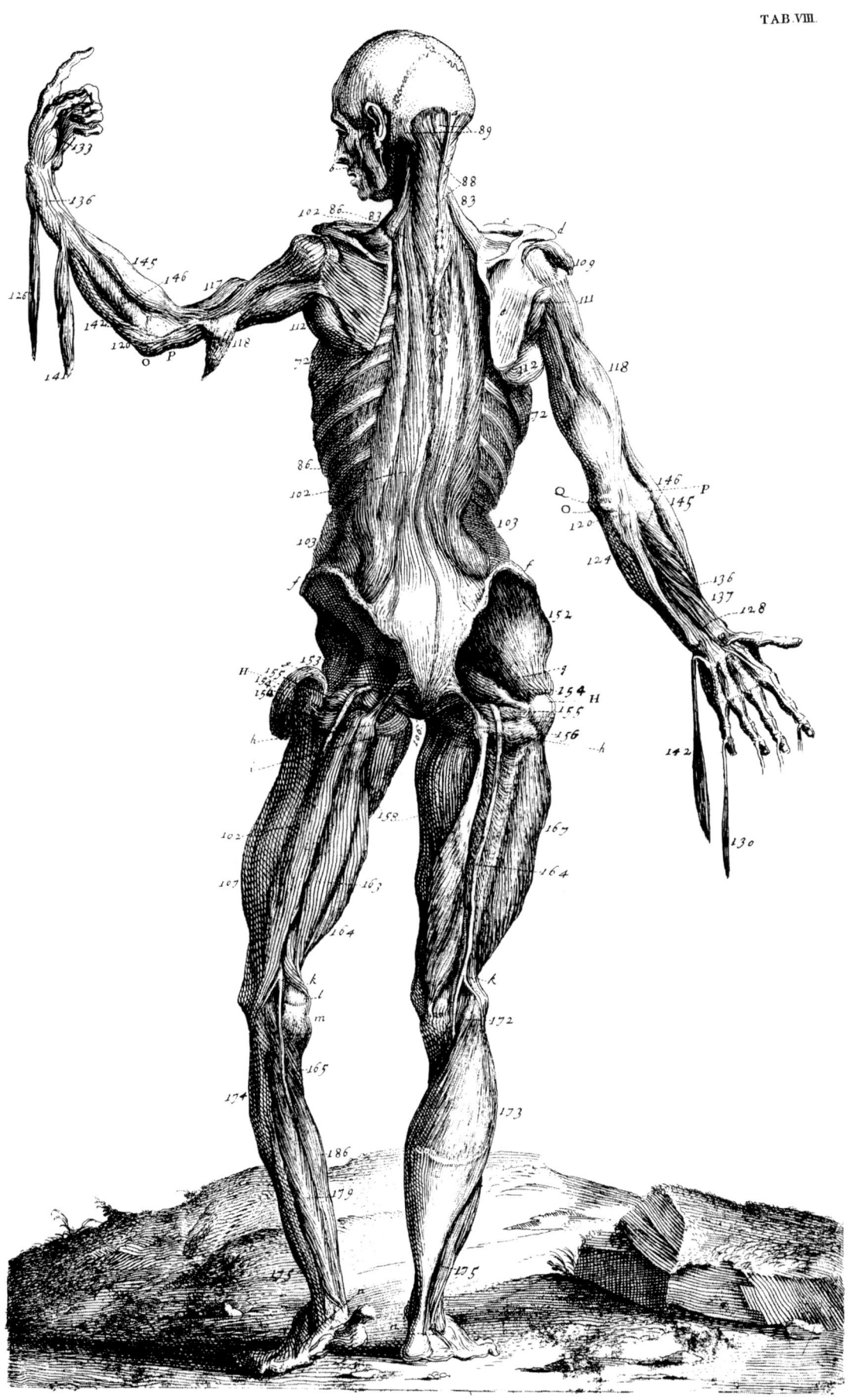

39. Skeleton and muscles, deep dissection.
Male figure, posterior view, by William Cowper
1666–1709

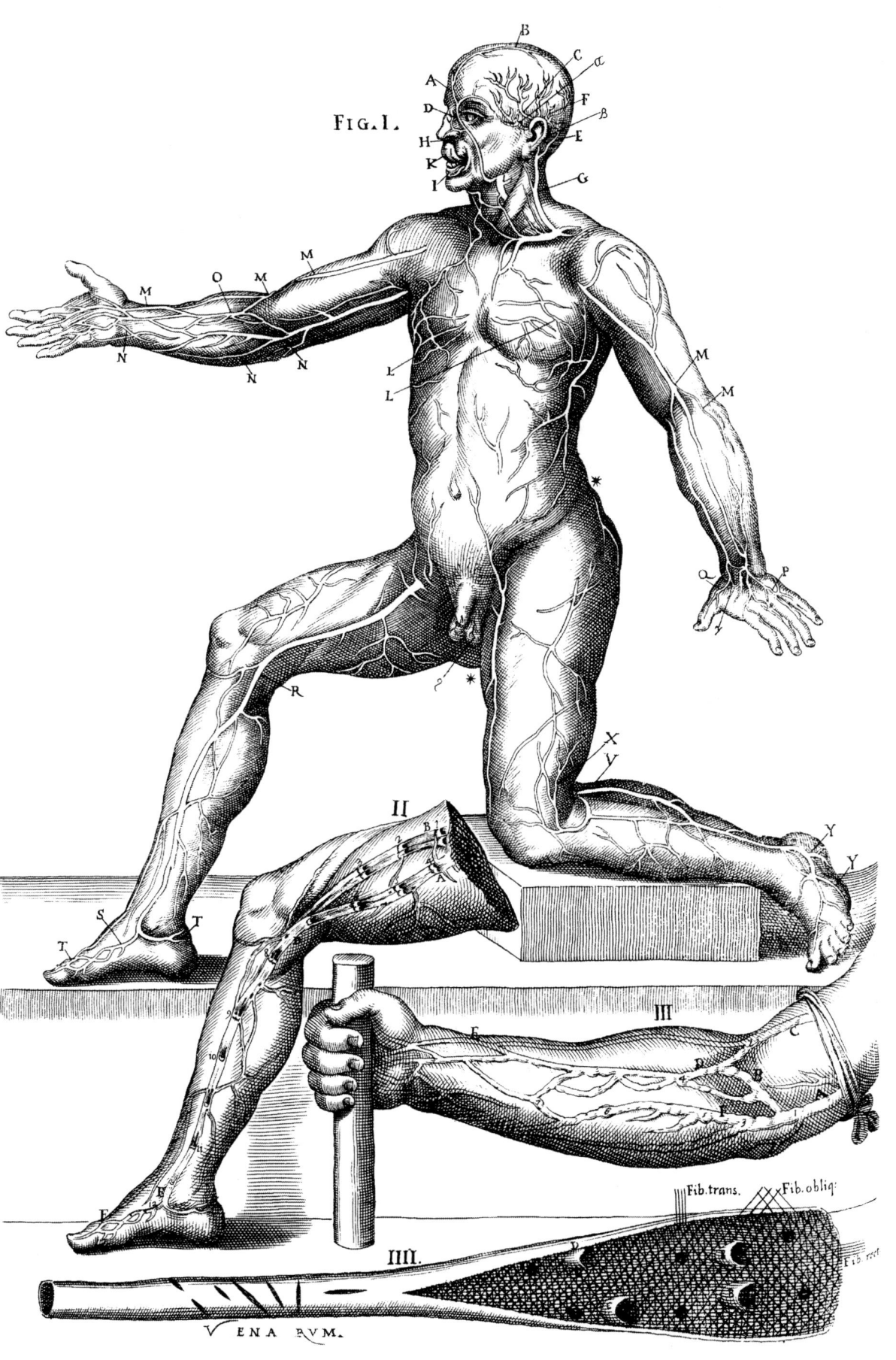

40. Ecorché figure kneeling with arm extended
by Pietro da Cortona. (1597–1669) 1741

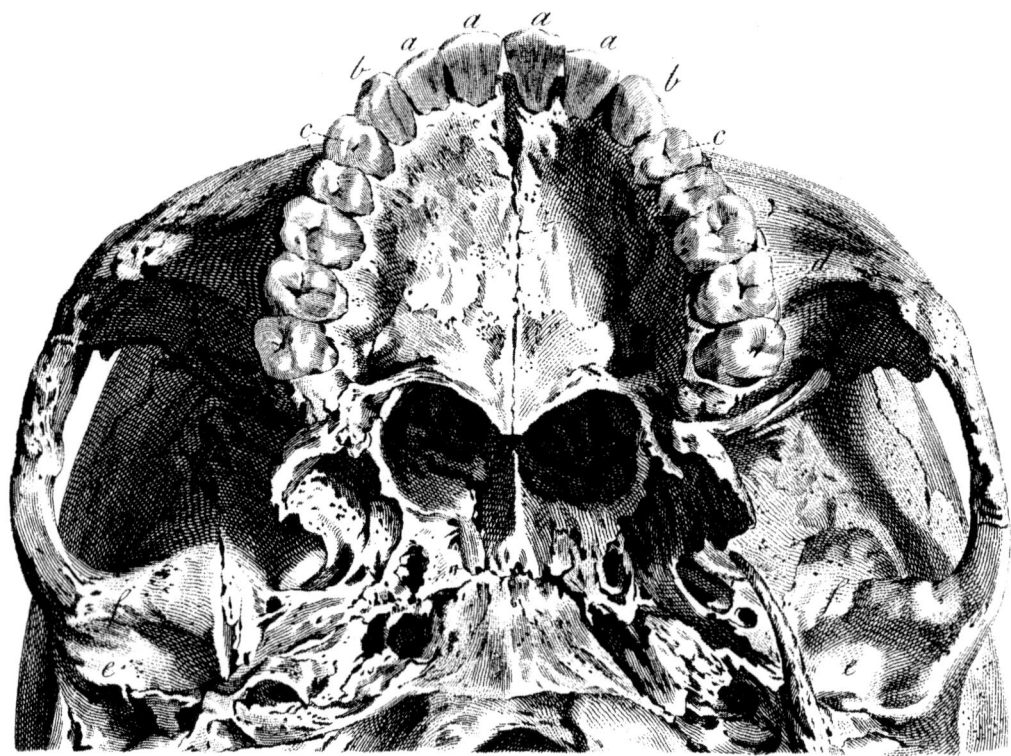

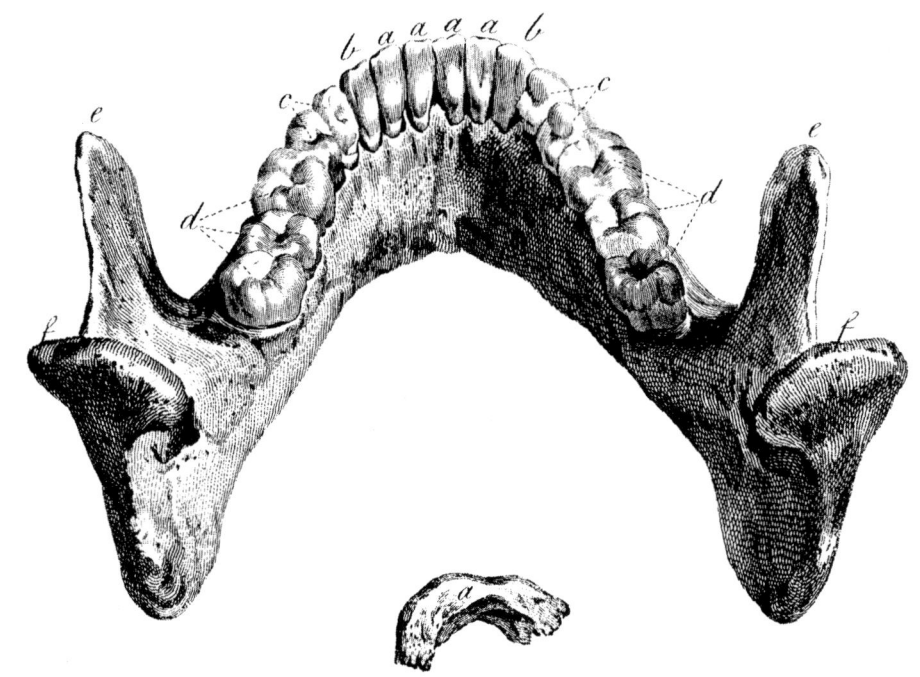

41. Base of skull, maxilla, mandible, cartilage and teeth by John Hunter, 1728–1793 pub. J Johnson

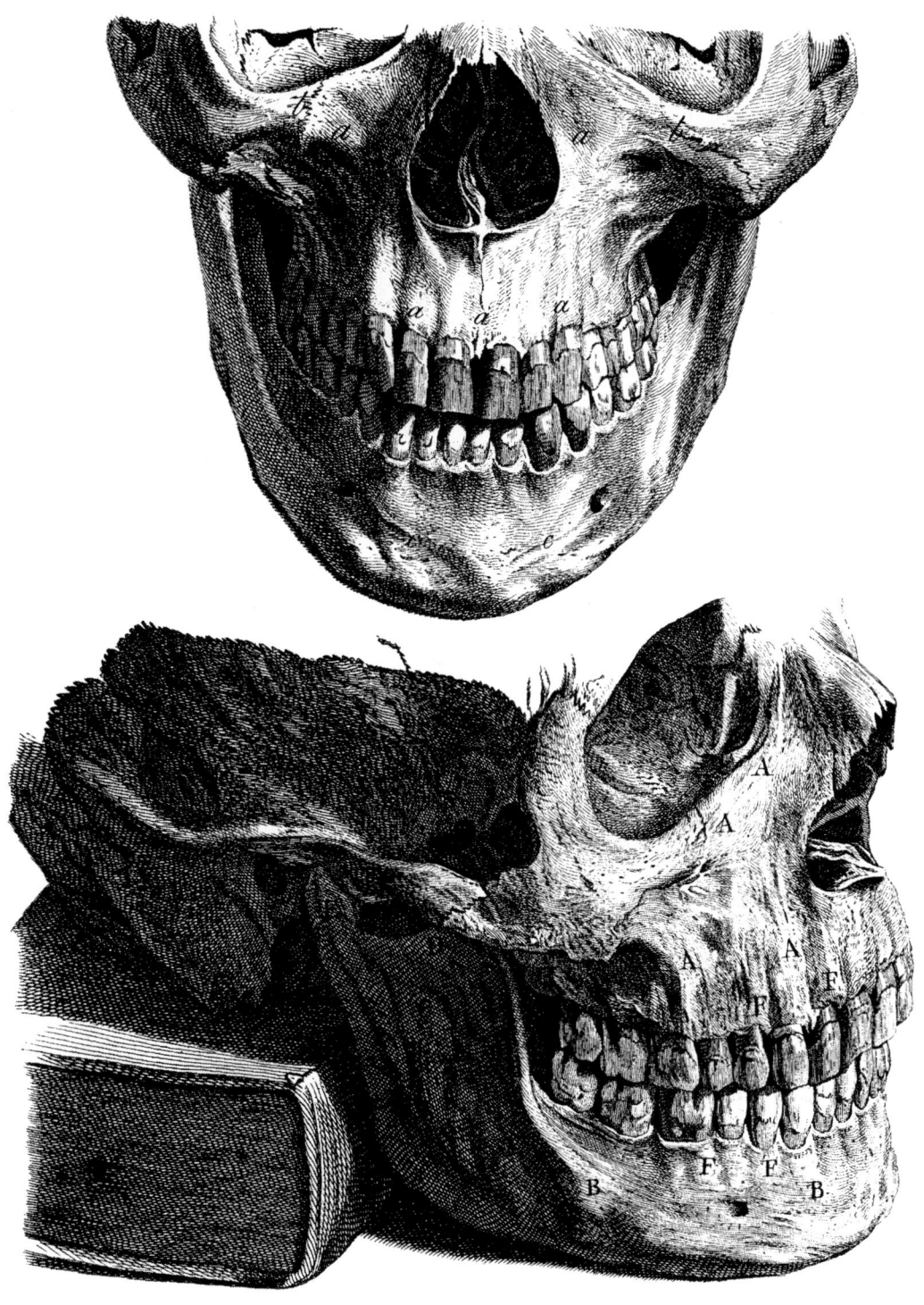

42. Skull and mandible by John Hunter, 1728–1793 pub. J Johnson

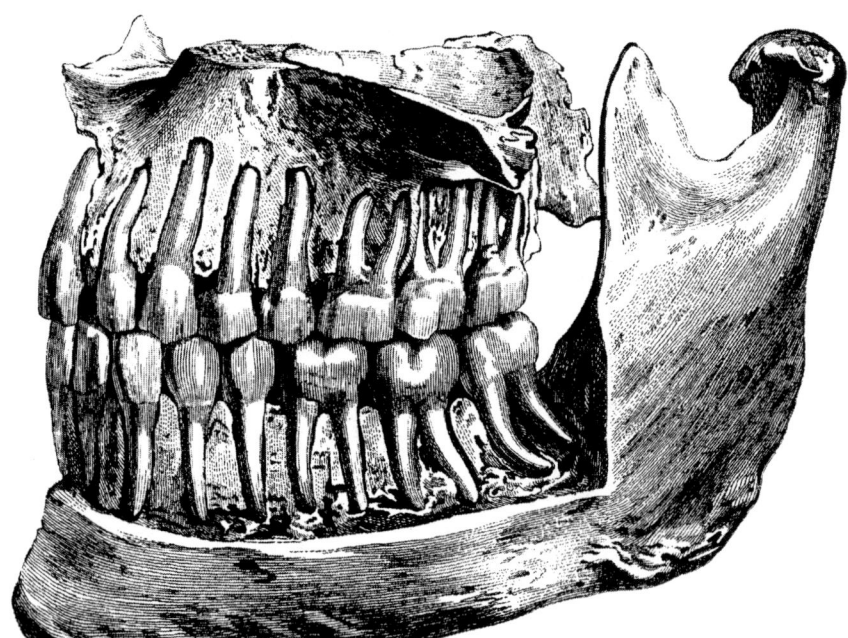
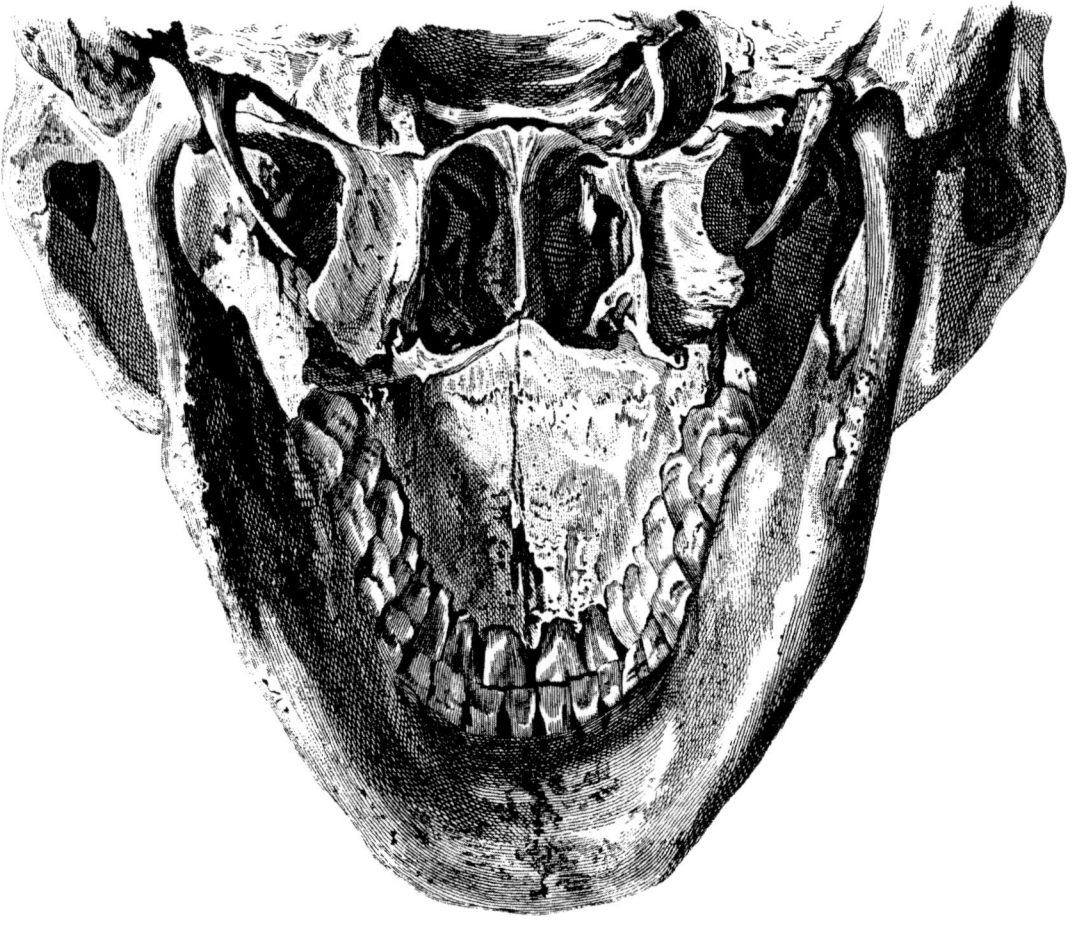

43. Maxilla, mandible and teeth by John Hunter,
1728–1793 pub. J Johnson

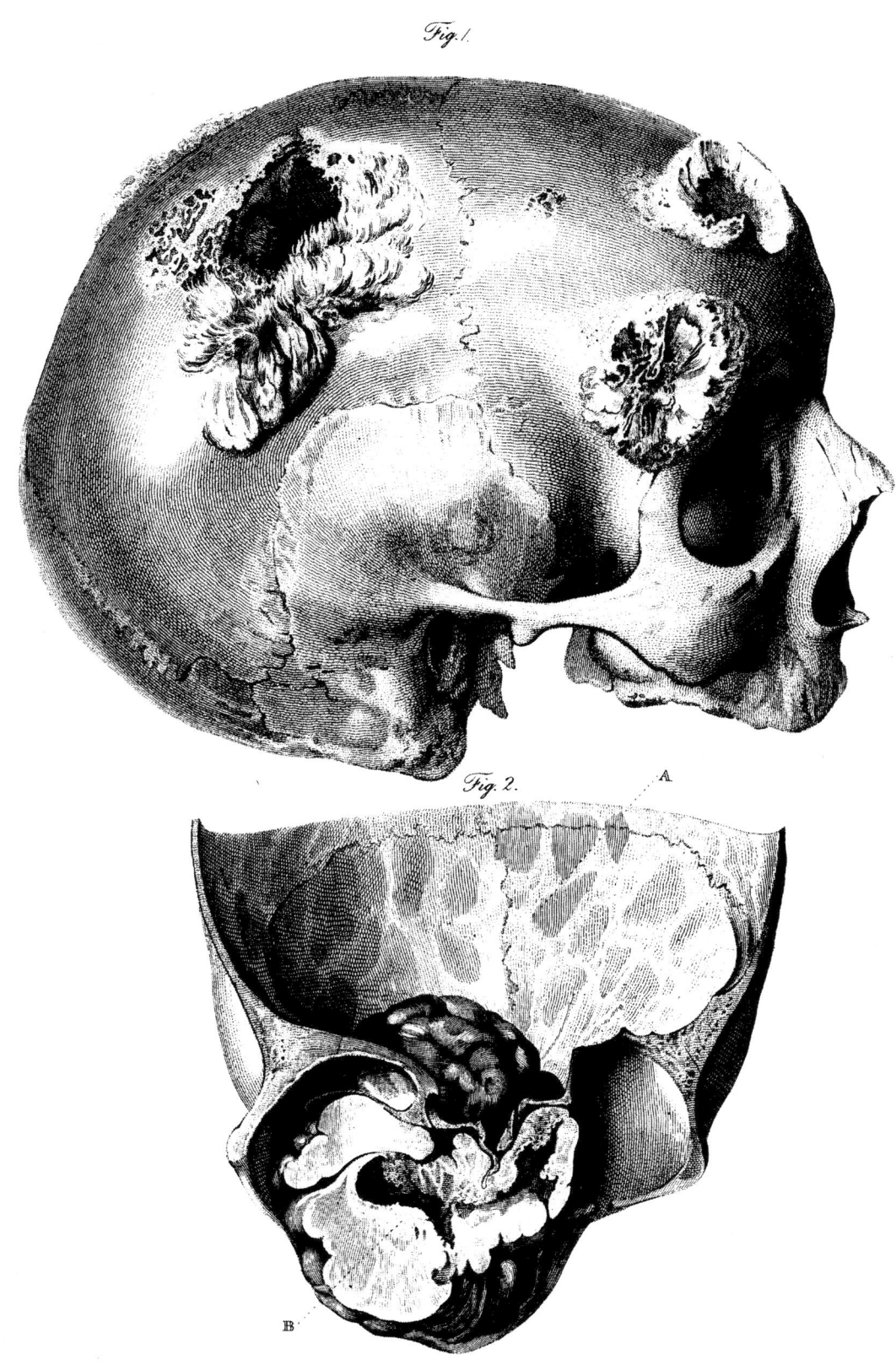

44. Skull with neoplasms by Matthew Baillie
1761–1823

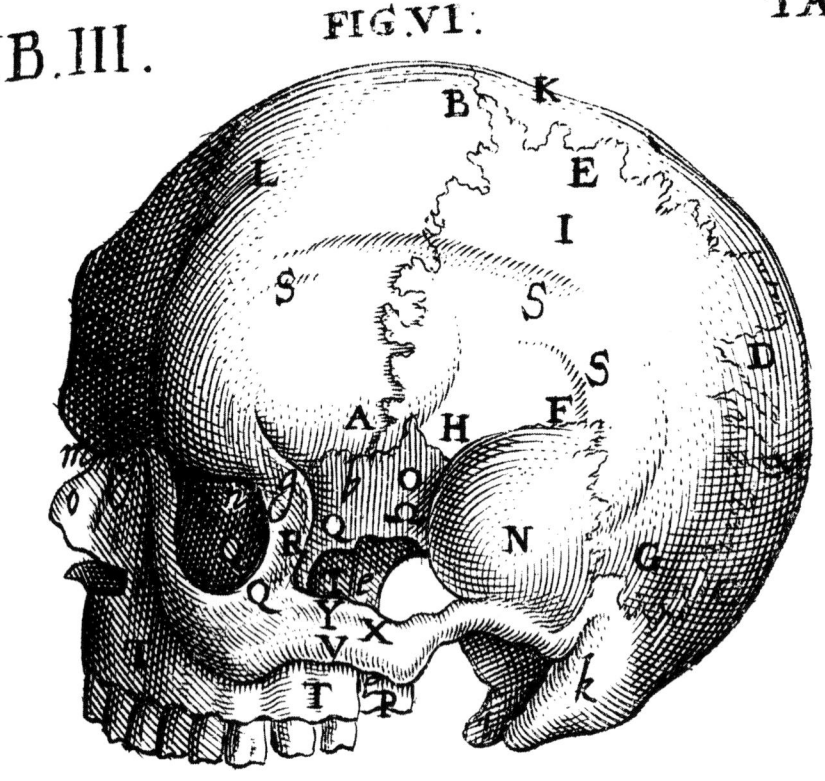
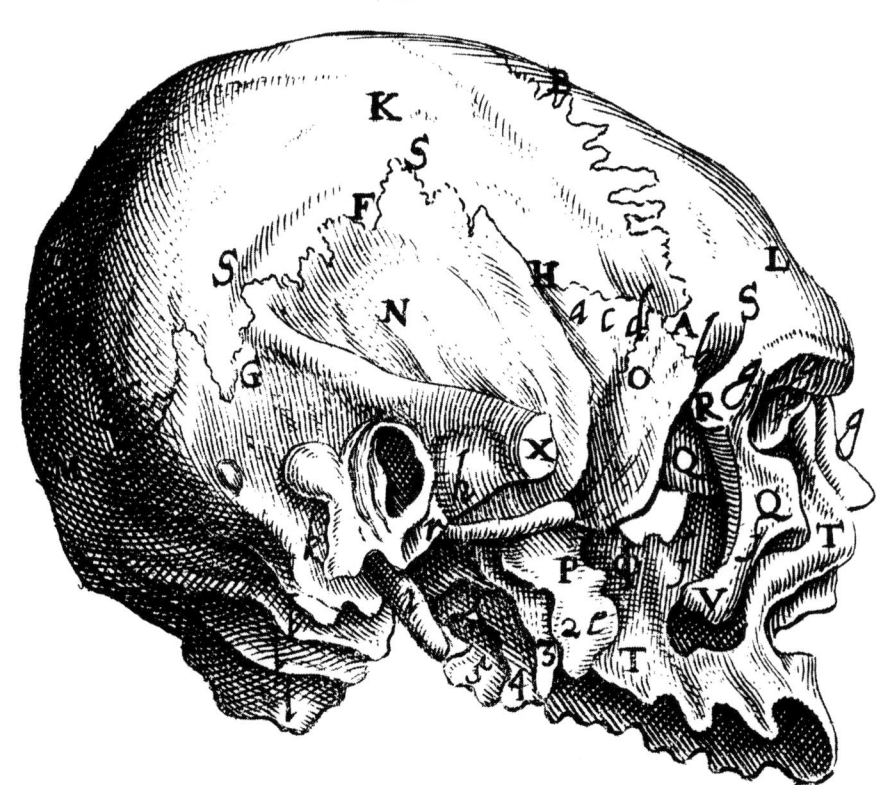

45. Skull fig 6 and 7 by Kaspar Bauhin, 1560–1624

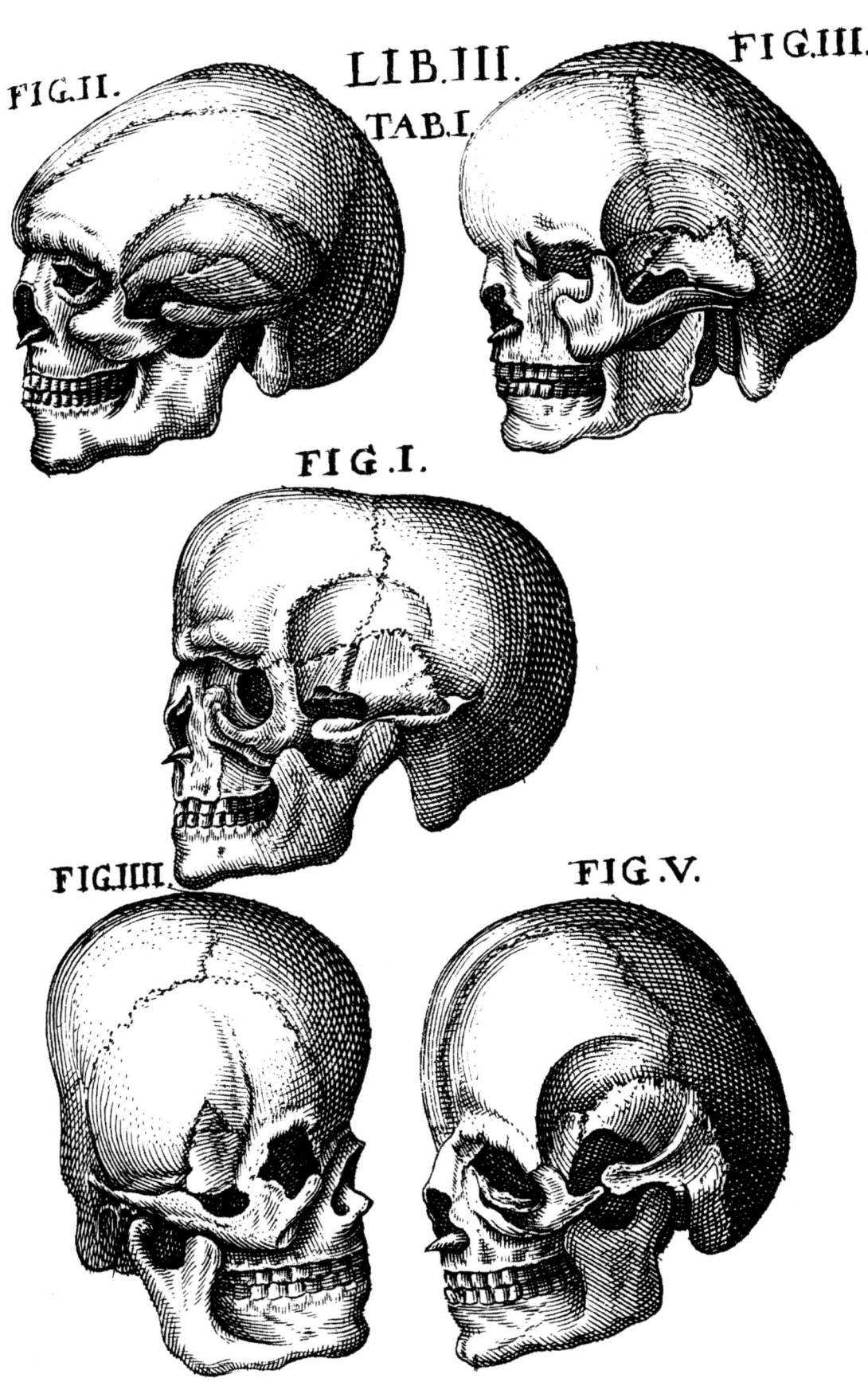

46. Skulls, abnormal by Kaspar Bauhin, 1560–1624

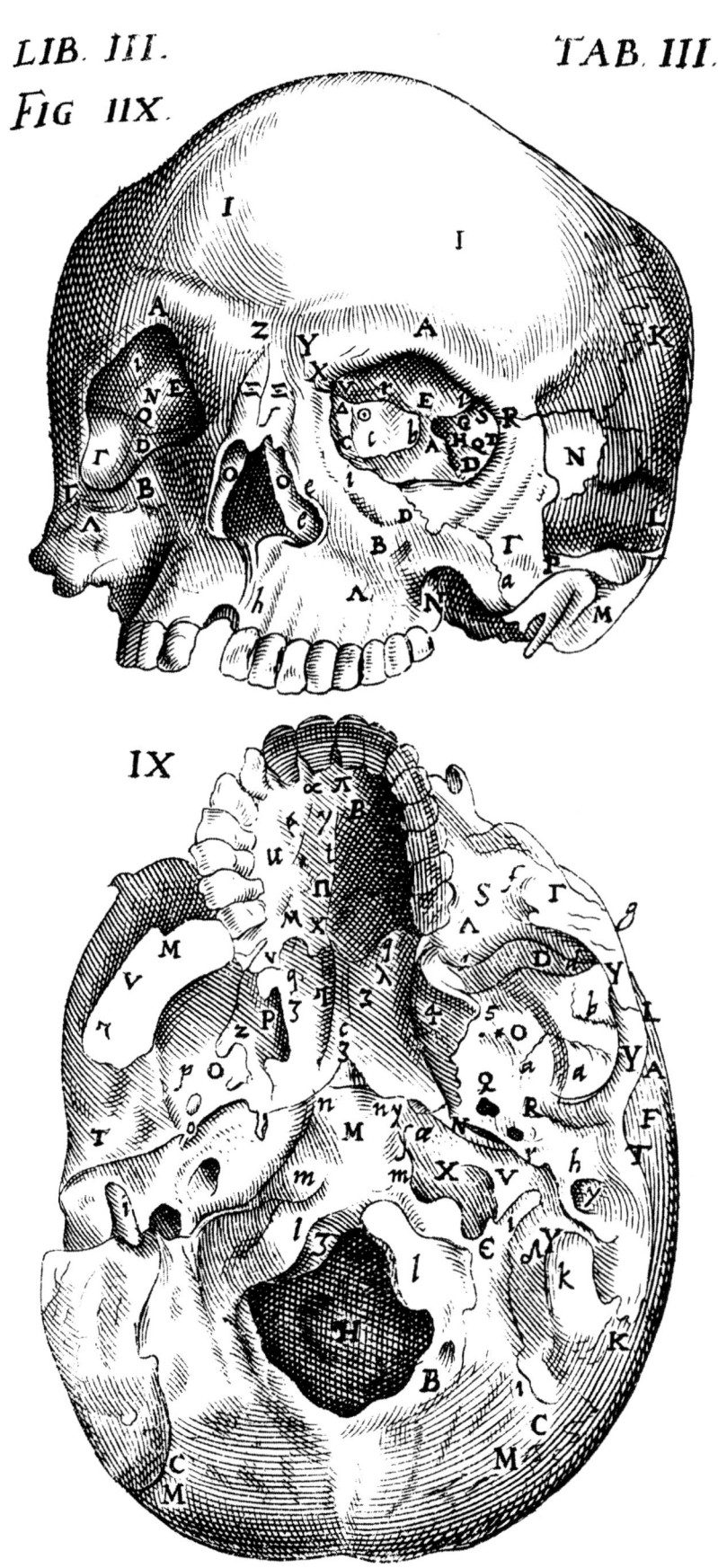

47. Skull fig 8 and 9 by Kaspar Bauhin, 1560–1624

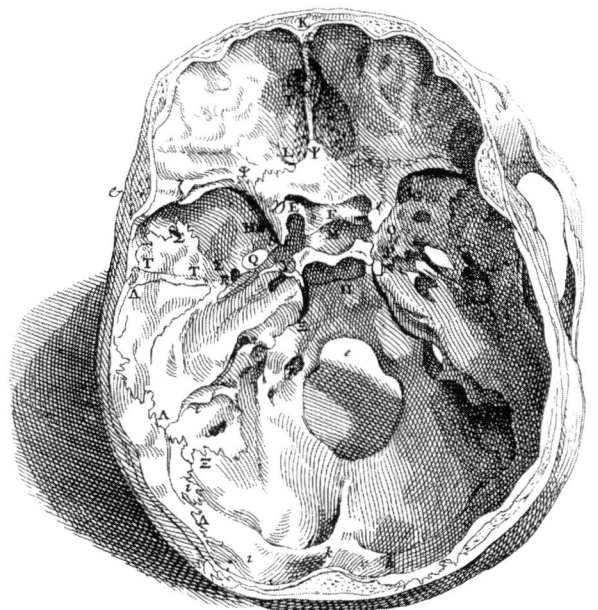
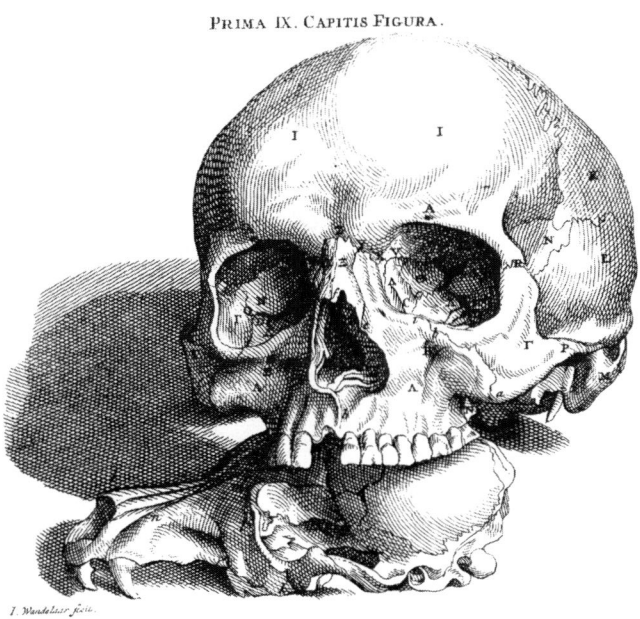
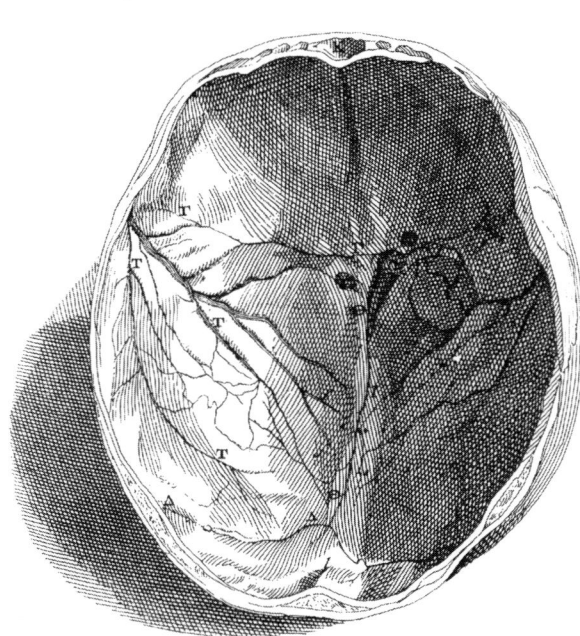
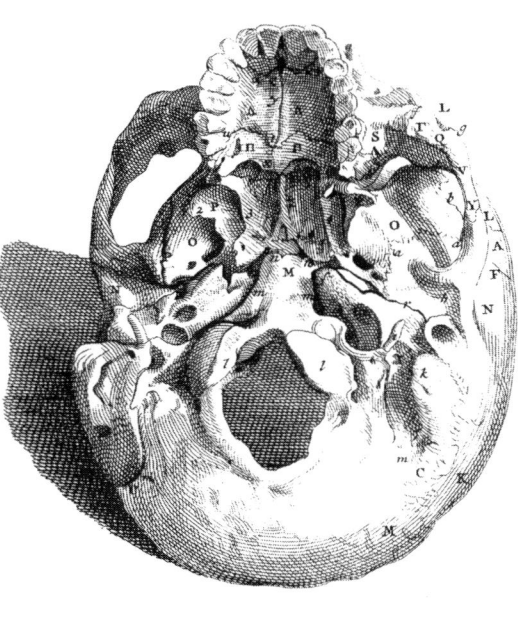

48. Base of skull, skullcap, by Andreas Vesalius, 1514–1564, reprinted 1725

49. Skull of a human and a dog, by Andreas Vesalius, 1514–1564, reprinted 1725

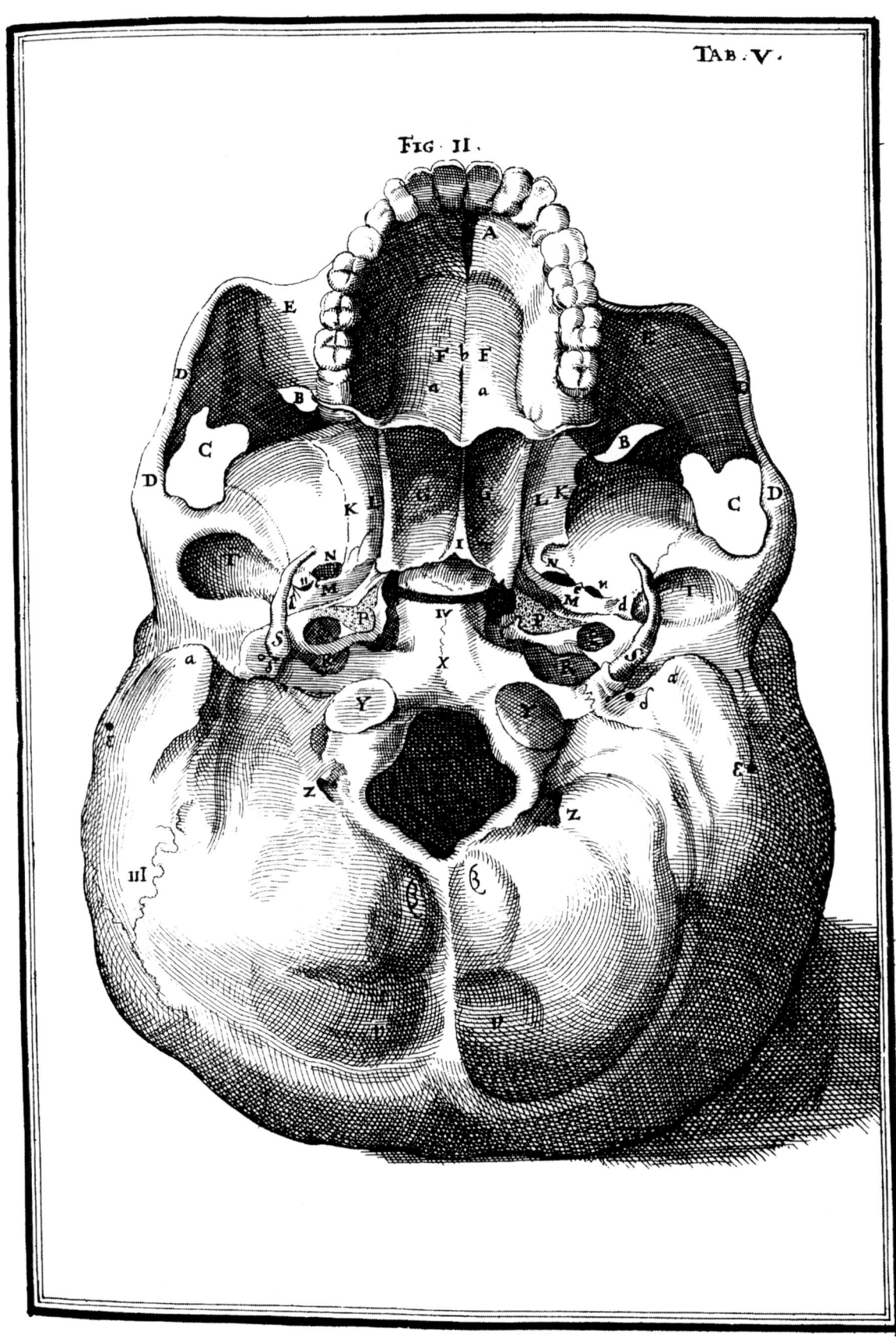

50. Skull and base of skull, tab 4, fig 2, by Adriaan van de Spiegel, engraved by Francesco Valesio, 1631

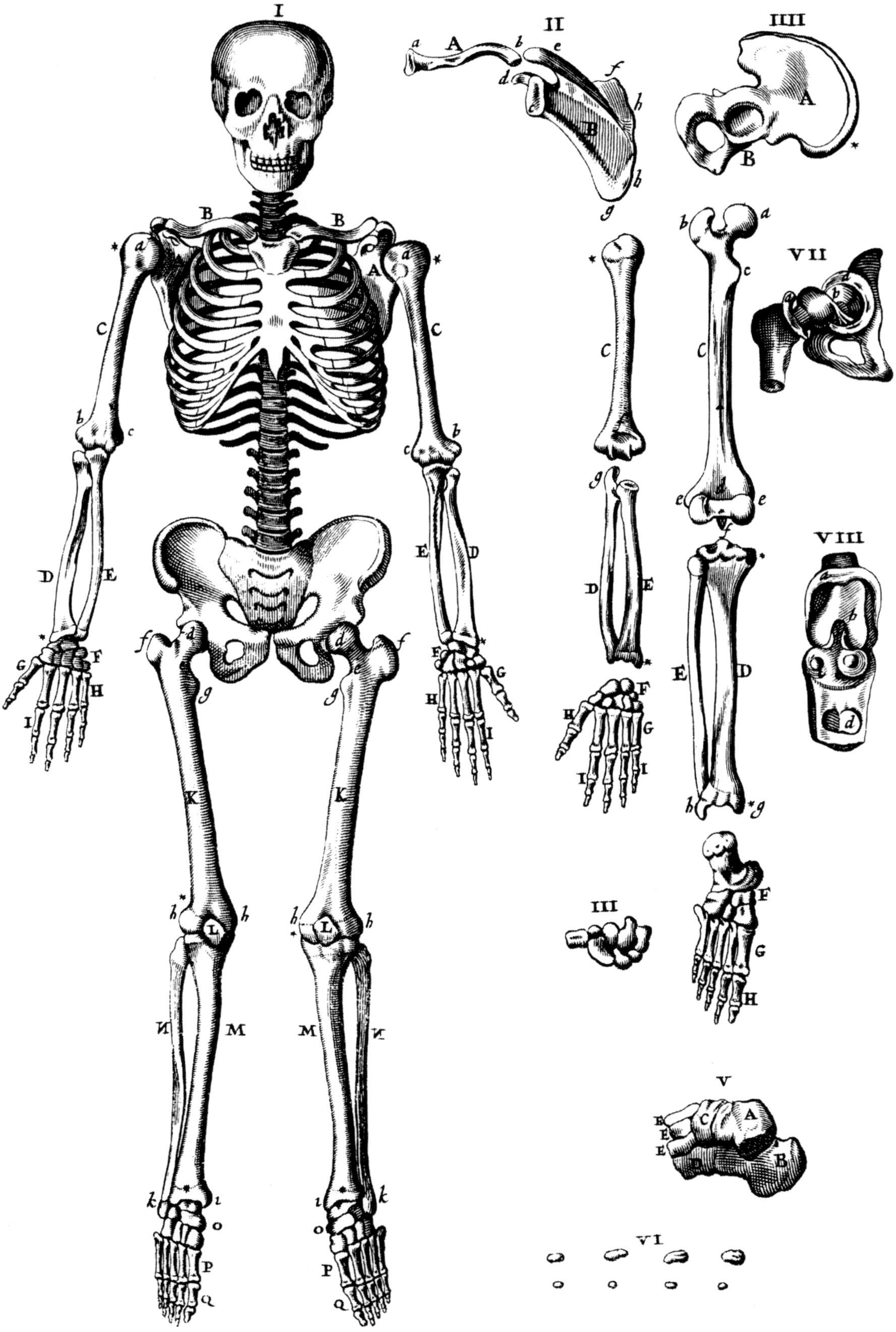

51. Skeleton, by Jean Riolan, 1649

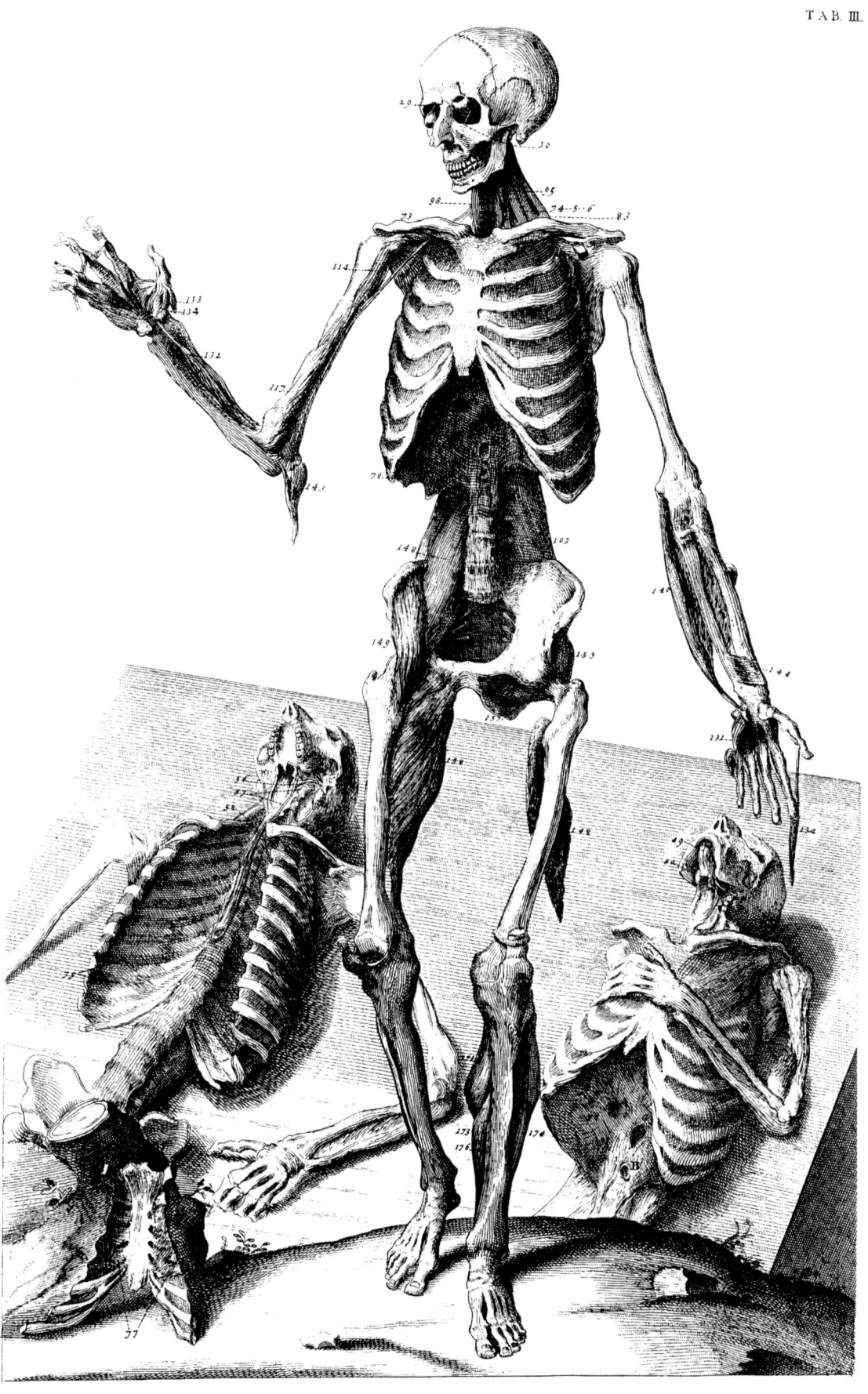

52. Skeleton, Muscles by William Cowper
1666–1709

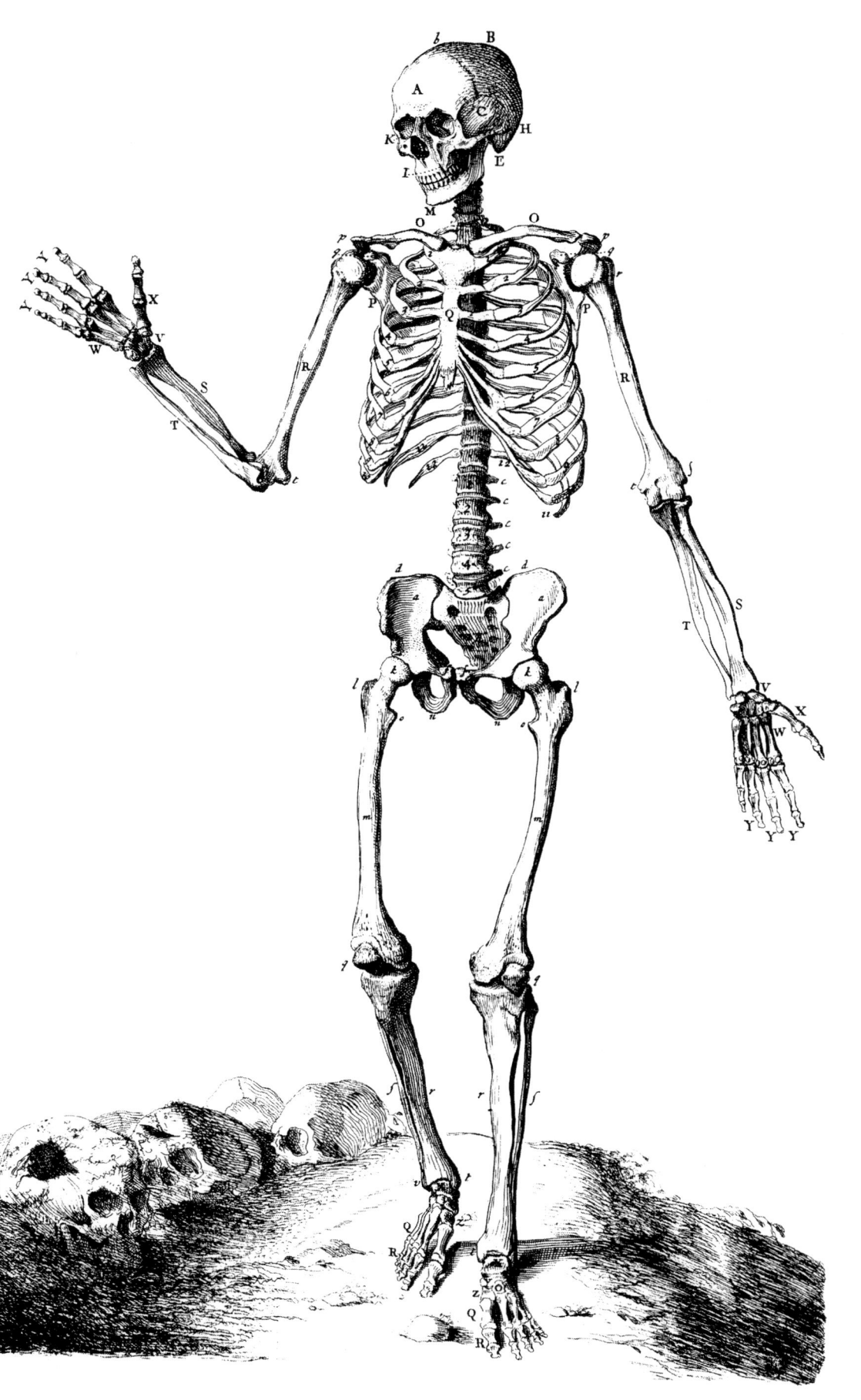

53. Skeleton (2) by William Cowper 1666–1709

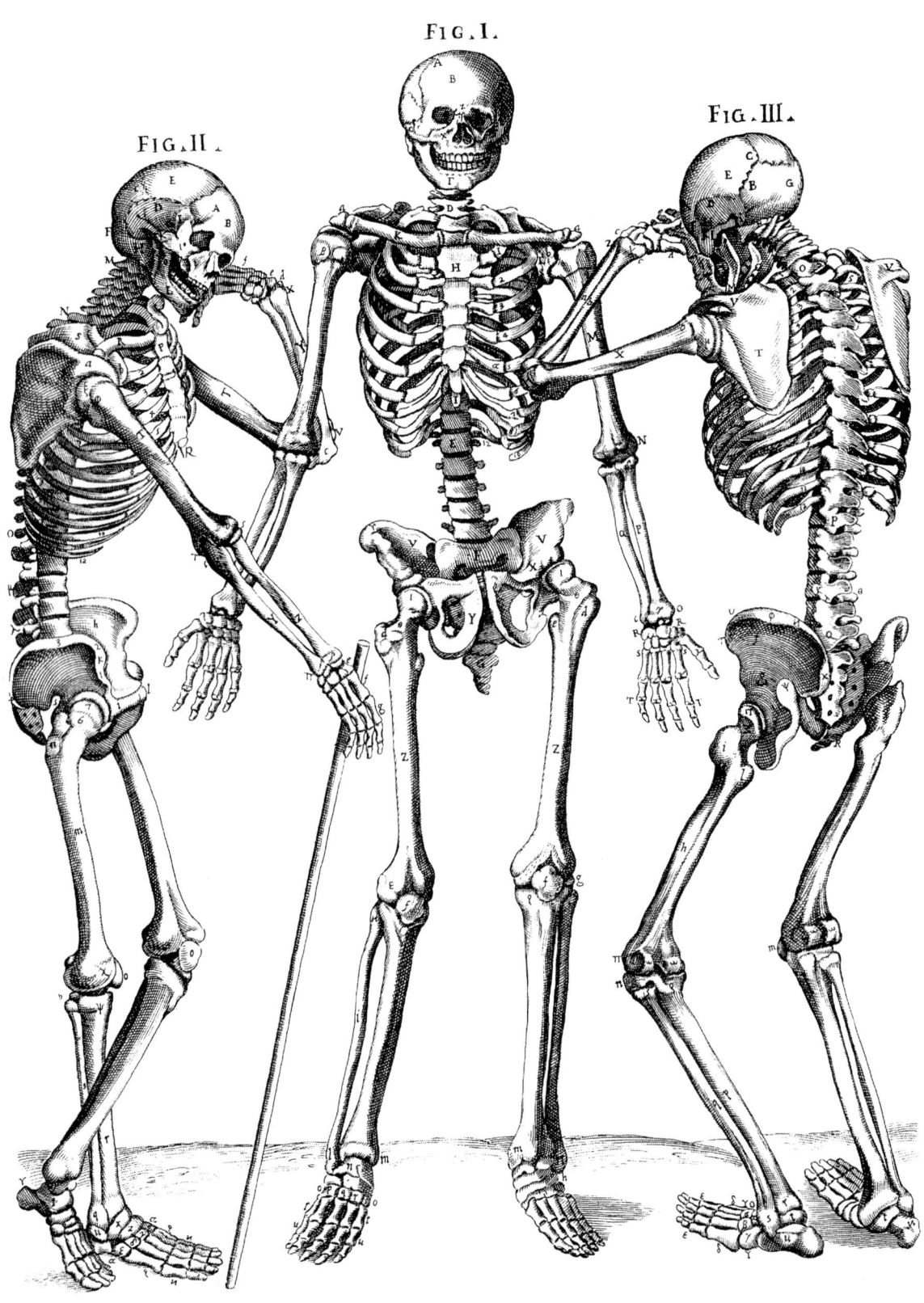

54. Three skeletons by Pietro da Cortona, (1597–1669) 1741

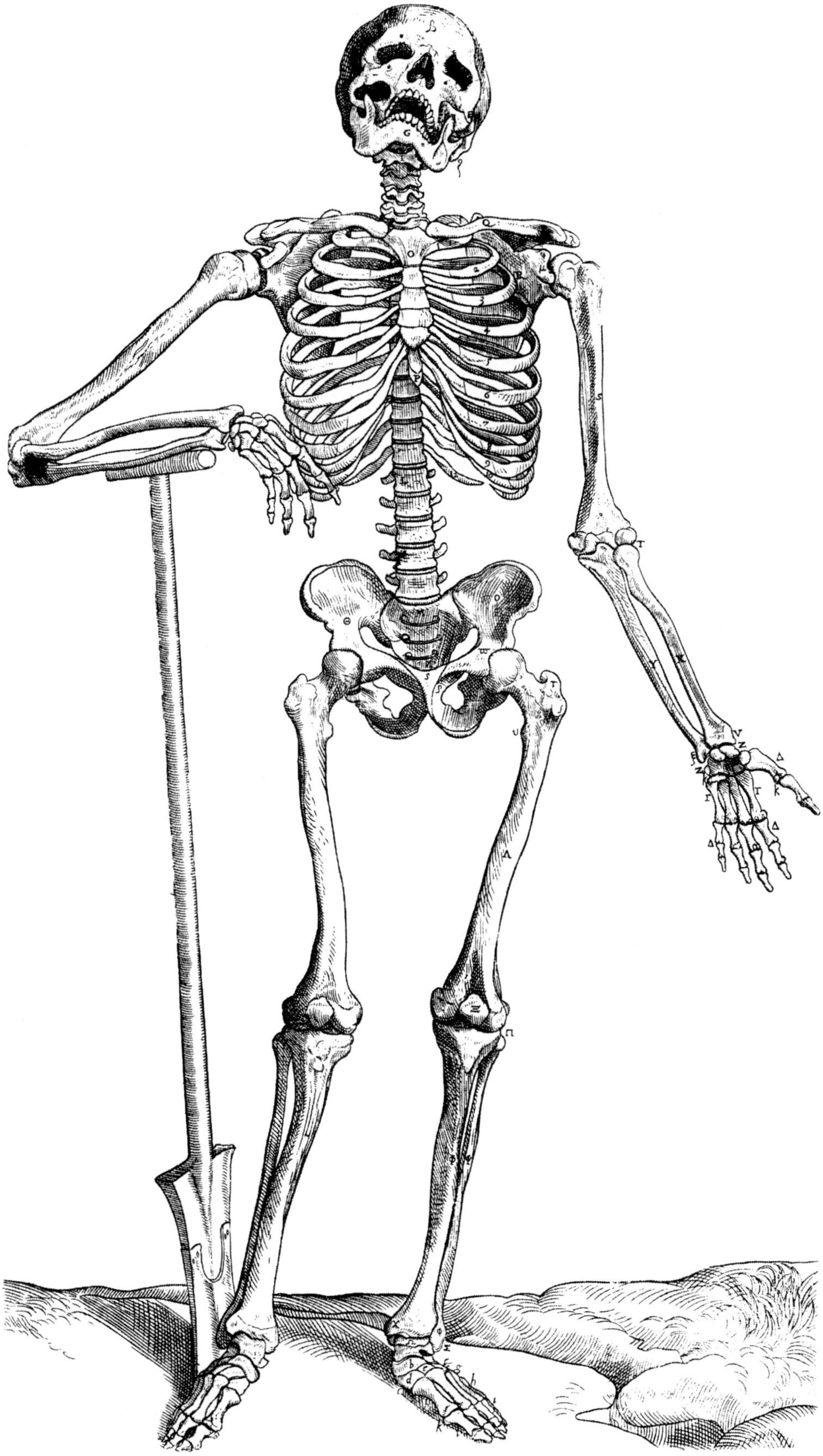

55. Skeleton, tab 1, by Thomas Geminus, d.1562

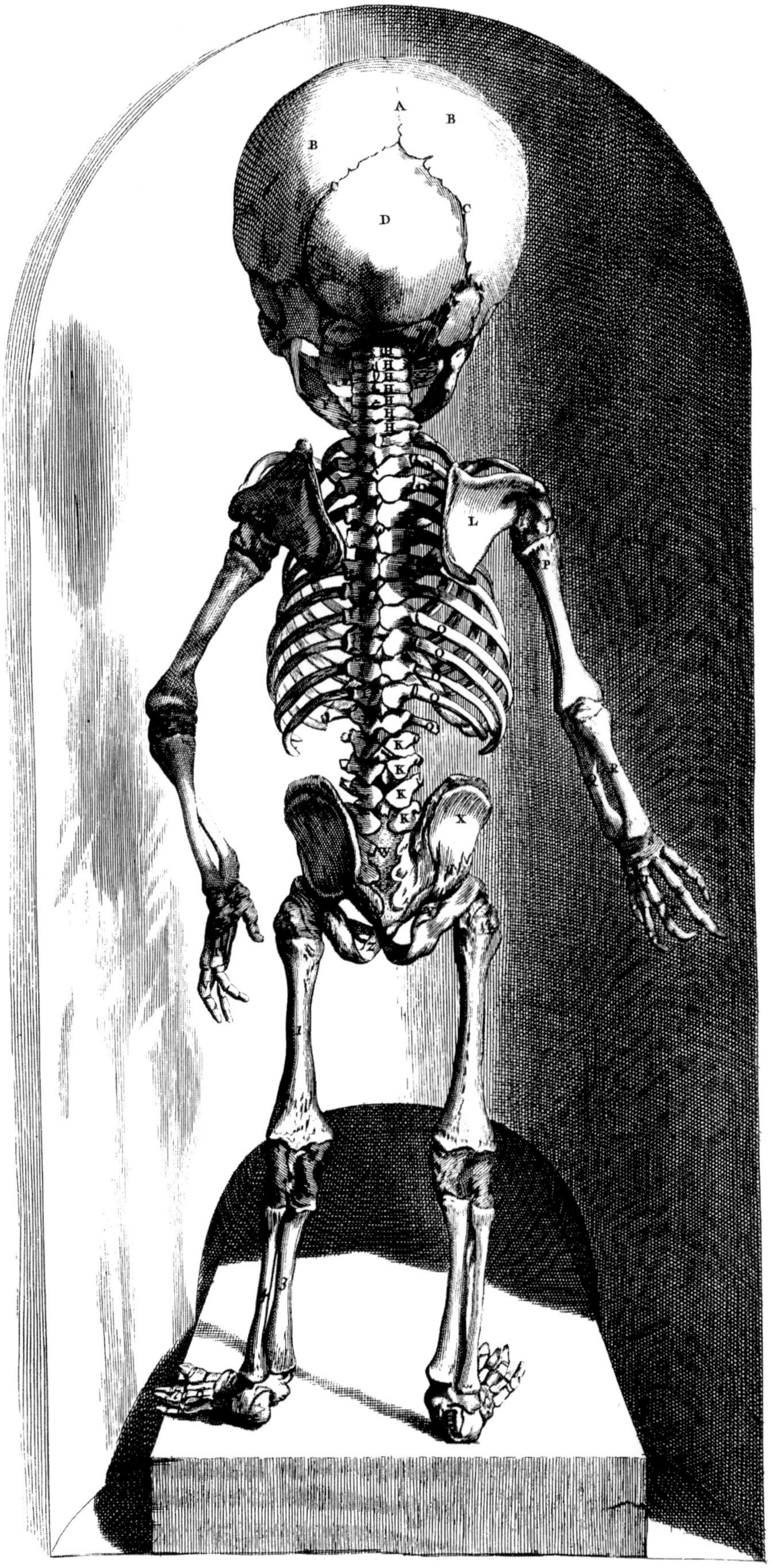

56. Skeleton of a fetus, tab 102, by Govard Bidloo, 1649–1713

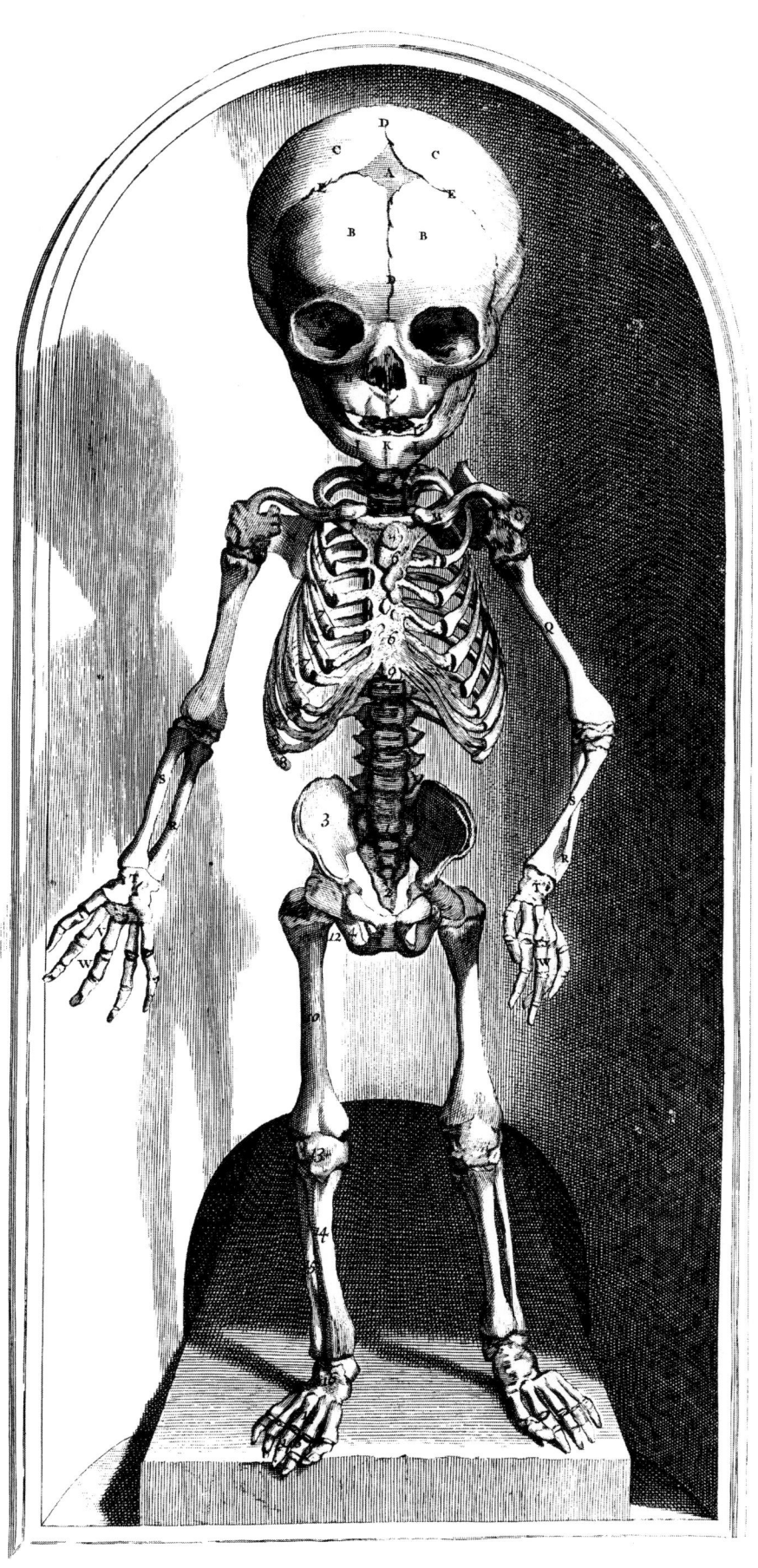

57. Skeleton of a fetus, tab 101, by Govard Bidloo, 1649–1713

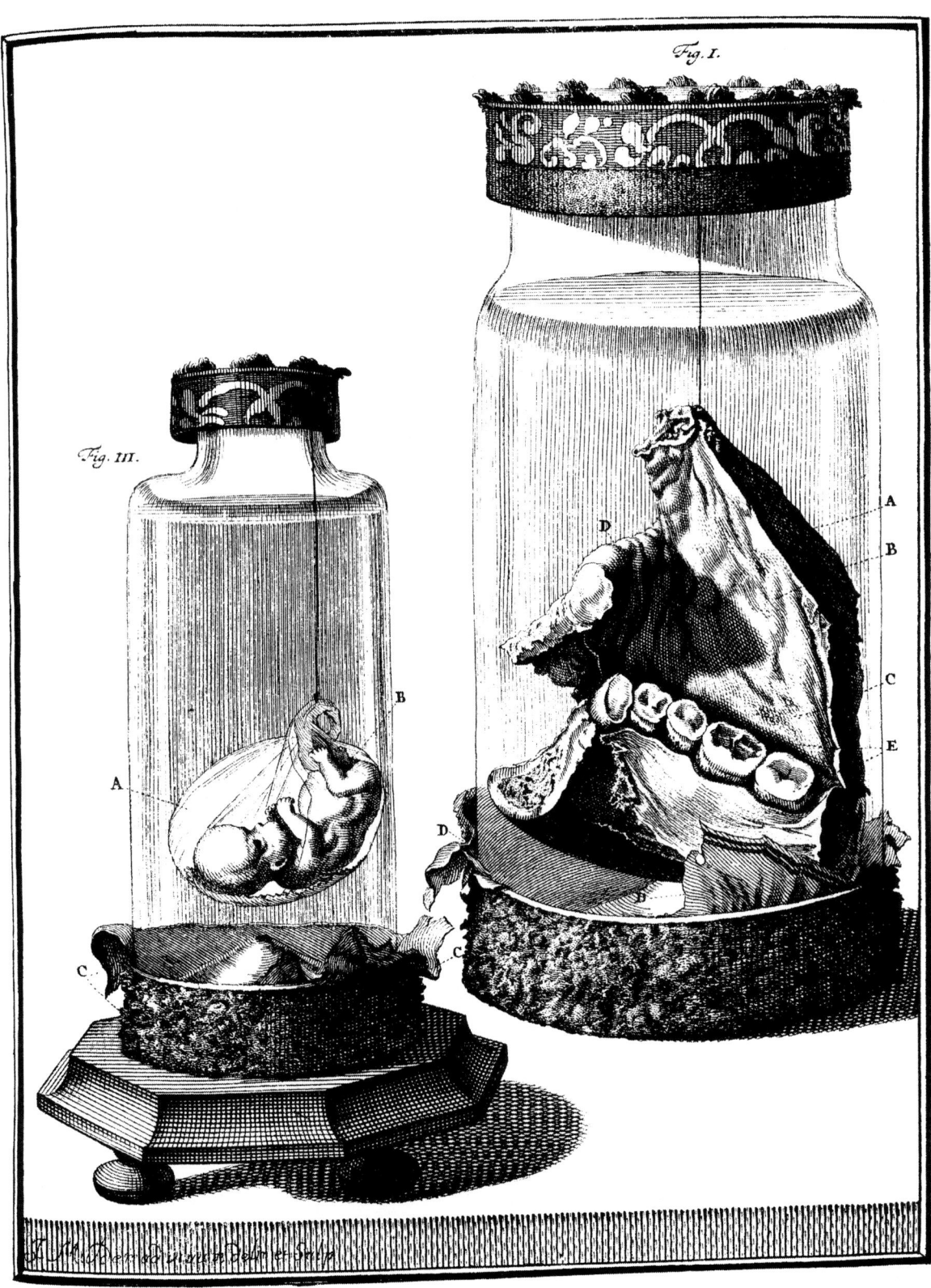

58. Jar containing a mandible, jar containing a human fetus, buccal epithelium Jar containing a mandible, by Frederik Ruysch 1638–1731

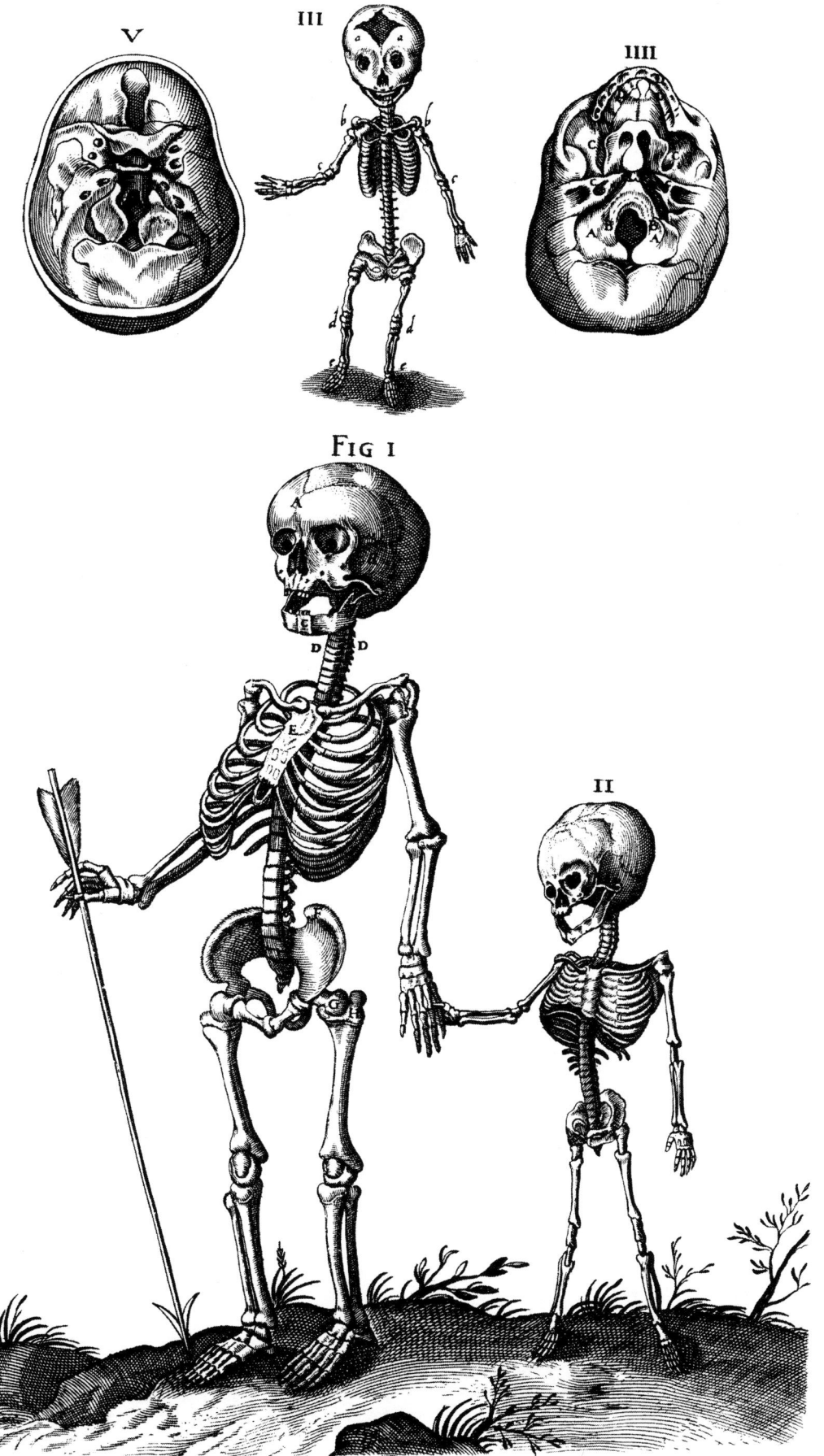

59. Skeleton and skull of the child by Andrãe Du Laurens 1558–1609, published 1627

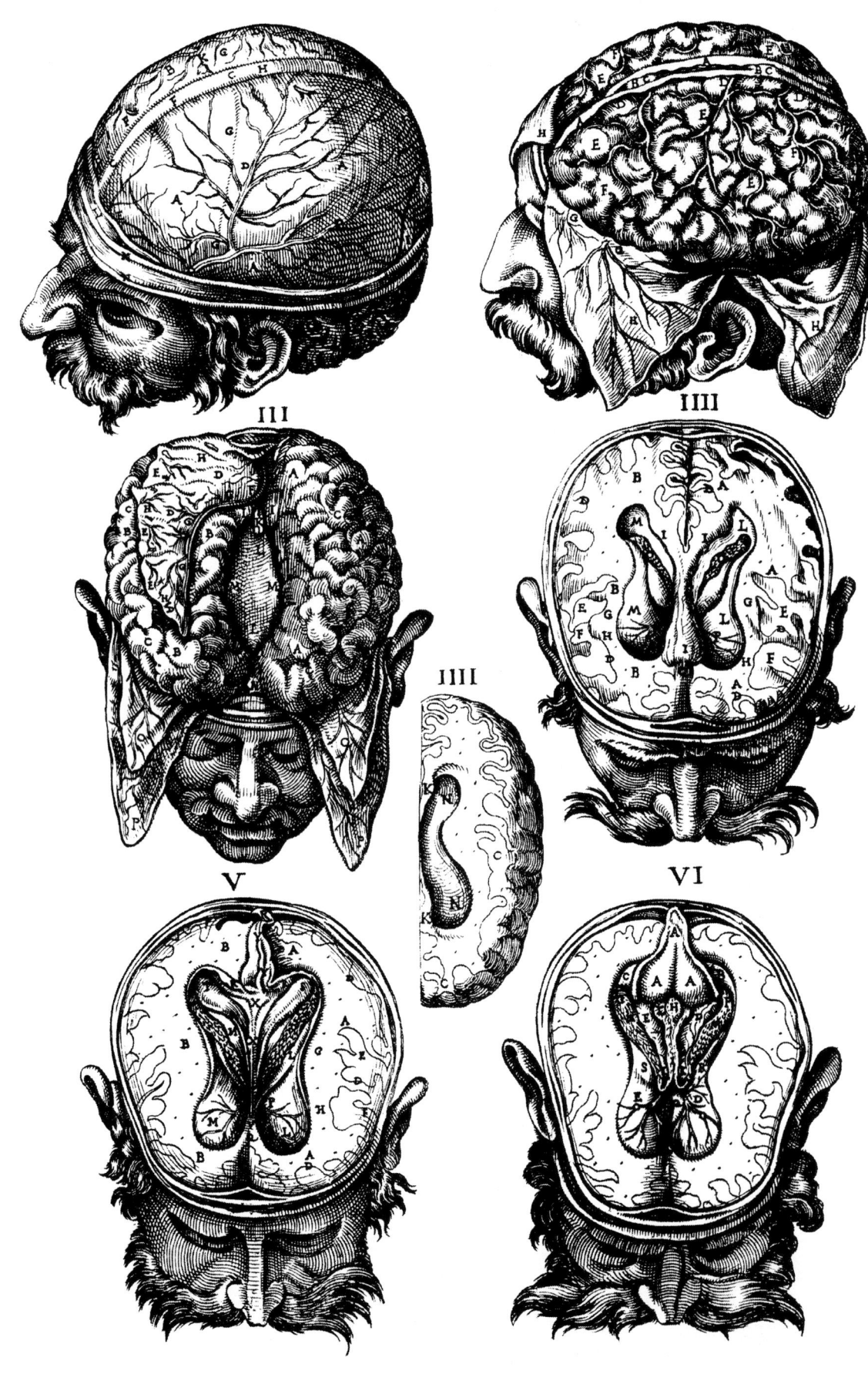

60. Dissection of the brain, fig 9,10,11,12 by Thomas Geminus, d.1562

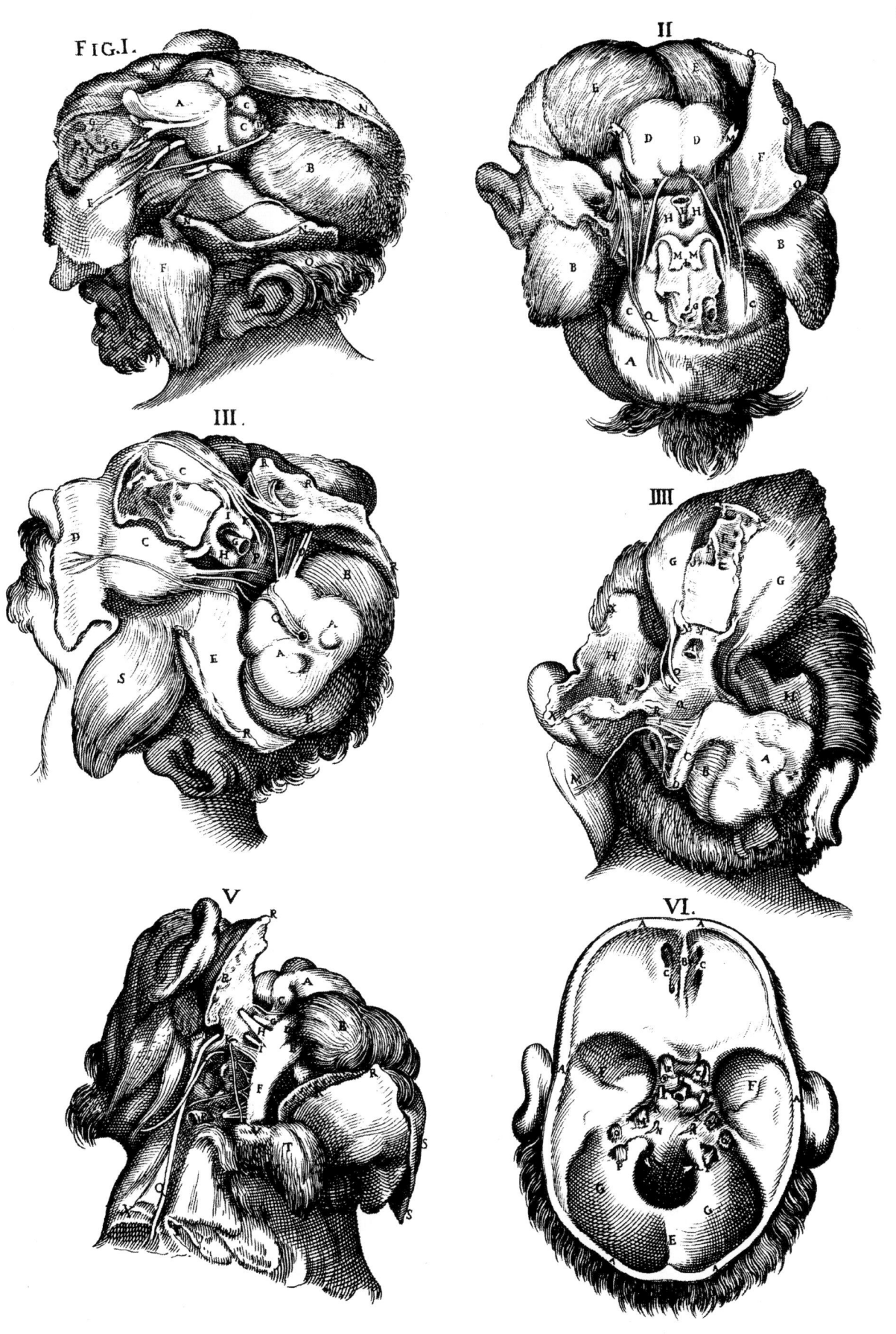

61. Images of heads from different angles by Pietro da Cortona, (1597–1669) 1741

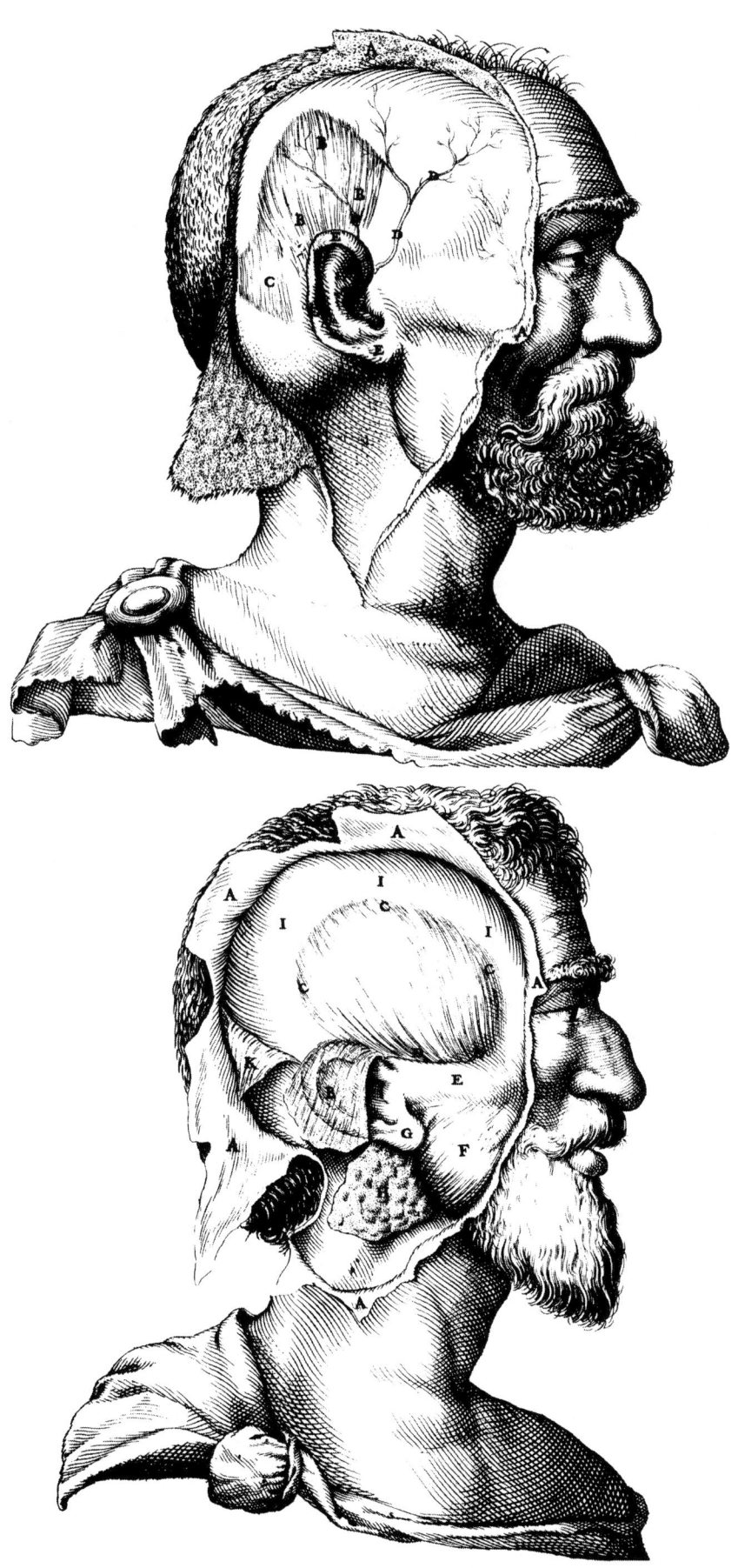

62. Dissection of the brain, fig 9,10,11,12 by Thomas Geminus, d.1562

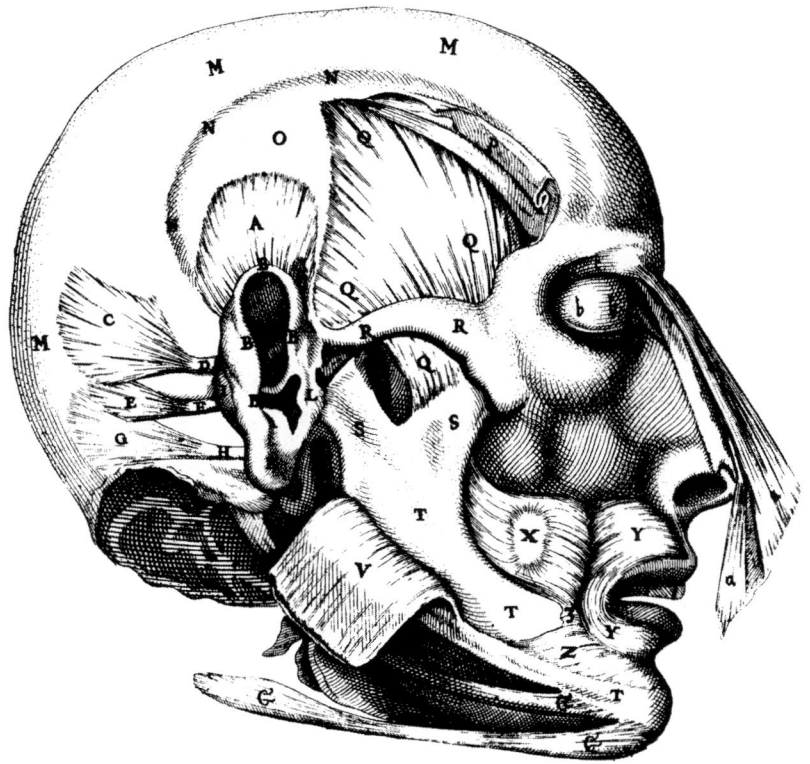

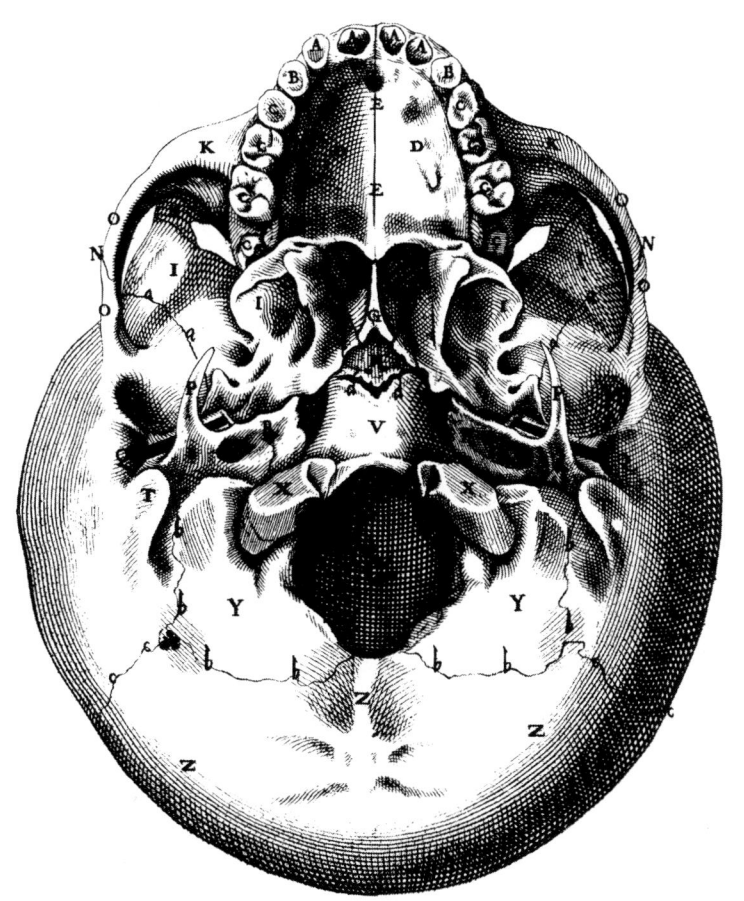

63. Images of heads from different angles by Pietro da Cortona, (1597–1669) 1741

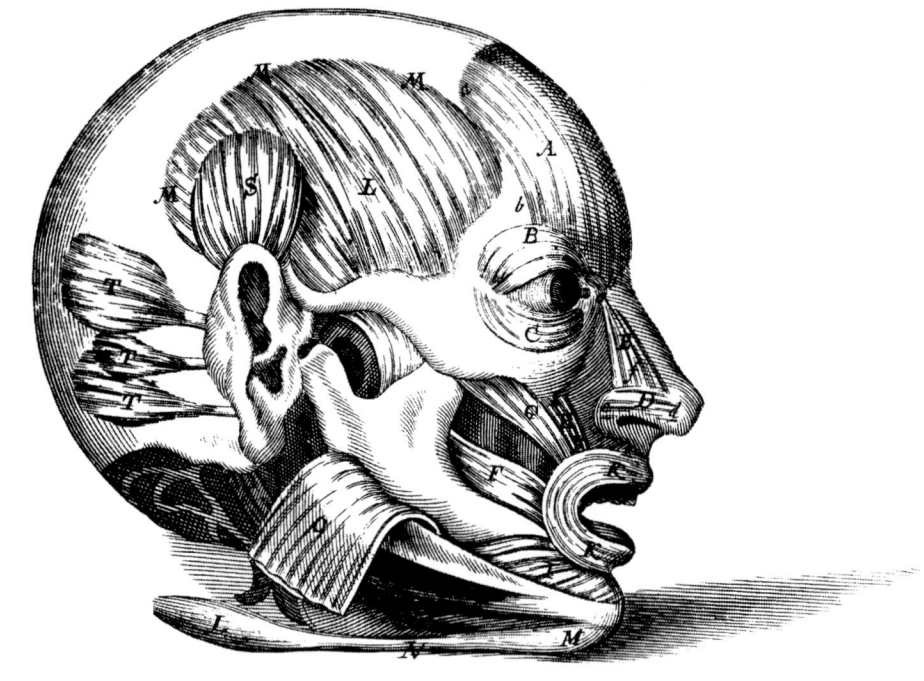

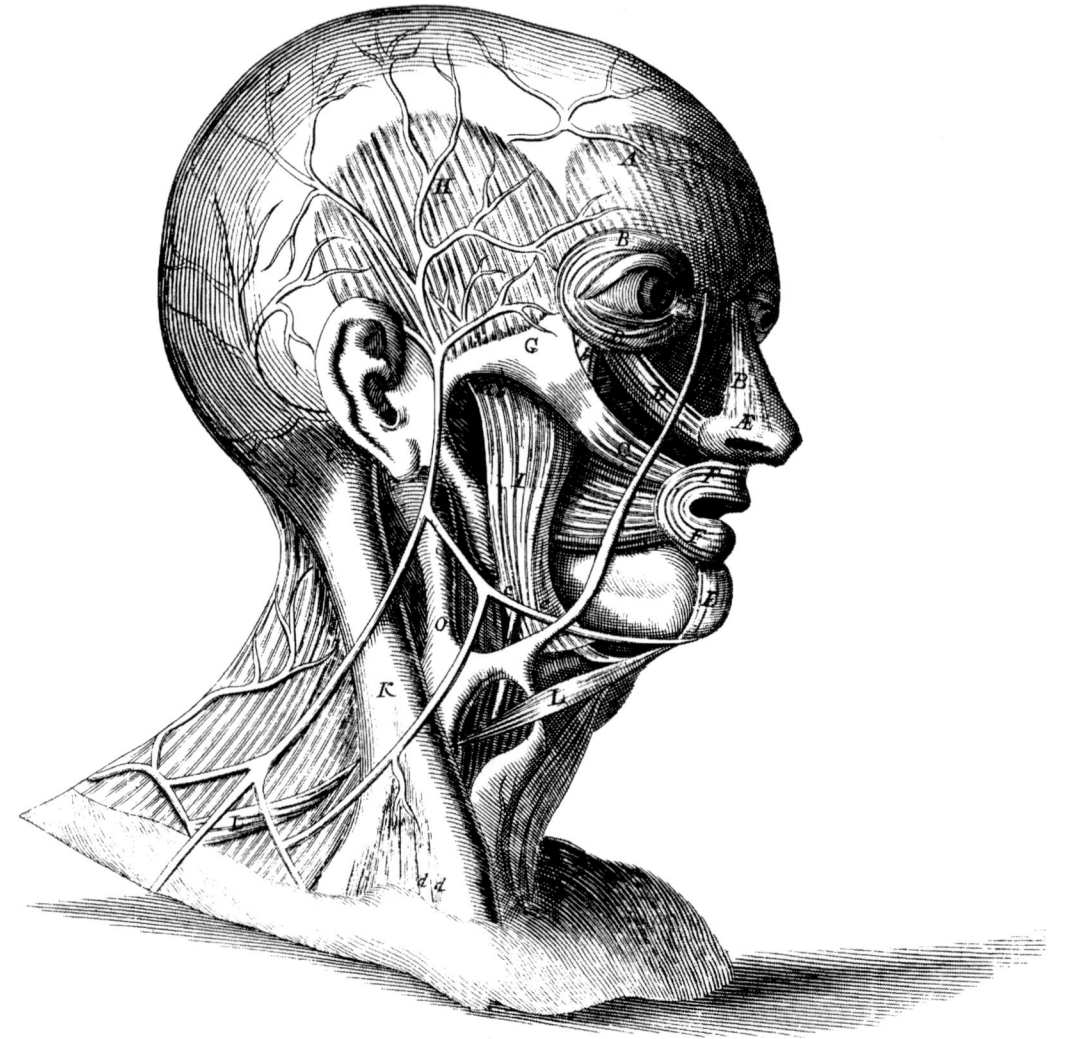

64. Facial muscles, masticatory muscles by John Browne 1642–ca. 1700

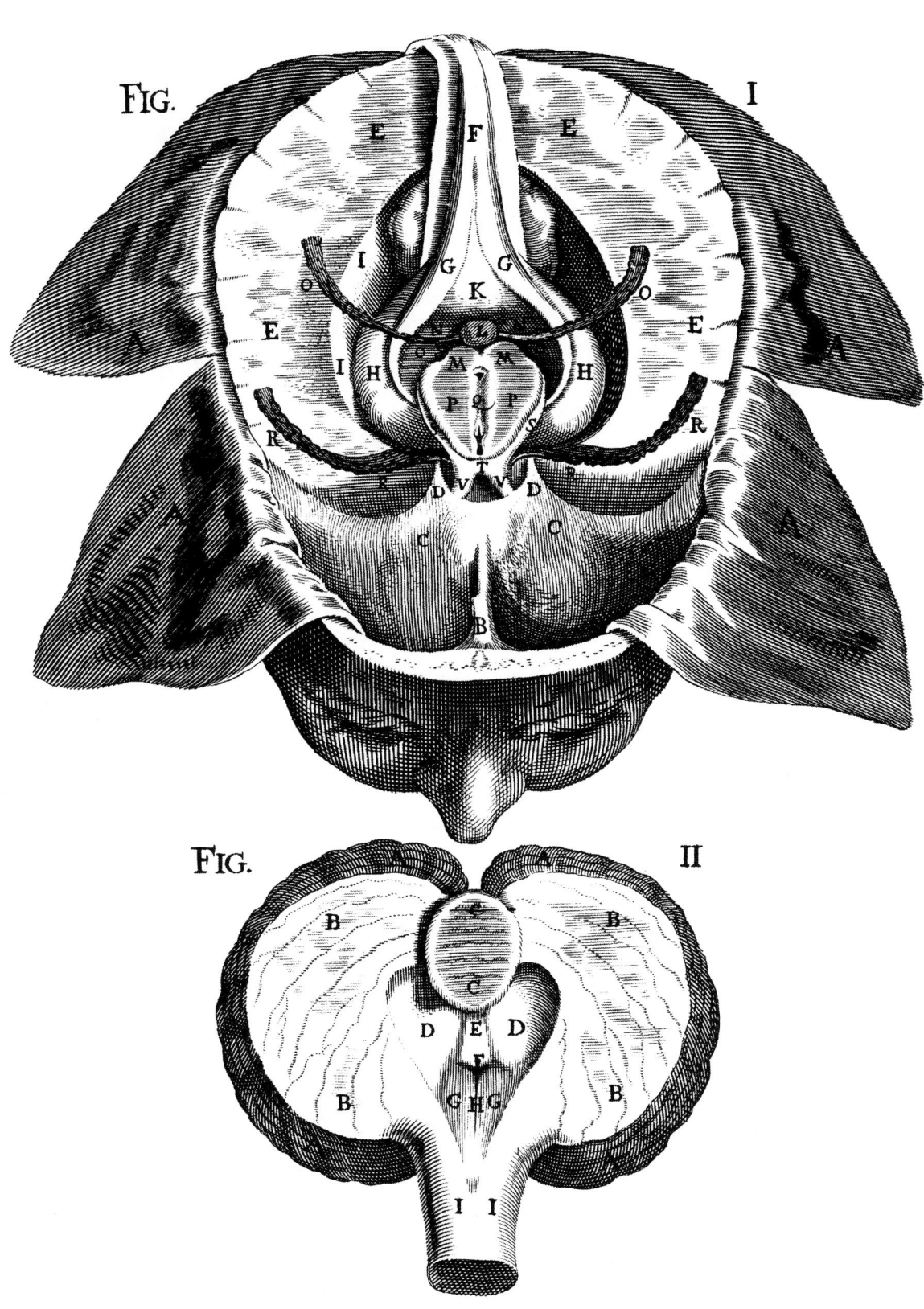

65. Dissection of the brain, fig 1, 2, by Jean Riolan, 1649

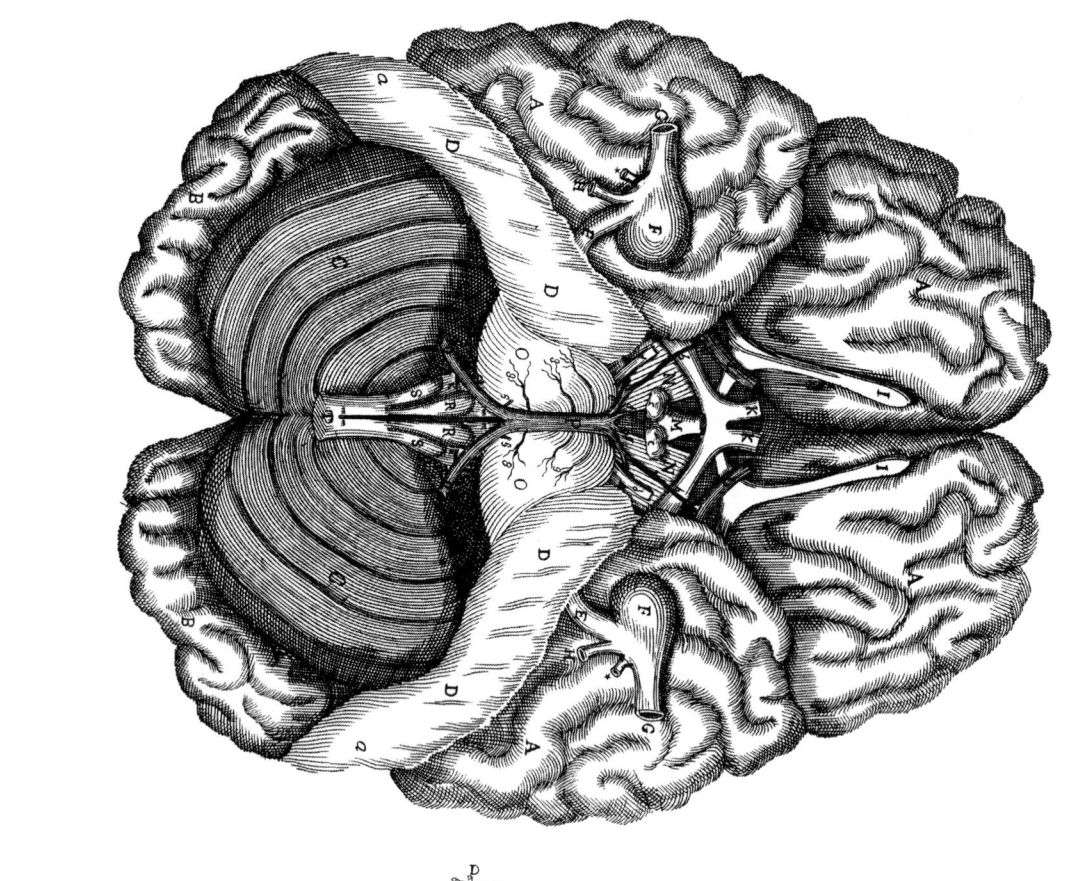

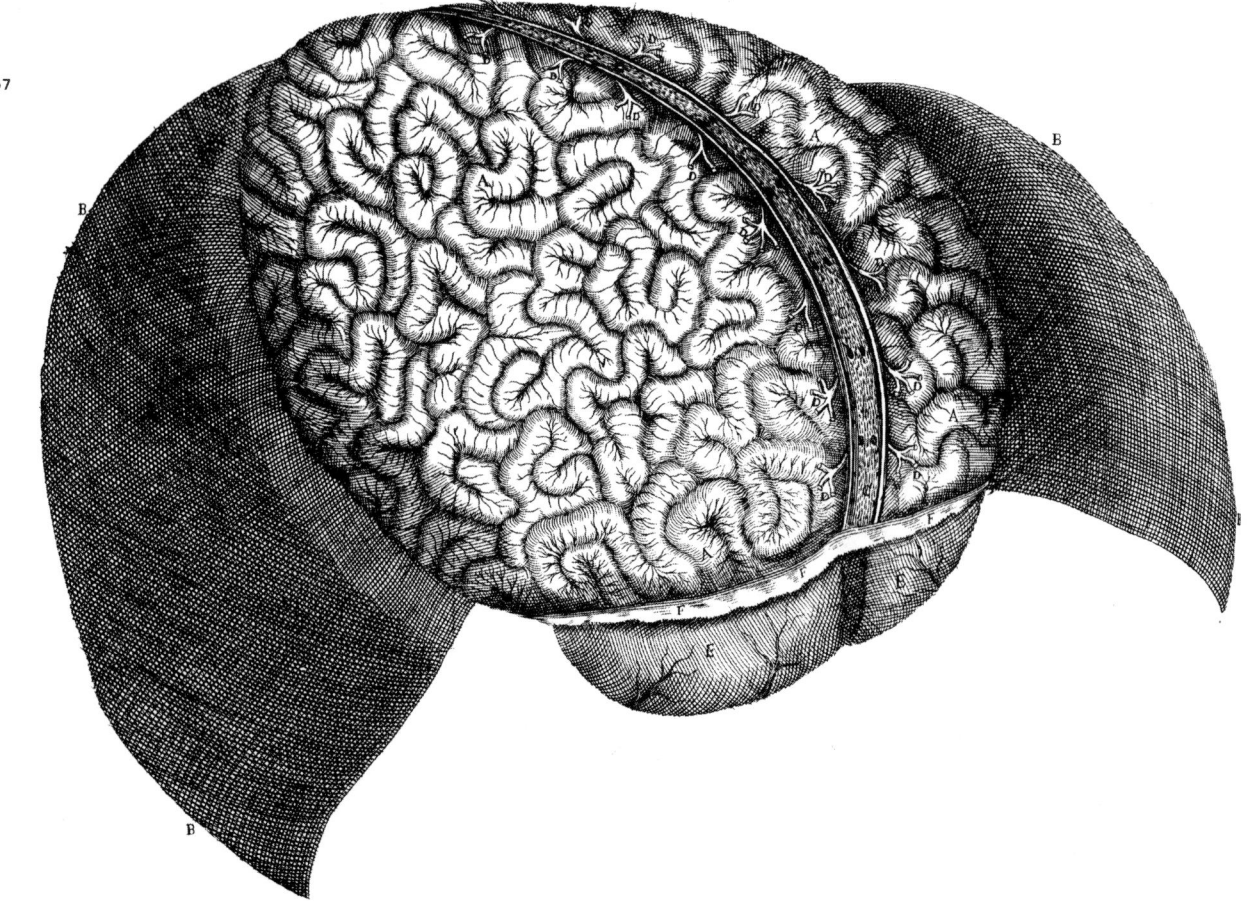

66. Dissection of the brain, Tab 4, by Raymond Vieussens, engravings by Beaudeau, 1685

67. Dissection of the brain, Tab 2, by Raymond Vieussens, engravings by Beaudeau, 1685

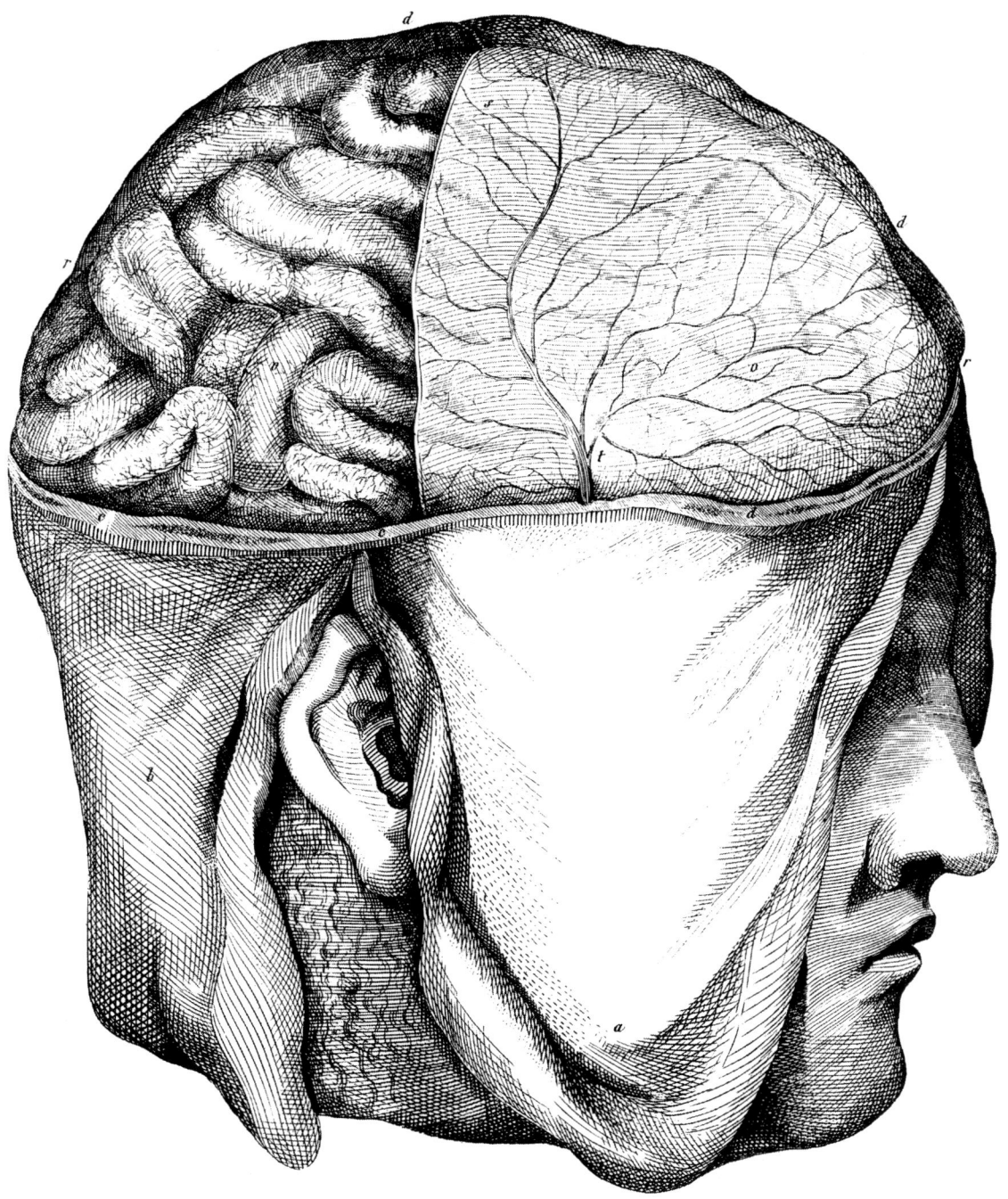

68. Dissection of the head and brain, Plate 1, by Fdelix Vicq-d'Azyr (1748–1794).

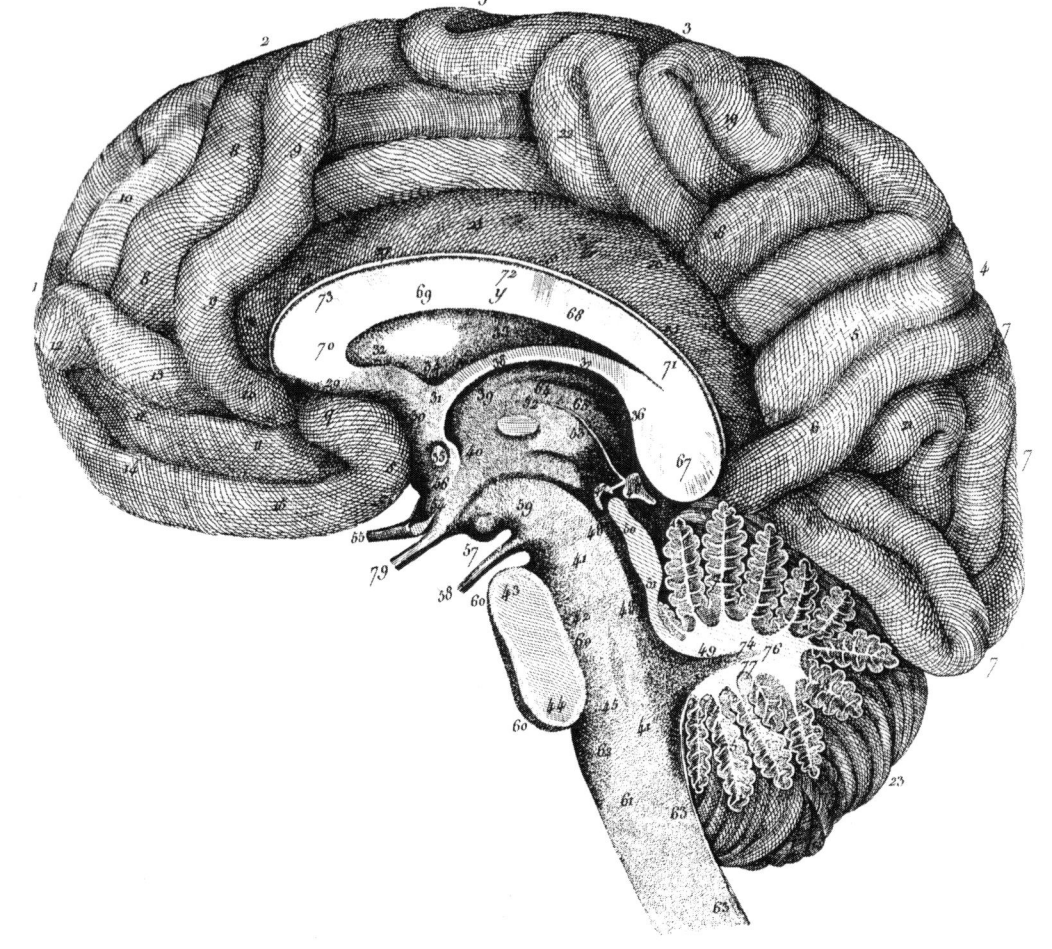

69. Dissection of the brain, Tab 5, by Raymond Vieussens, engravings by Beaudeau, 1685

70. Brain, Fig 1, by Fdelix Vicq-d'Azyr (1748–1794)

71. Brain, Fig 22, by Fdelix Vicq-d'Azyr (1748–1794)

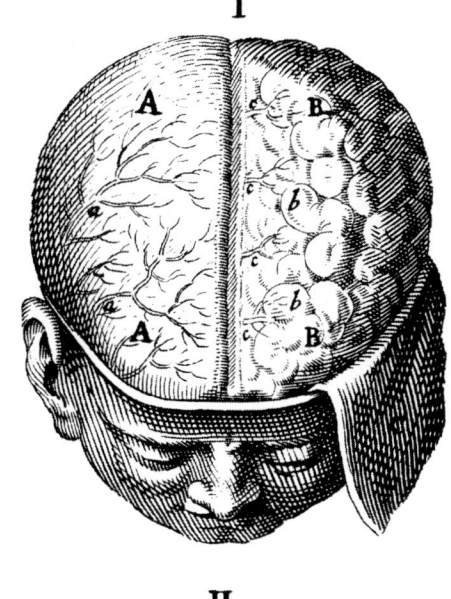
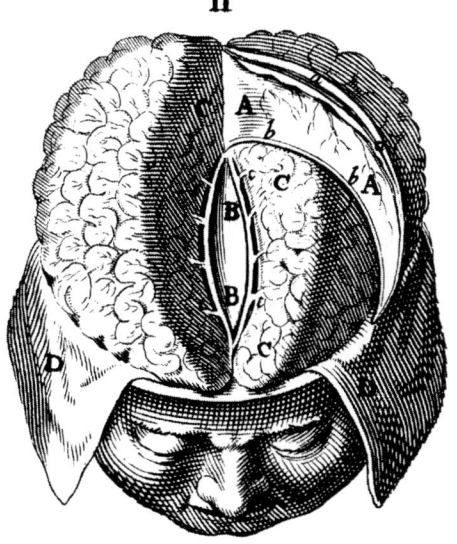
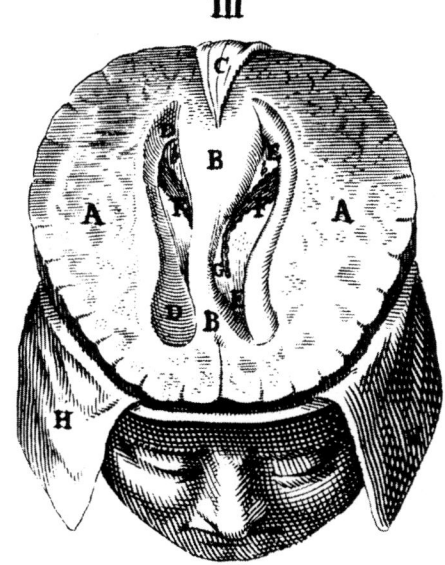
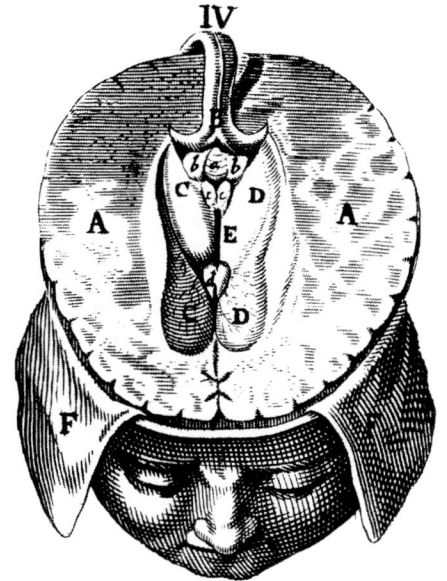
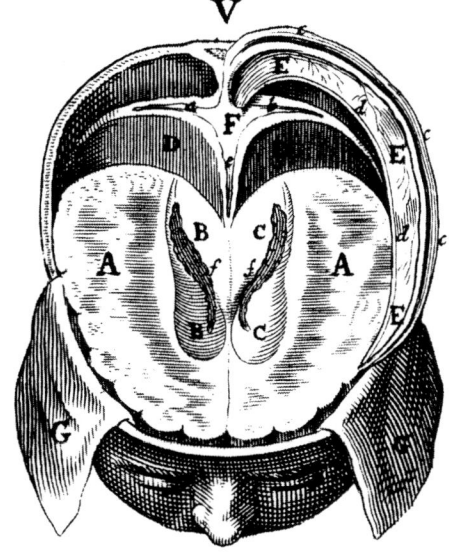
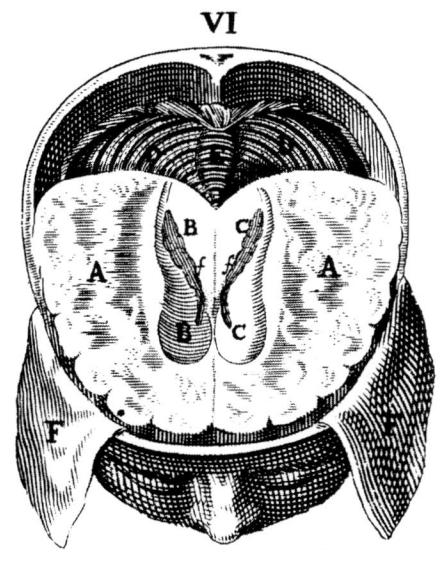

72. Six figures showing cross sections of the brain.

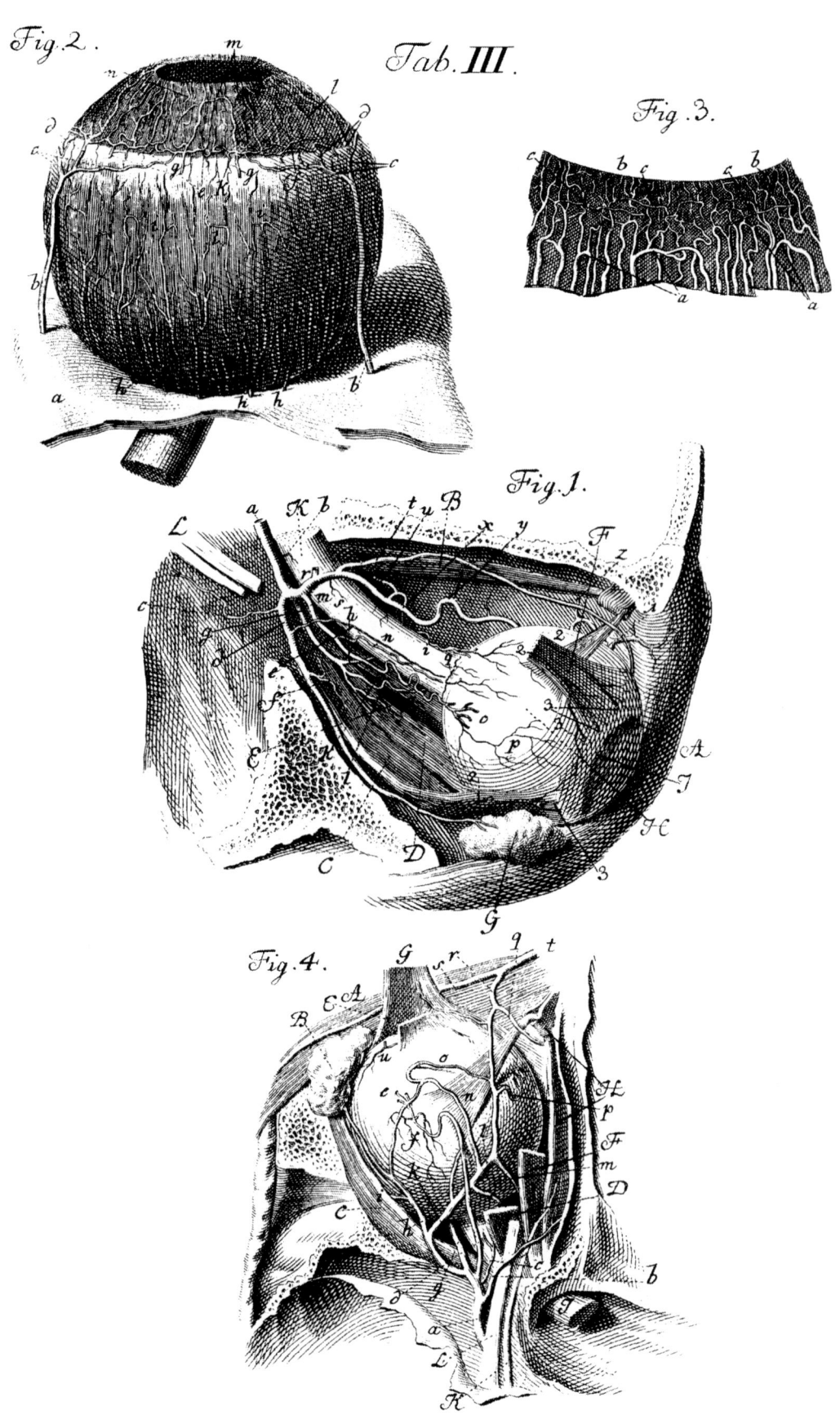

73. Dissection of the eye by Johann Gottfried Zinn, 1727–1759

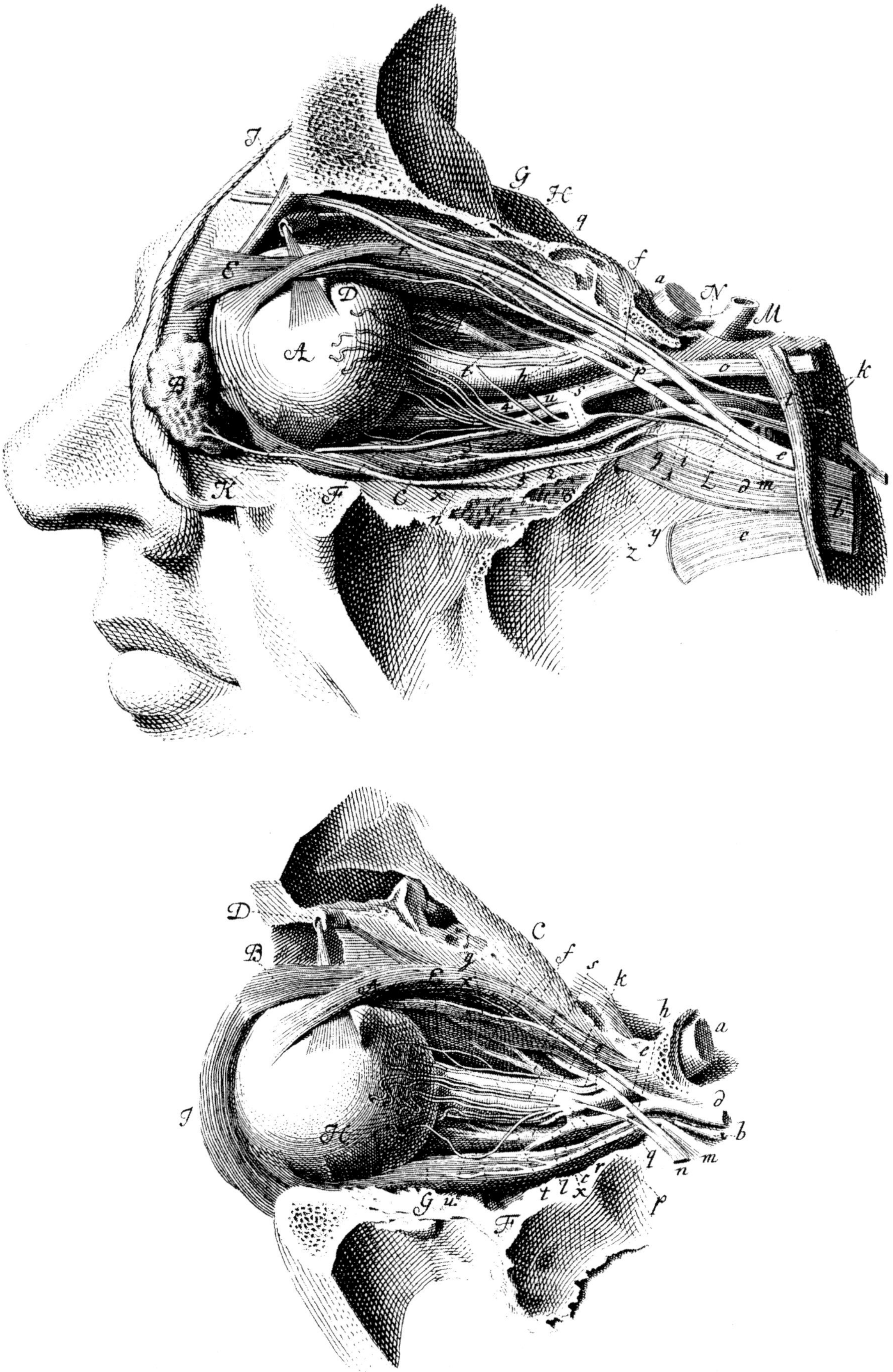

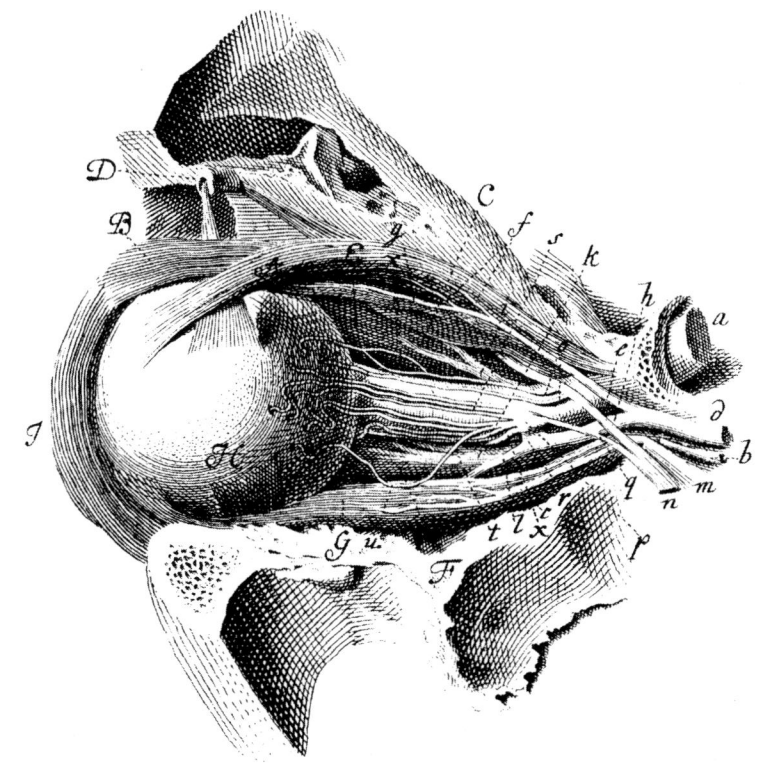

74. Dissection of the eye and skull; optic nerve, oculomotor muscles by Johann Gottfried Zinn, 1727–1759

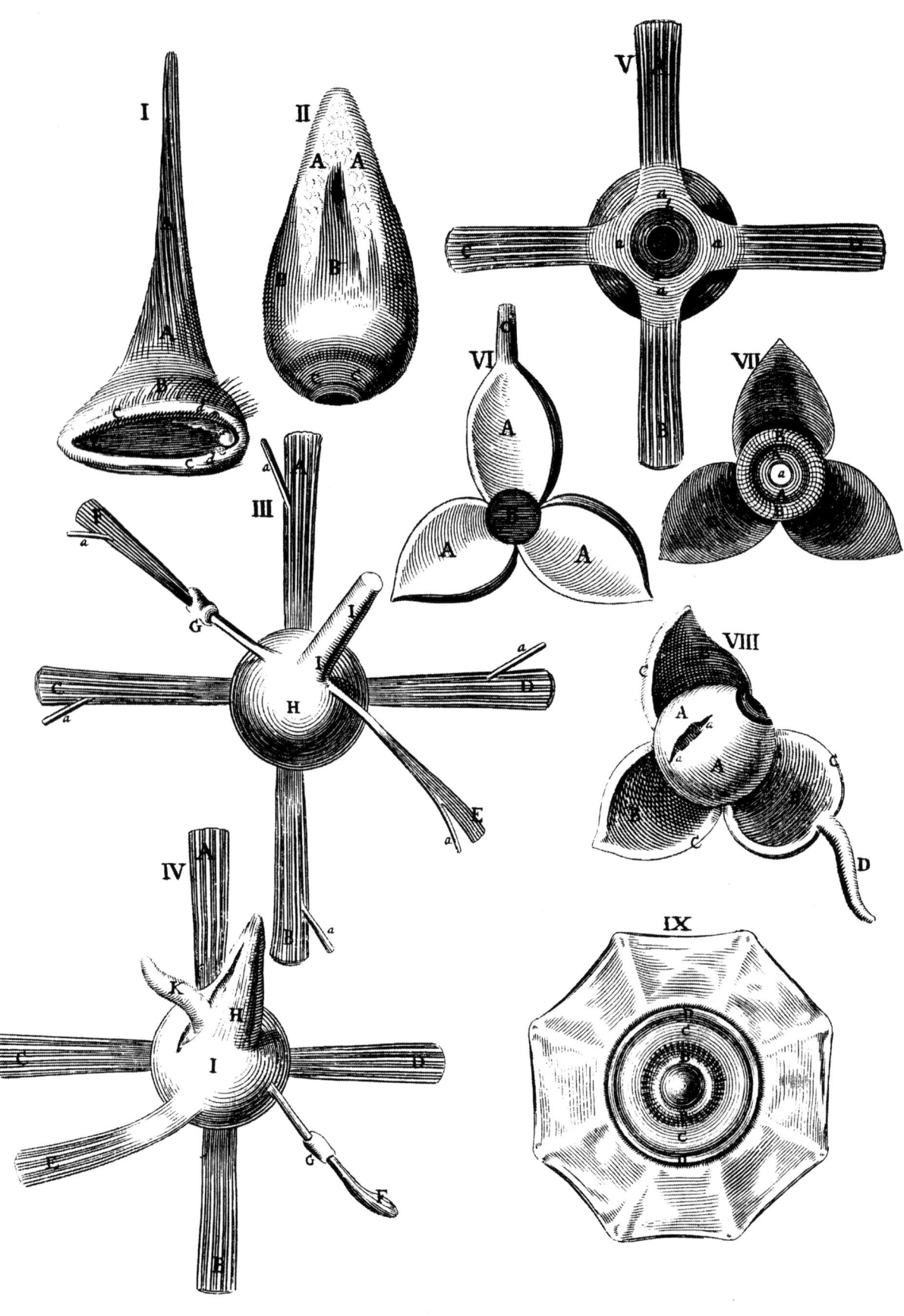

75. Eye, by Jean Riolan, 1649

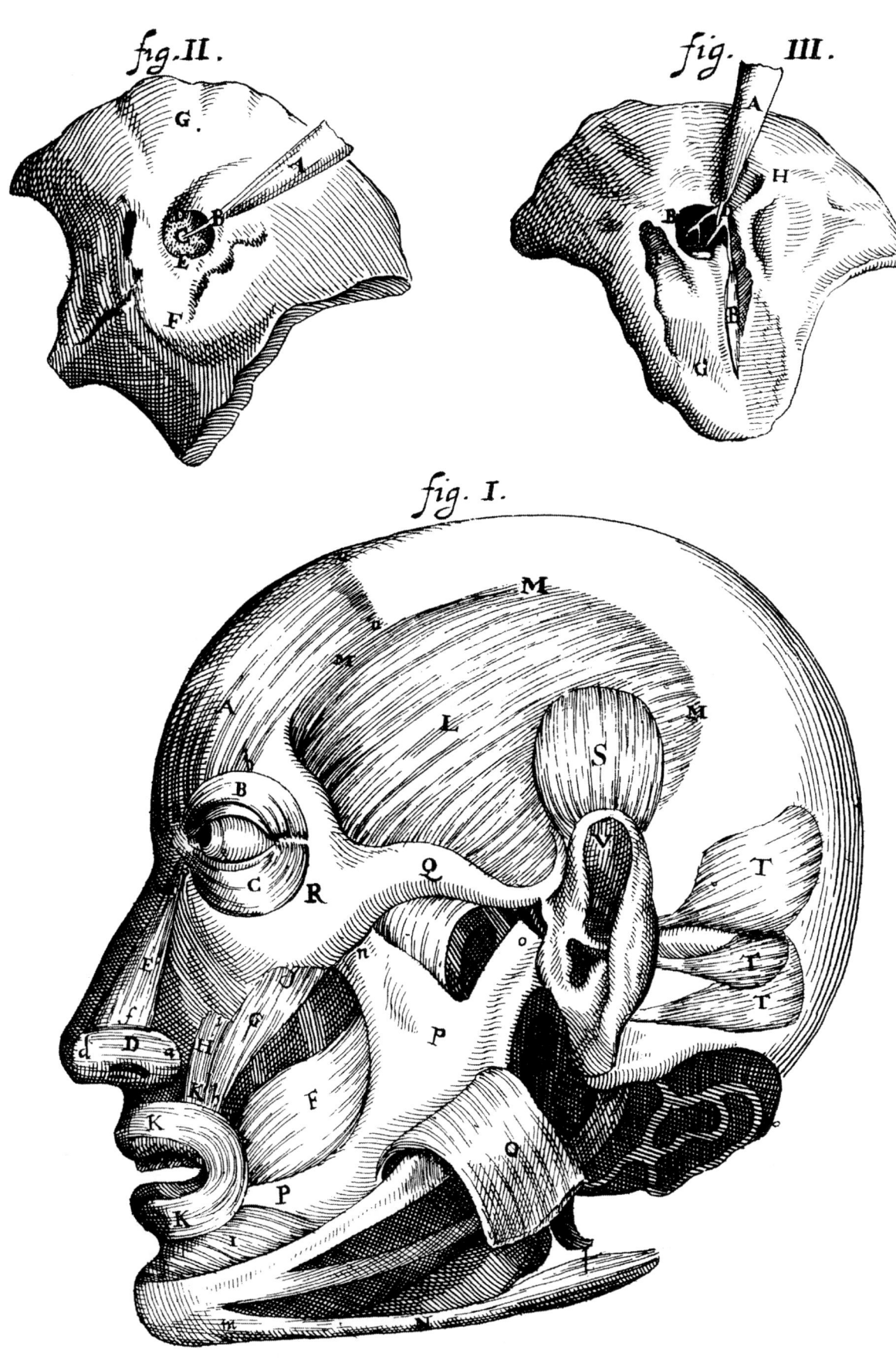

76. Middle ear, masticatory muscles and facial muscles by Adriaan van de Spiegel, illustrated by Giulio Casseri, 1631

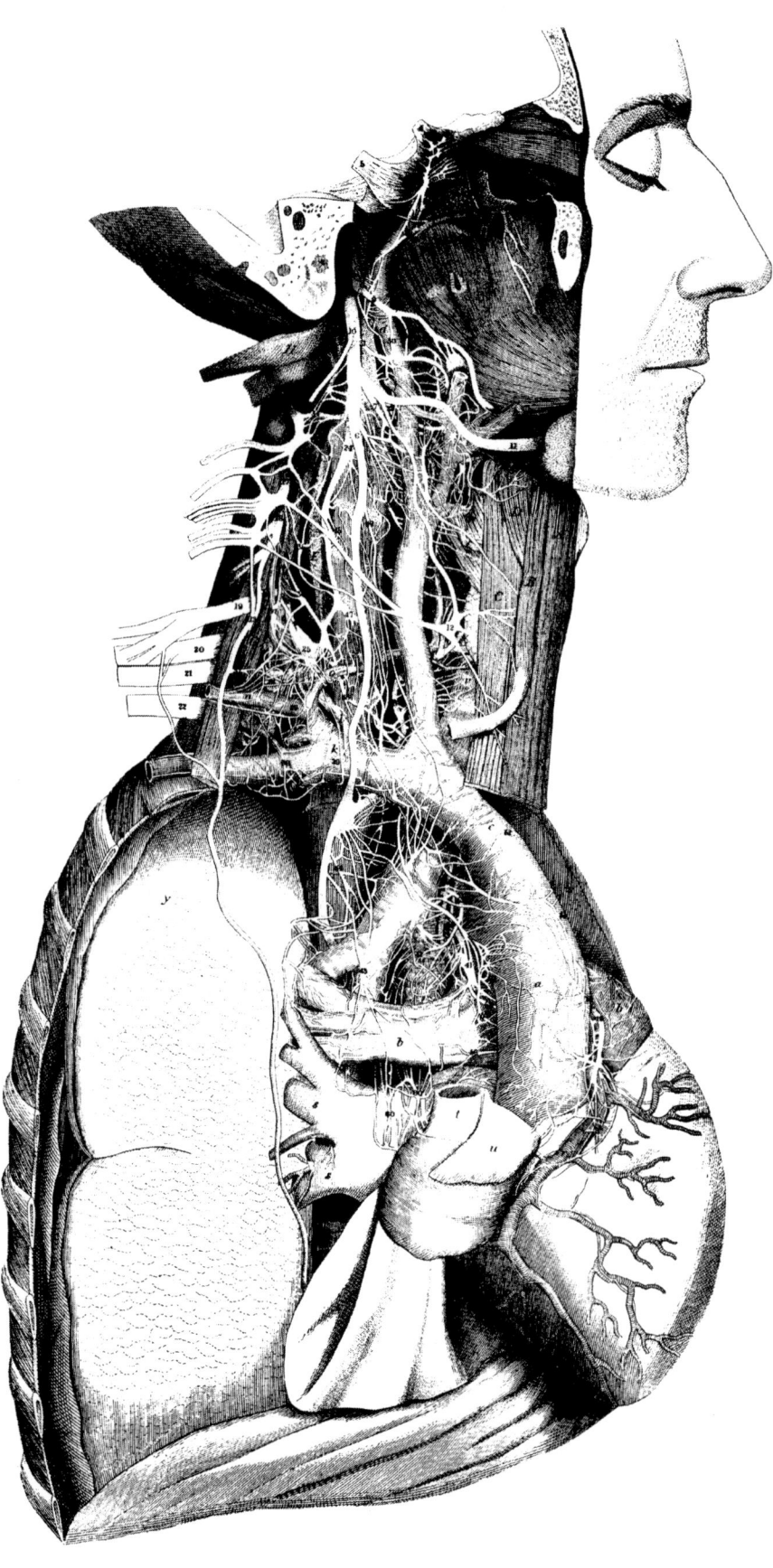

77. Nerves of the head, neck and thorax, plate 1,
drawn by E. West, engraved by Finden, 1834

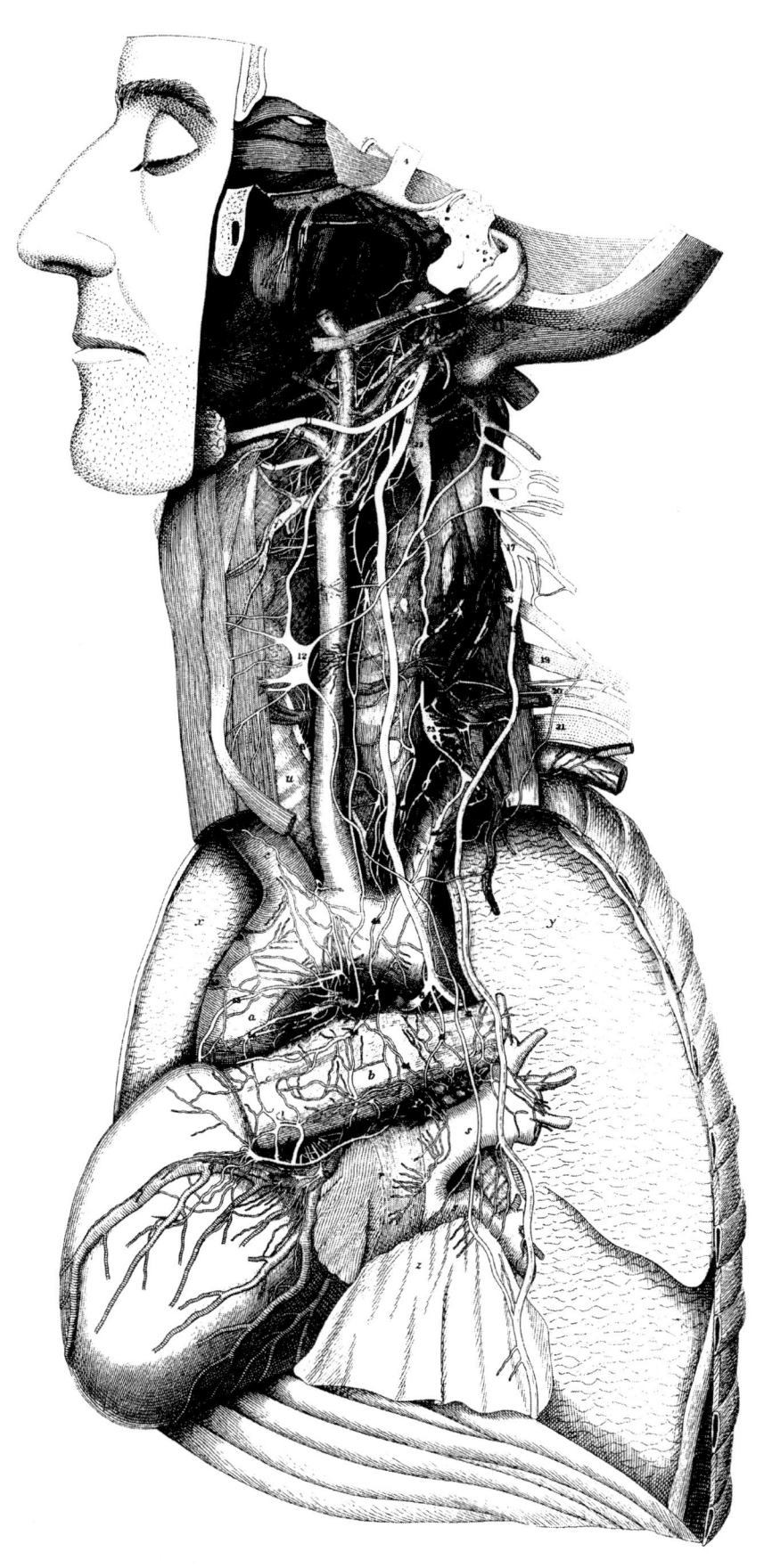

78. Nerves of the head, neck and thorax, plate 2, drawn by E. West, engraved by Finden 1834

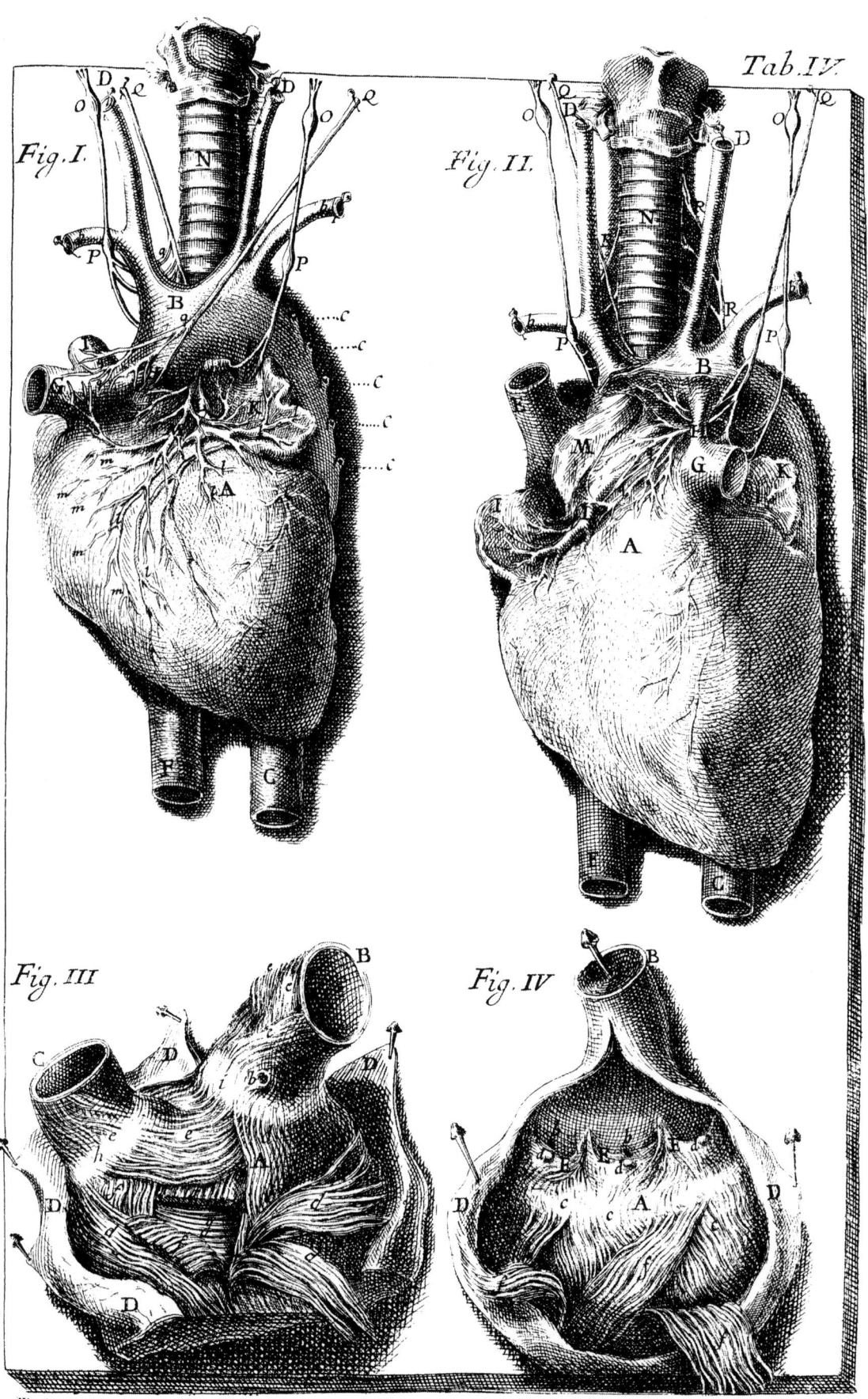

79. Heart, tab 4, by Giovanni Maria Lancisi, illustrated by Niccolo Ricciolini, engraved by Niccolo Oddi and F. Mastrozziso, 1738

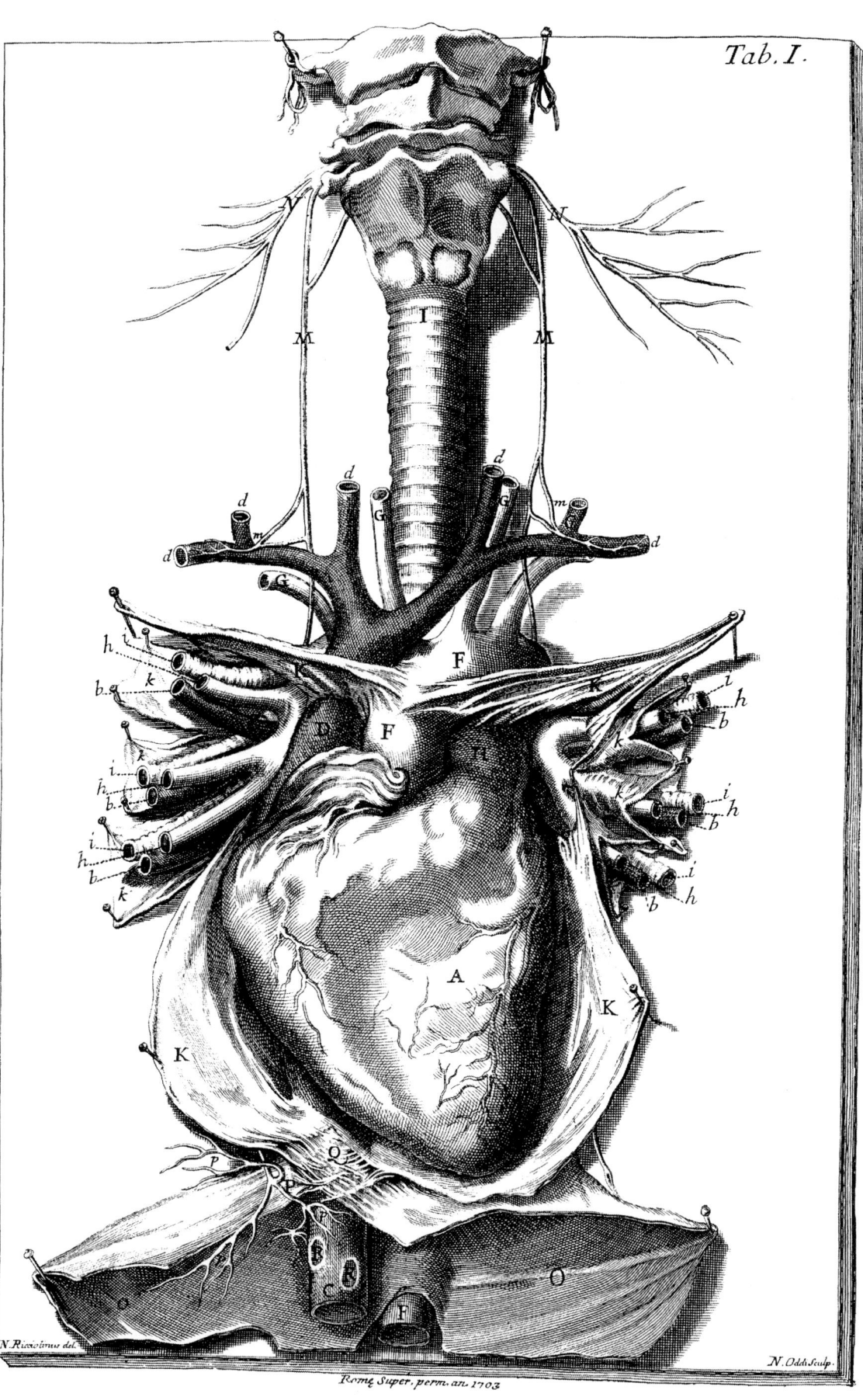

80. Heart, with blood vessels and larynx, tab 1, by Giovanni Maria Lancisi, illustrated by Niccolo Ricciolini, engraved by Niccolo Oddi, 1738

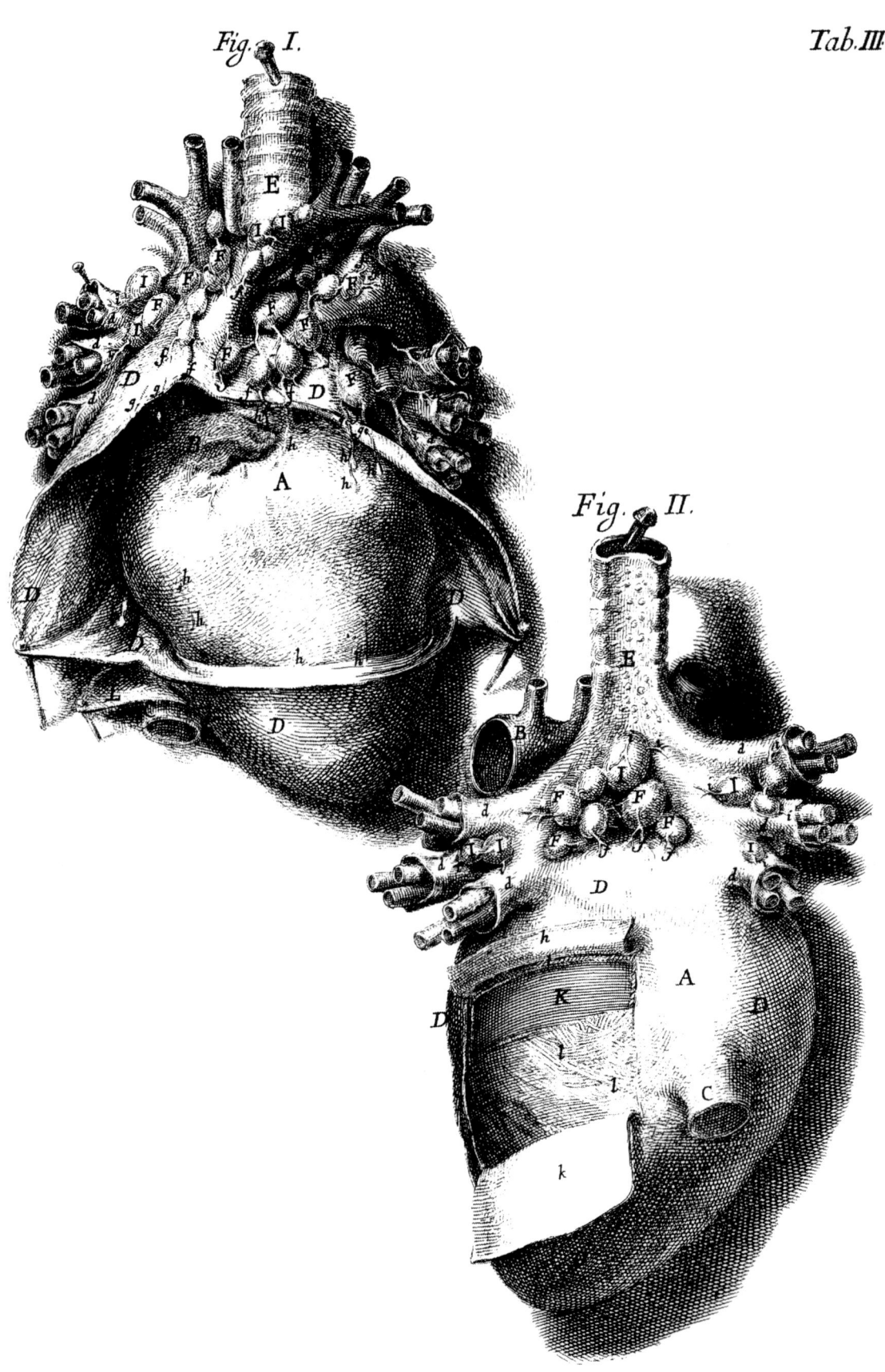

81. Heart, lymph nodes and lymphatic vessels
tab 3, by Giovanni Maria Lancisi, illustrated by
Niccolo Ricciolini, engraved by Niccolo Oddi, 1738

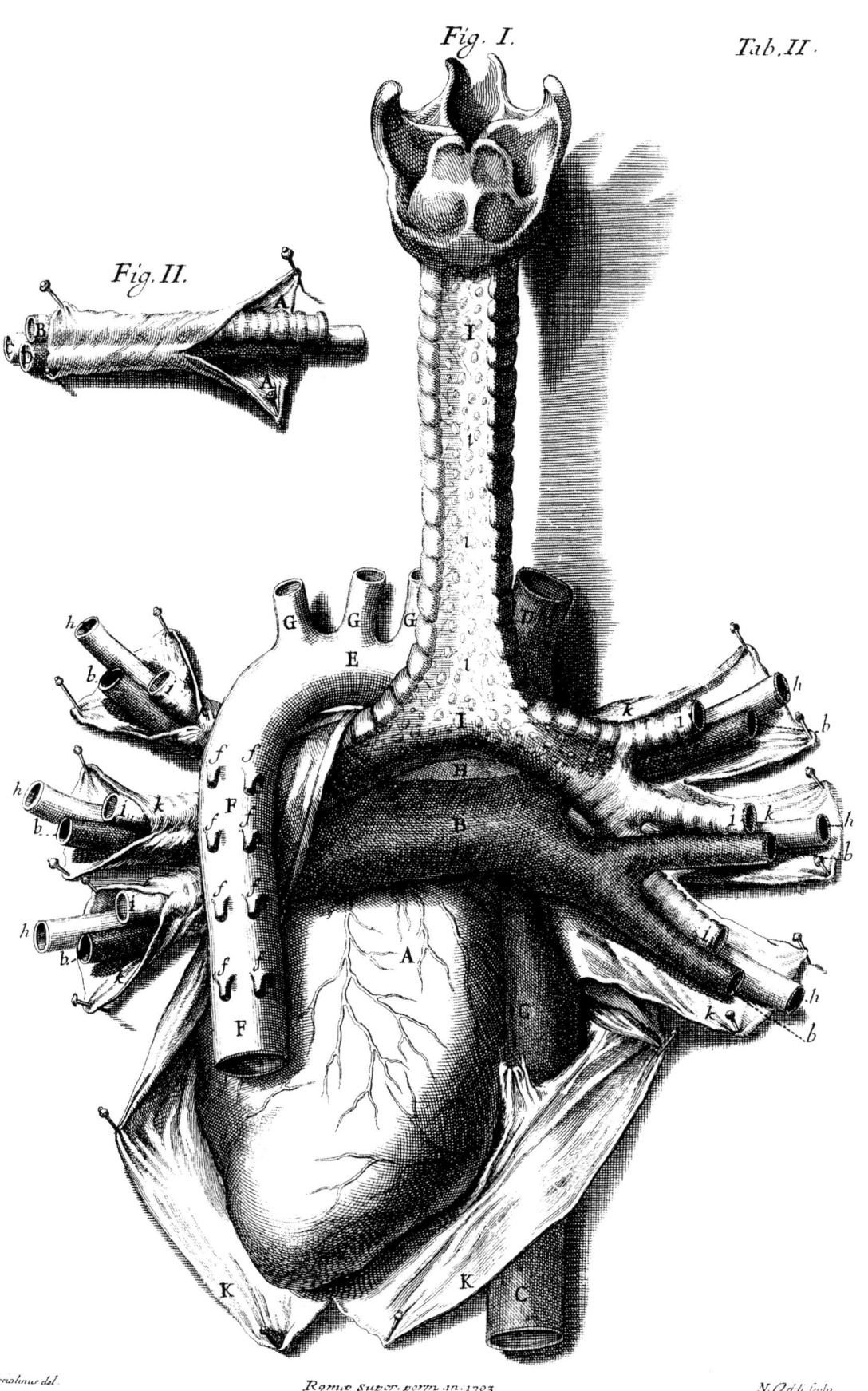

82. Heart, with blood vessels and larynx, tab 2, by Giovanni Maria Lancisi, illustrated by Niccolo Ricciolini, engraved by Niccolo Oddi, 1738

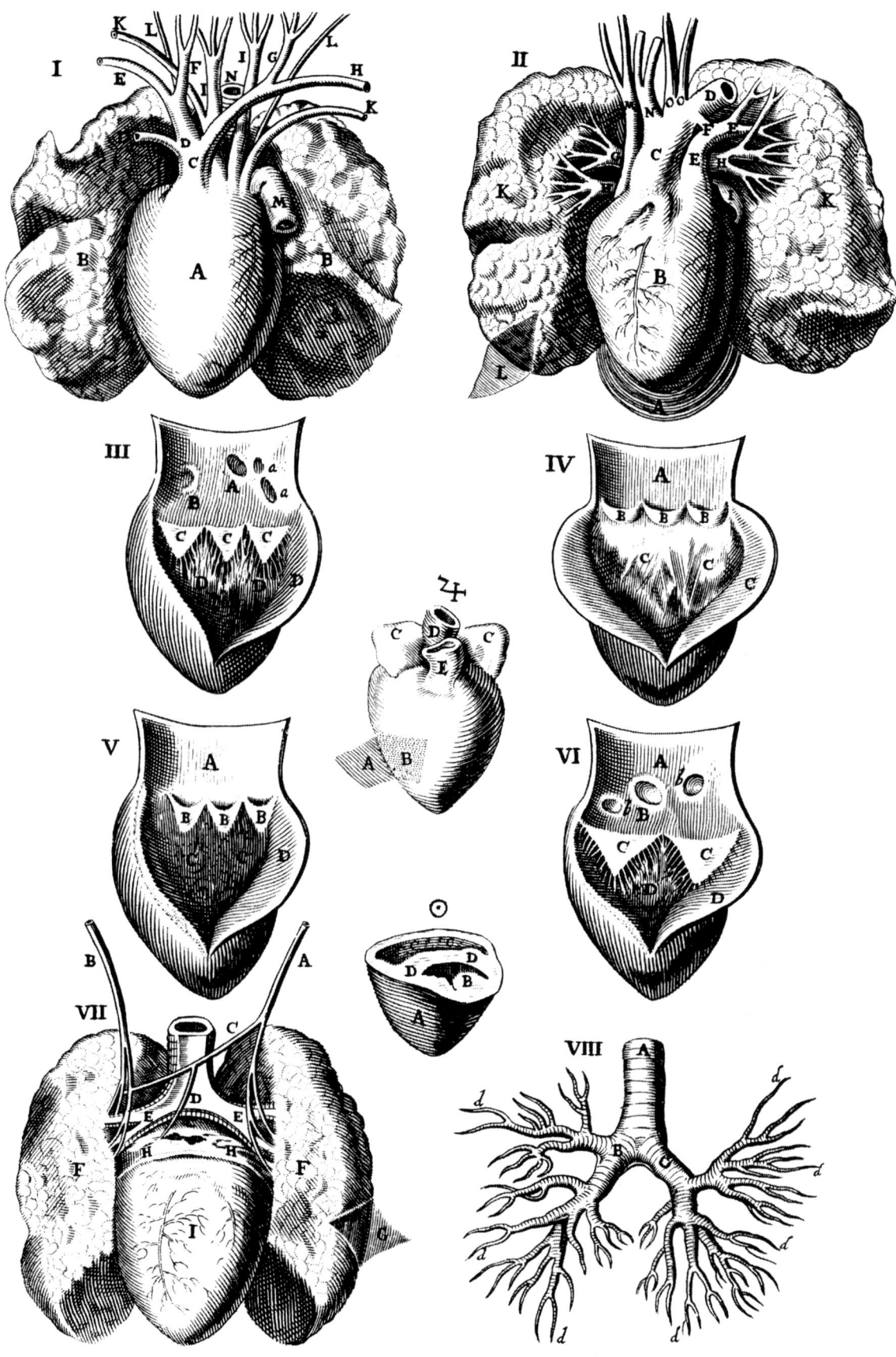

83. Heart and lungs by Jean Riolan, 1649

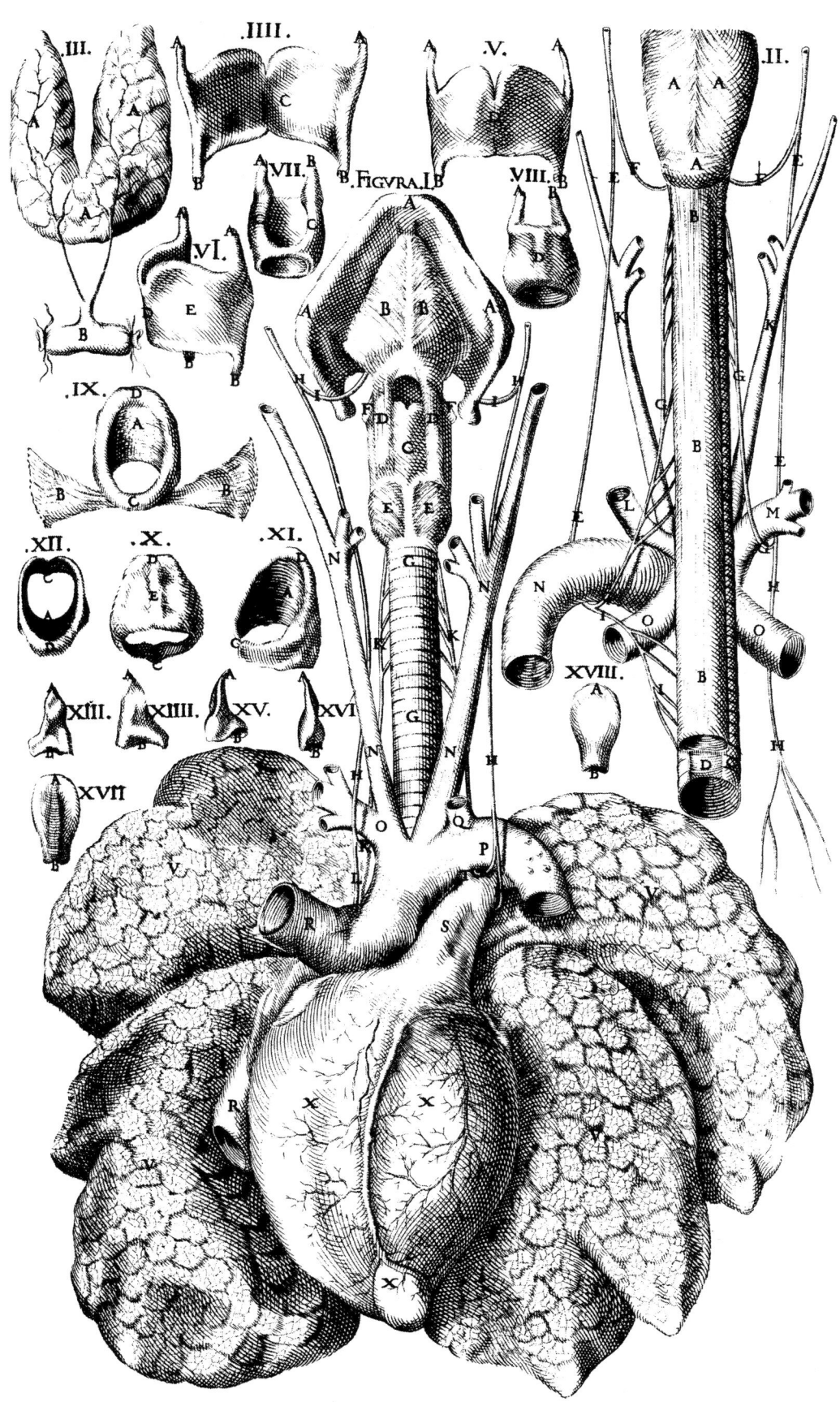

84. Laryngeal cartilages, thyroid, heart and lungs, laryngeal cartilages by Giulio Cesare Casseri, engraved by Joseph Maurer, 1600–1601

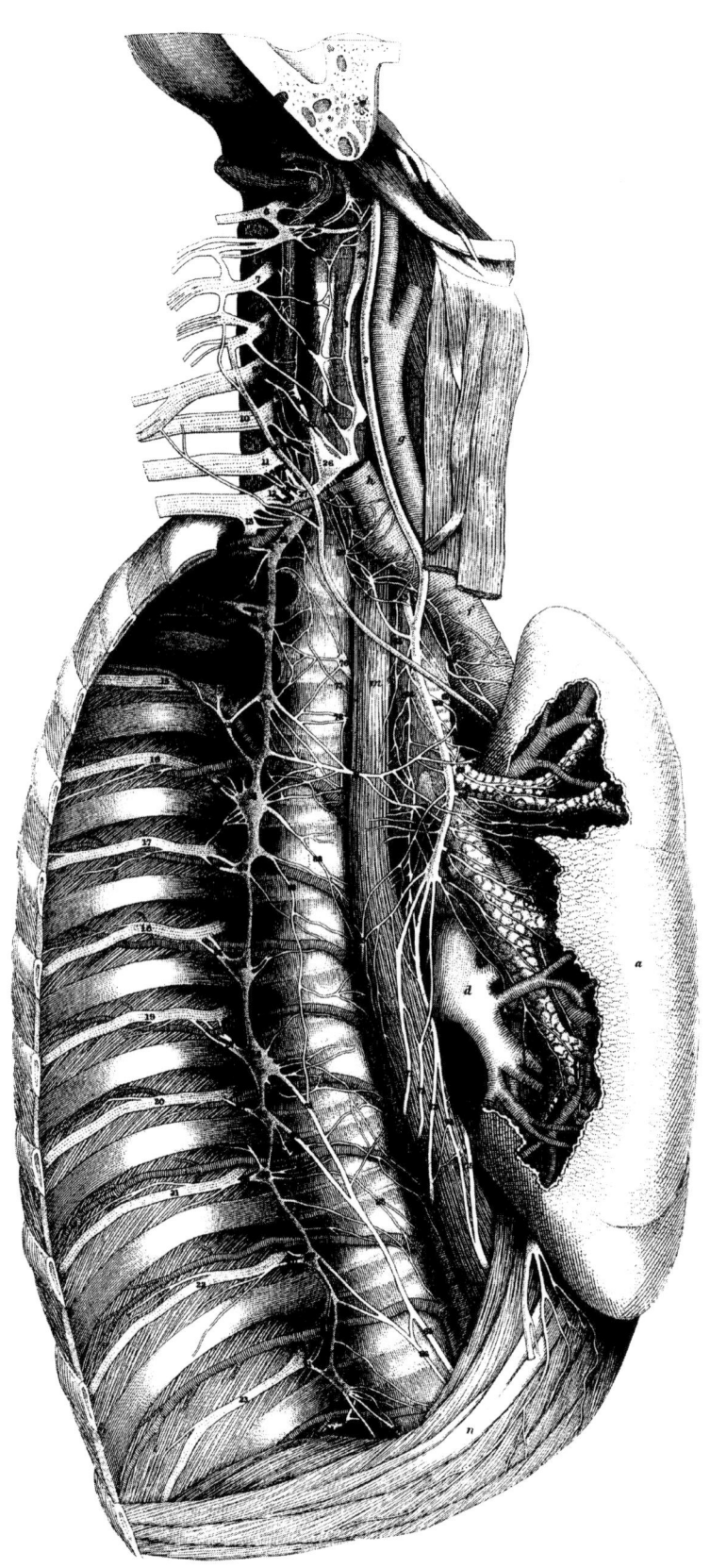

85. Nerves of the thorax, drawn by E. West, plate 3, engraved by Finden, 1834

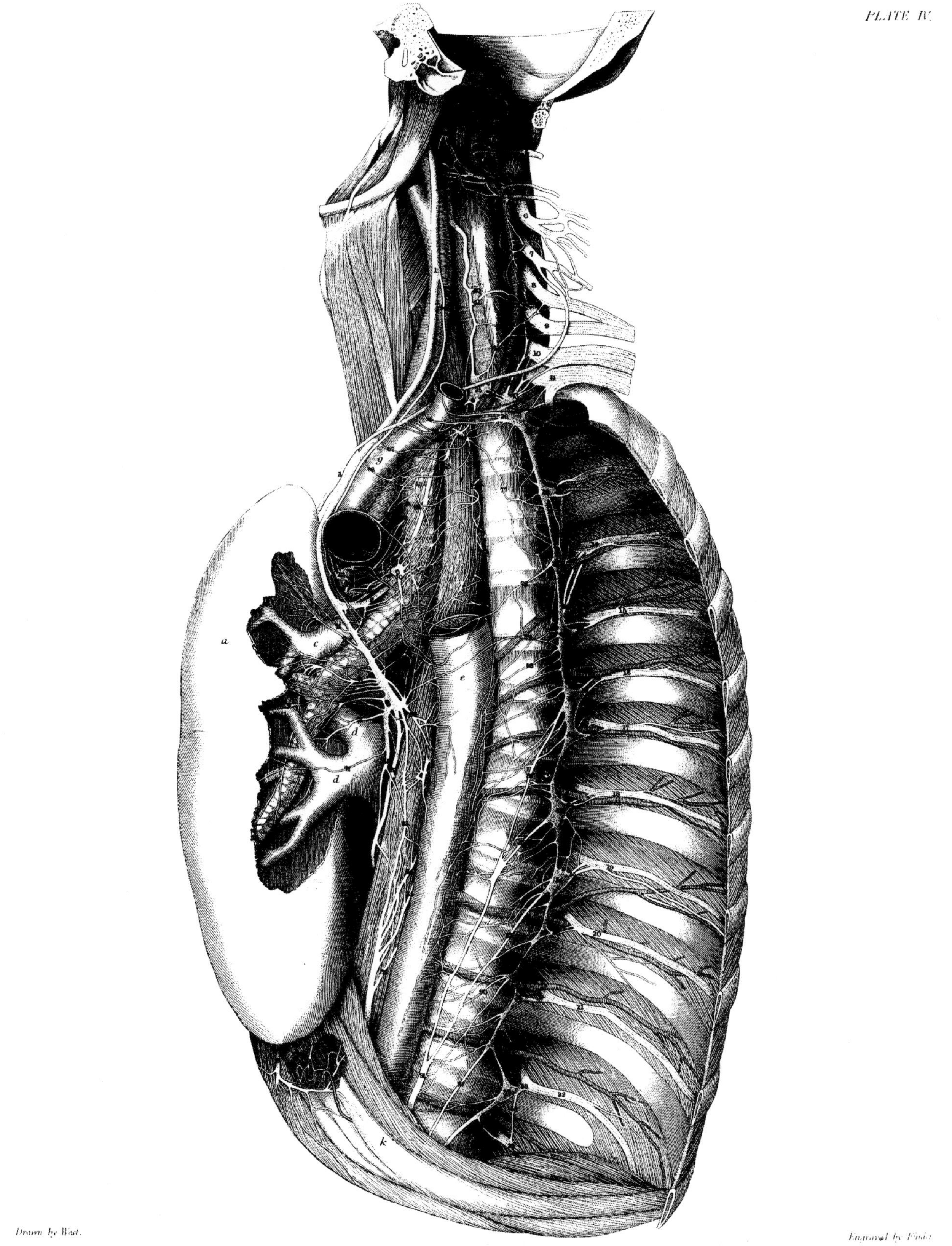

86. Nerves of the thorax, plate 4, drawn by E. West, engraved by Finden, 1834

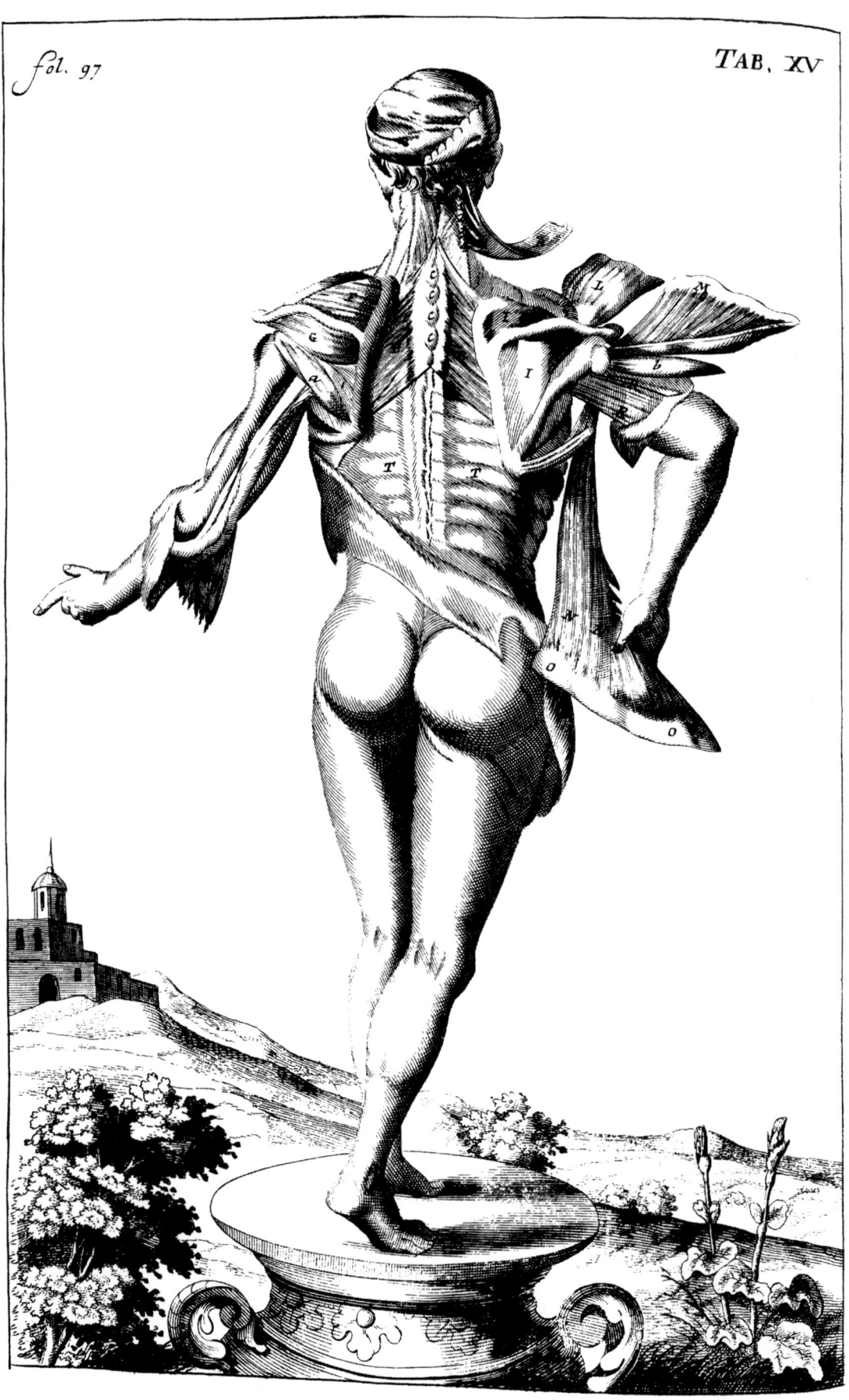

87. Back muscles tab 15, by John Browne
1642–ca. 1700

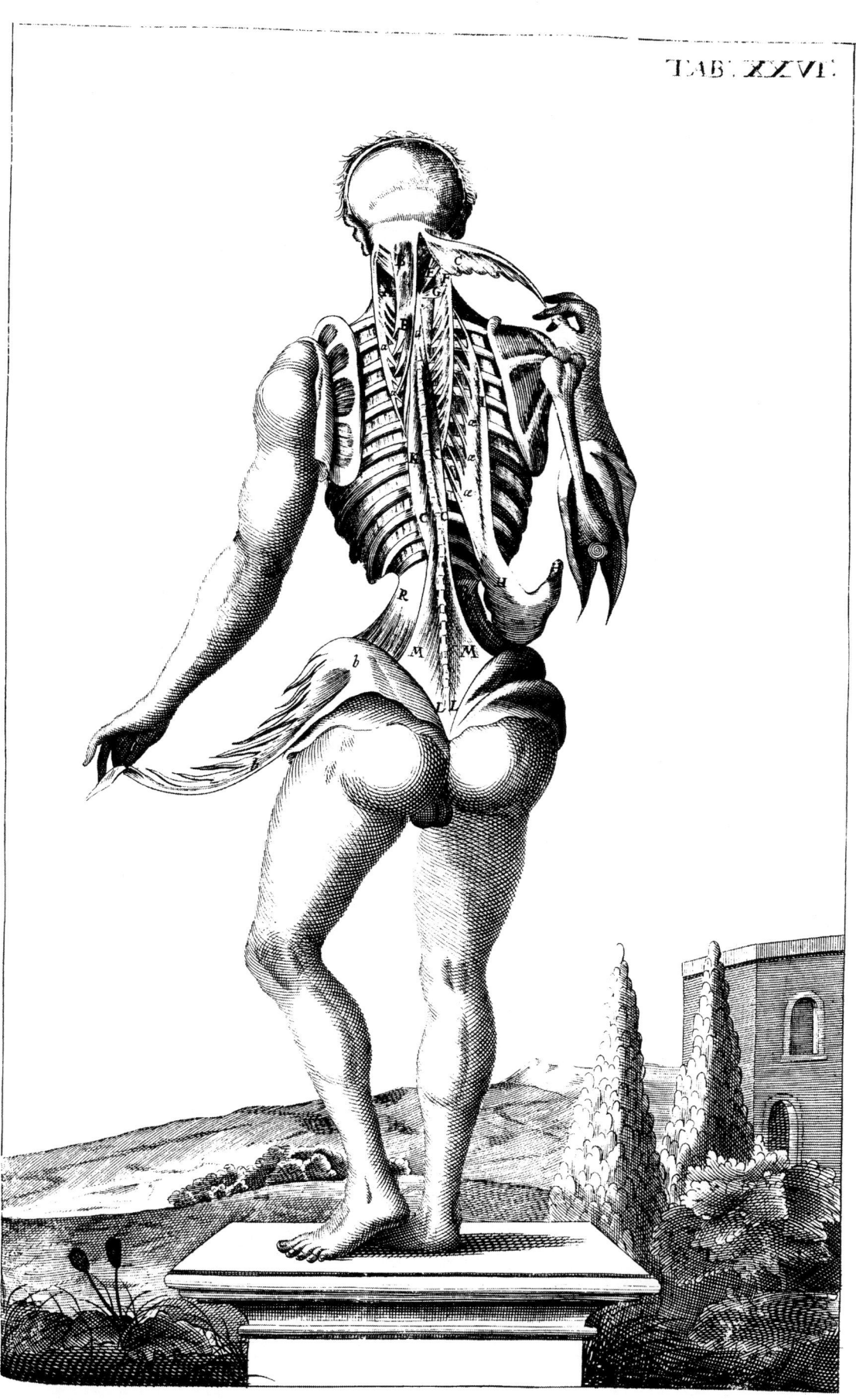

88. Back muscles tab 26, by John Browne
1642–ca. 1700

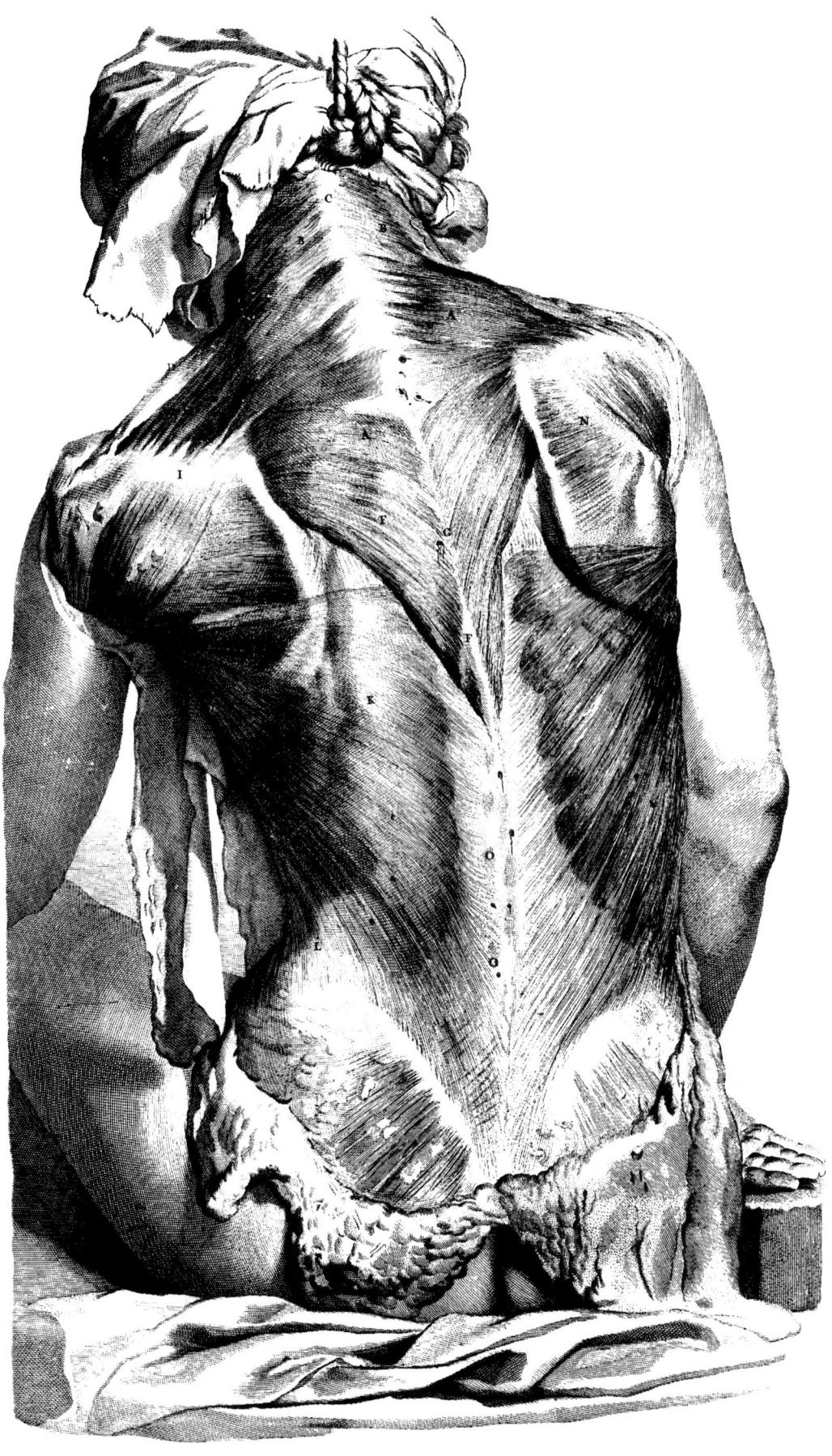

89. Back muscles by Govard Bidloo, 1649–1713

90. Back muscles tab 28 by Govard Bidloo,1649–1713

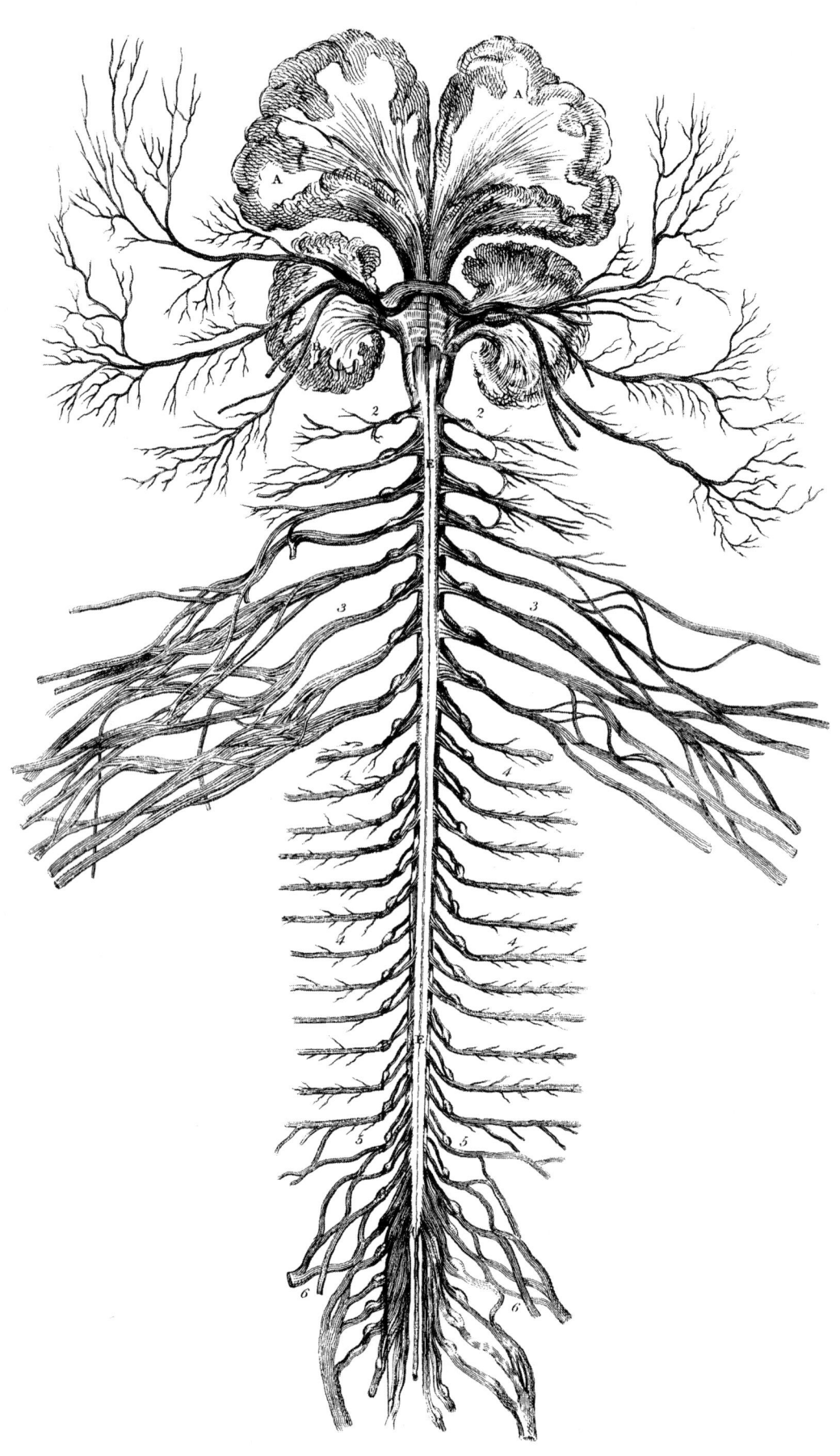

91. Cross-section of brain with brainstem, spinal cord, spinal nerves, brachioplexus, and trigeminal nerves by Sir Charles Bell, 1824

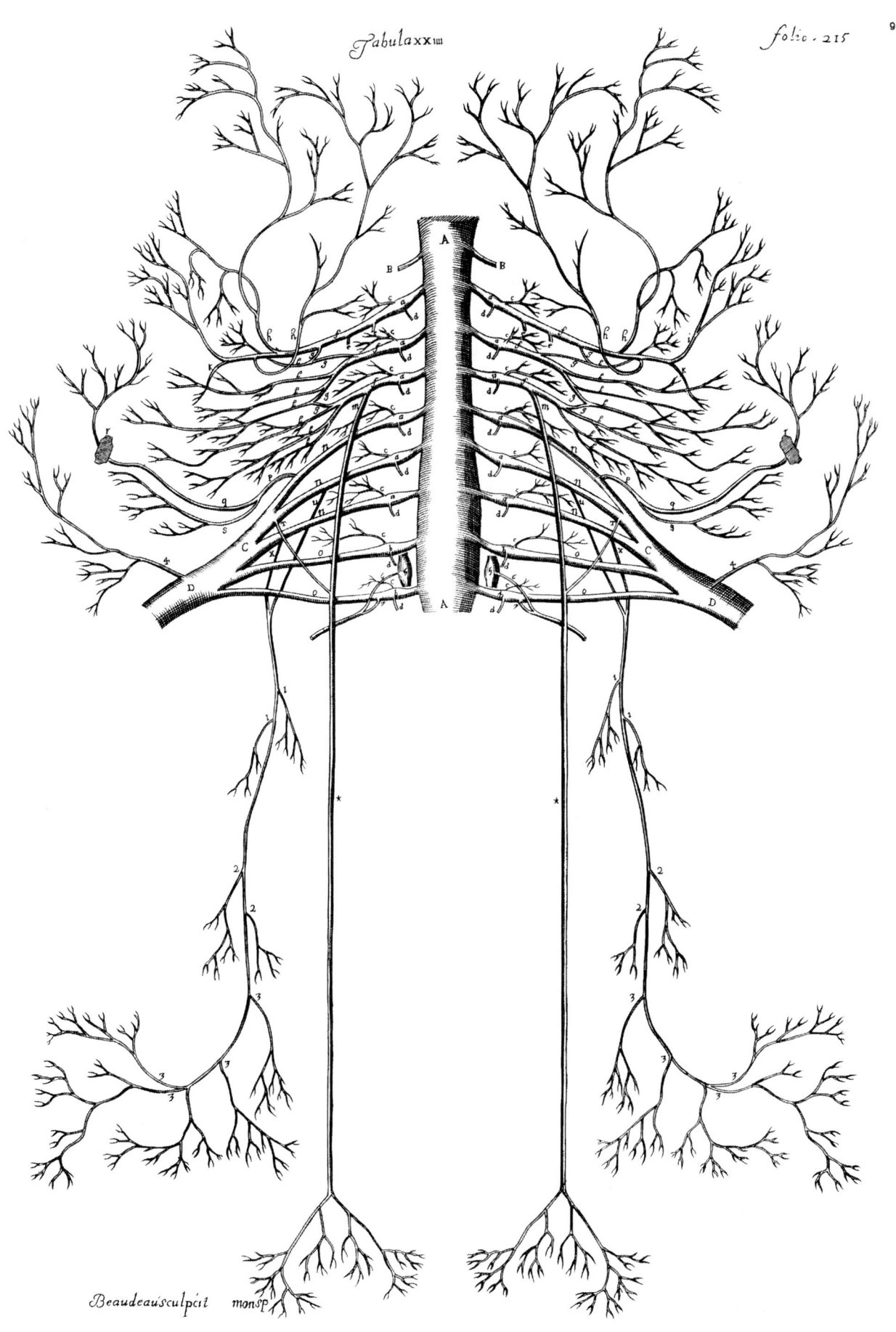

92. Spinal cord, cervical plexus and phrenic nerve, and brachial plexus by Raymond Vieussens, engravings by Beaudeau, 1685

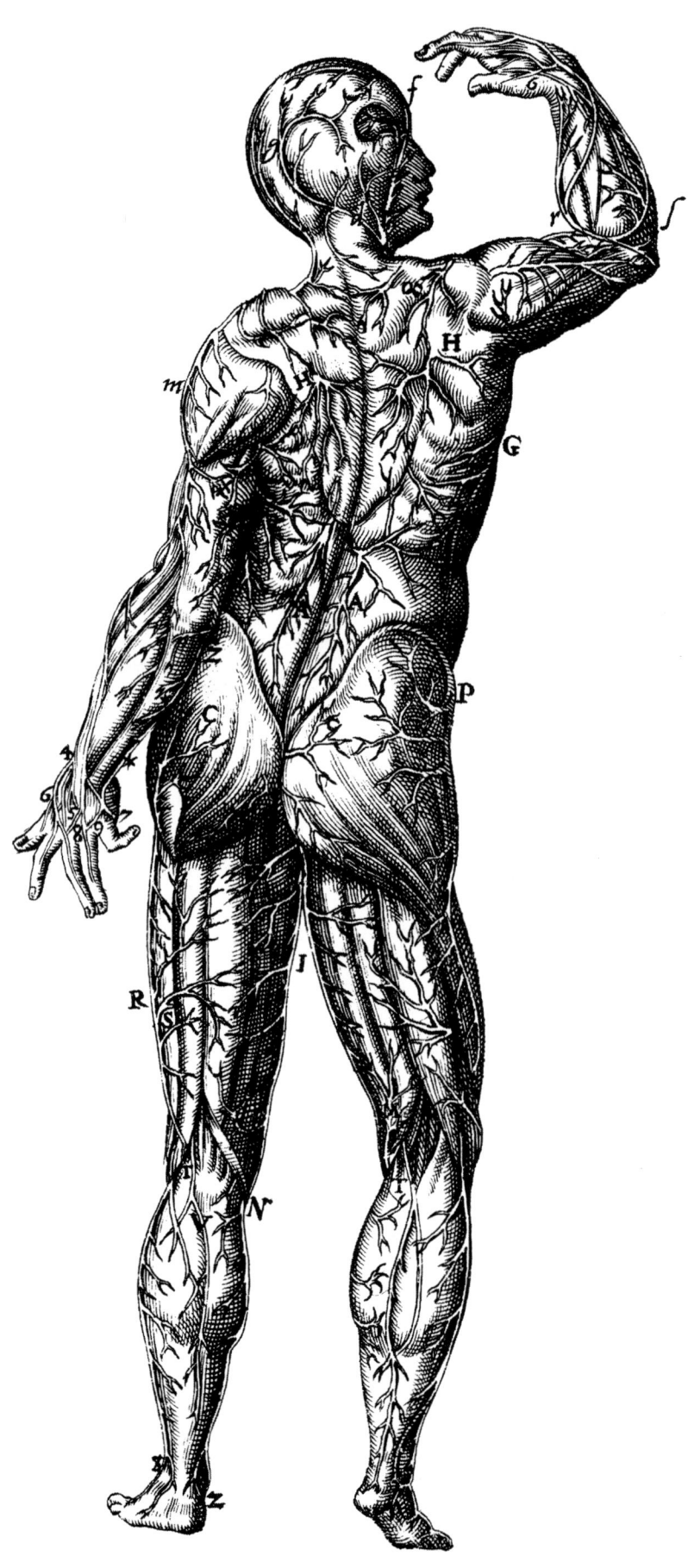

93. Muscles, skeletal, and superfical veins from Novis

94. Veins of the body, by Thomas Geminus, d.1562

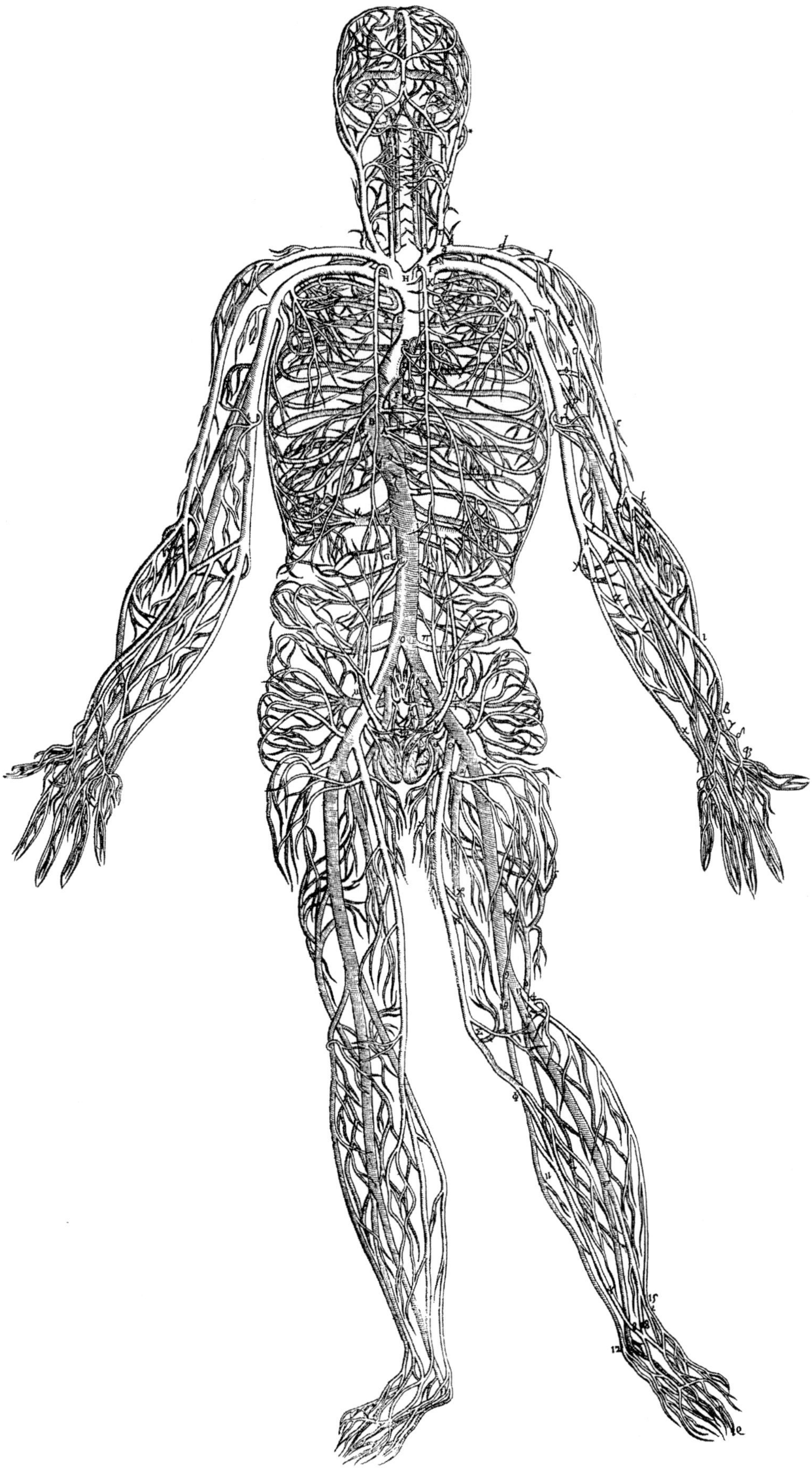

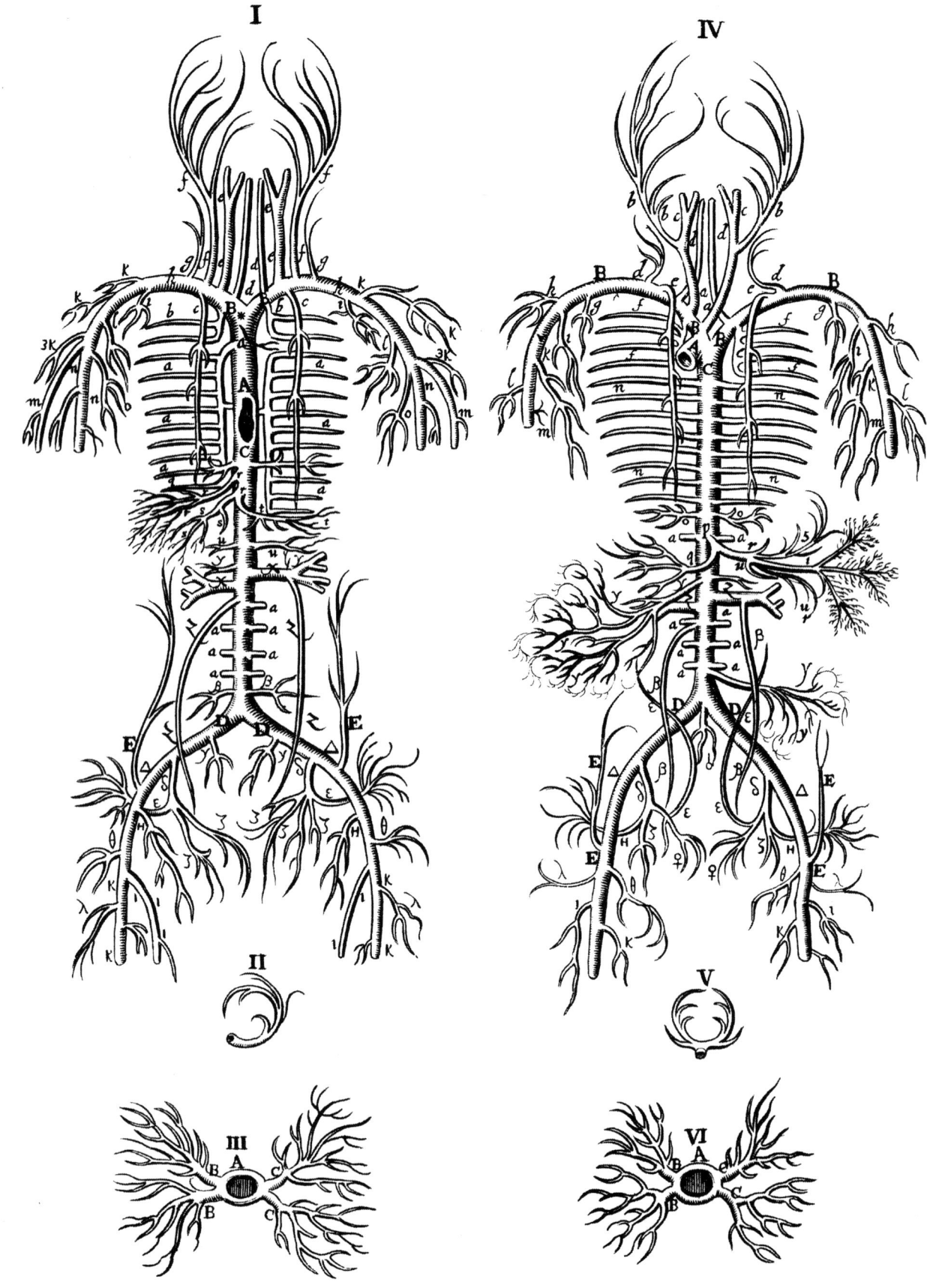

95. Arteries and veins of the body by Jean Riolan, 1649

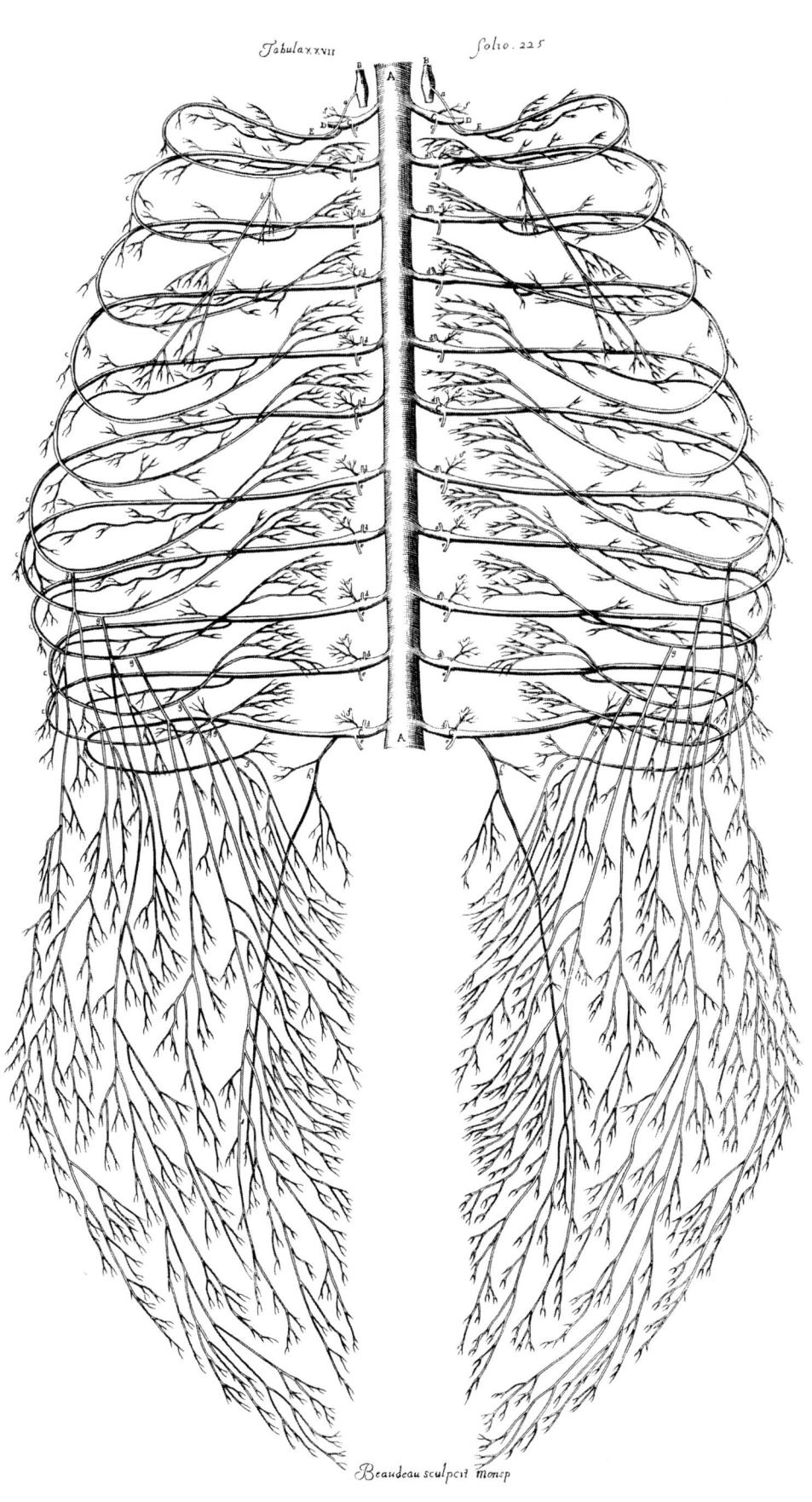

96. Spinal cord and intercostal nerves by Raymond Vieussens, engravings by Beaudeau, 1685

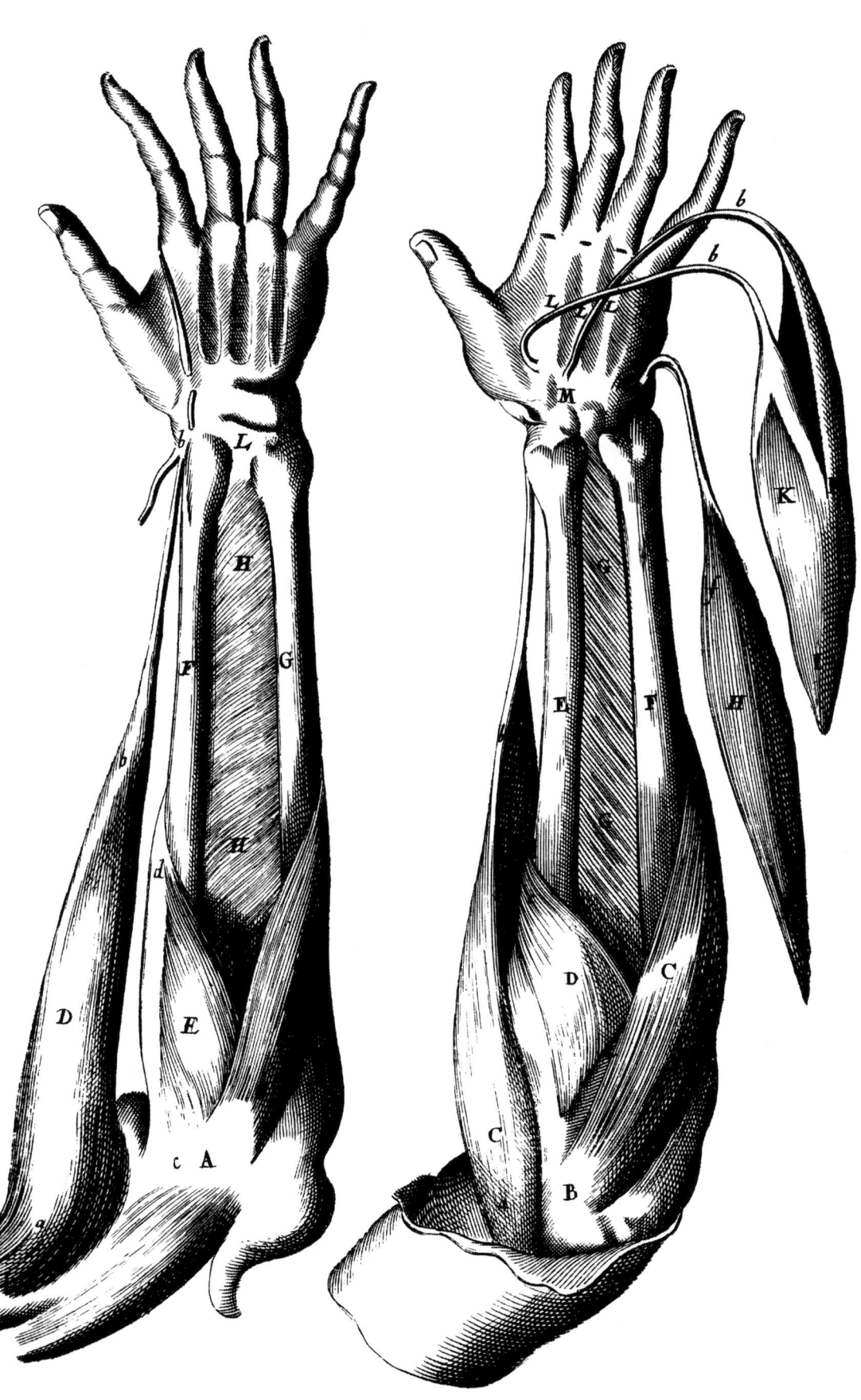

97. Bones and Muscles of the lower arm and hand by John Browne 1642–ca. 1700

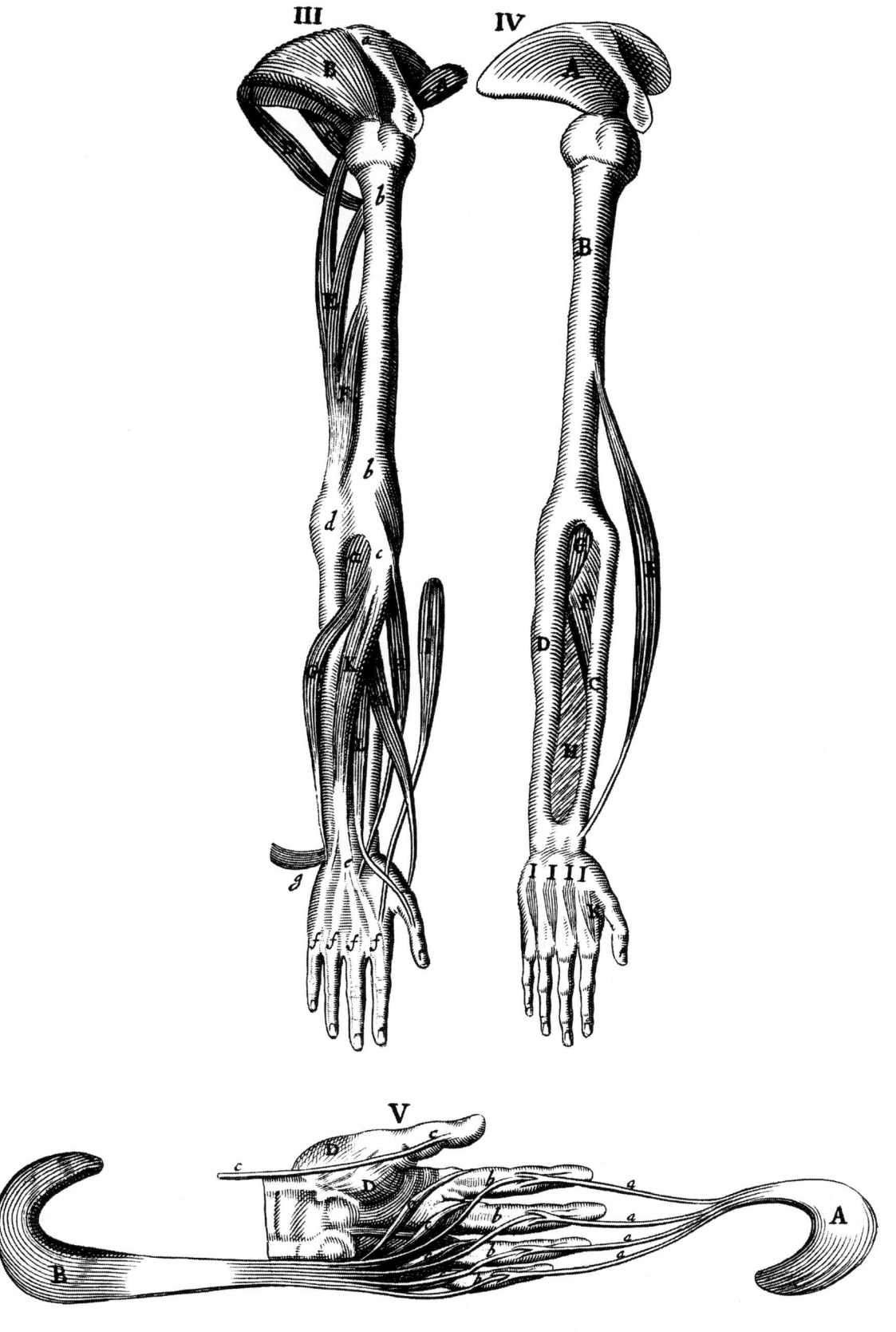

98. Bones and muscles of the arm and hand, by Jean Riolan, 1649

99. Muscles and tendons of the hand, tab 27, by Adriaan van de Spiegel, illustrated by Giulio Casseri, 1631

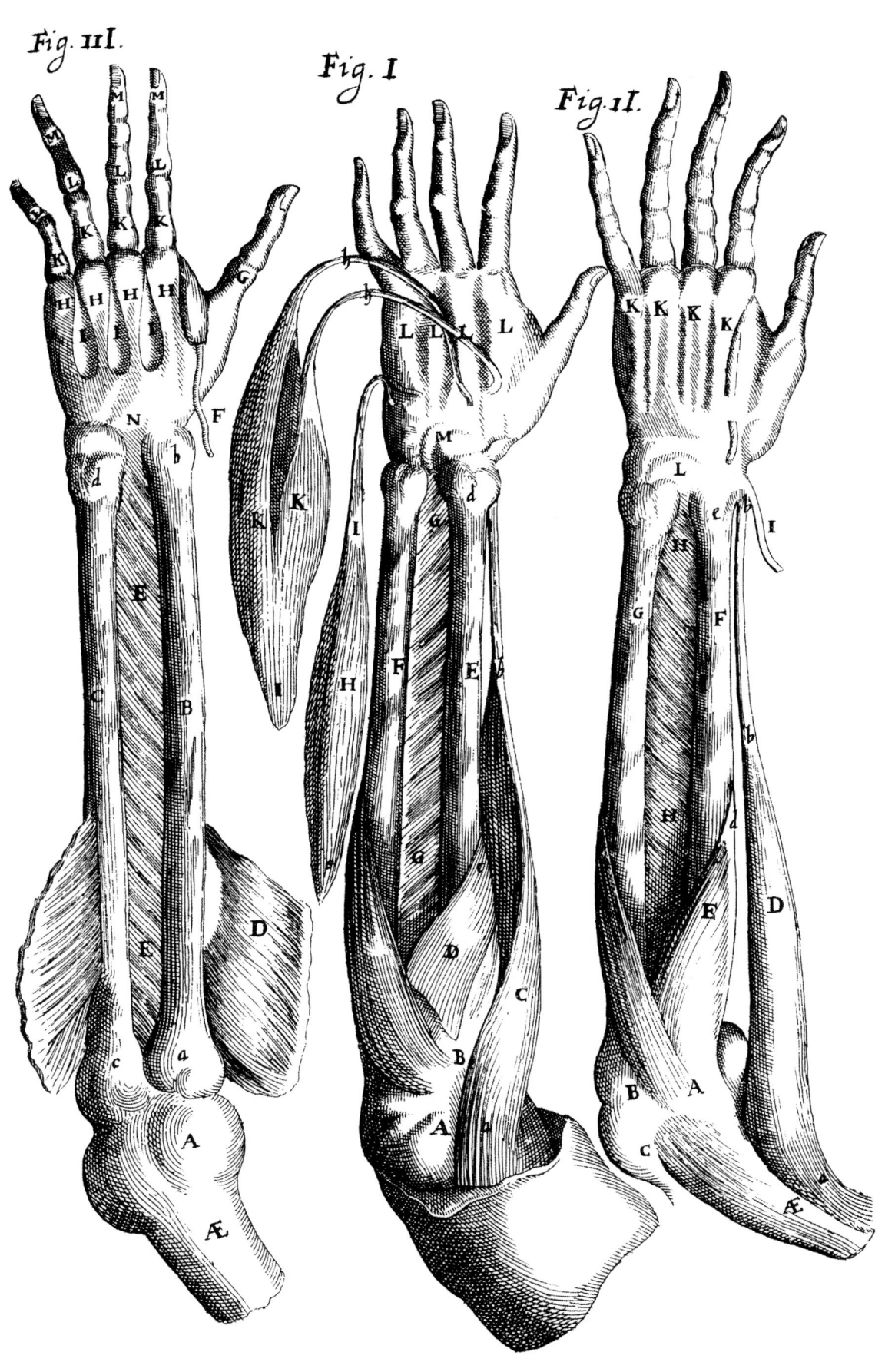

100. Muscles and tendons of the hand, tab 28, by Adriaan van de Spiegel, illustrated by Giulio Casseri and Odoardo Fialetti, 1631

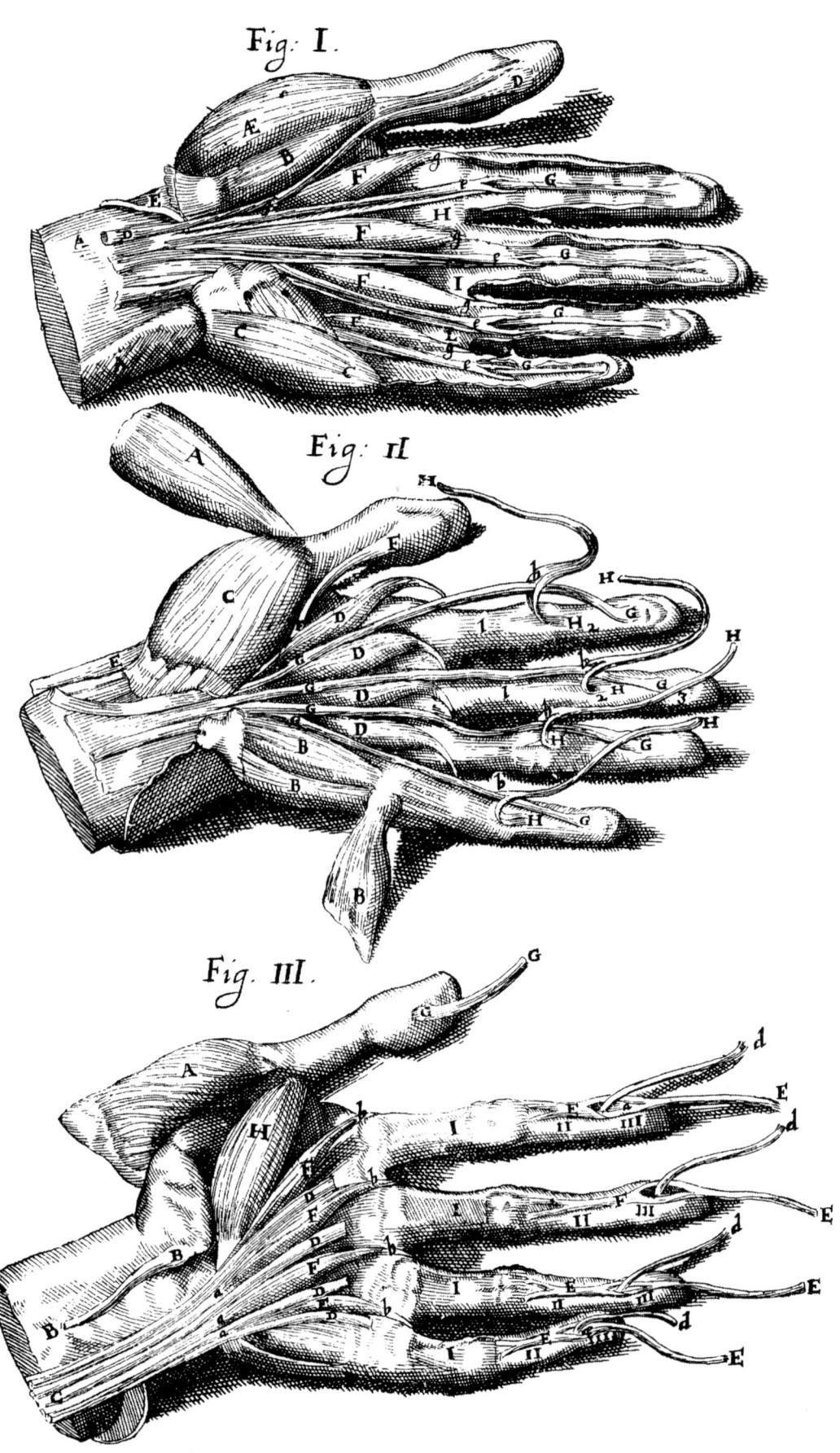

101. Muscles and tendons of the hand, tab 25, by Adriaan van de Spiegel, illustrated by Giulio Casseri and Odoardo Fialetti, 1631

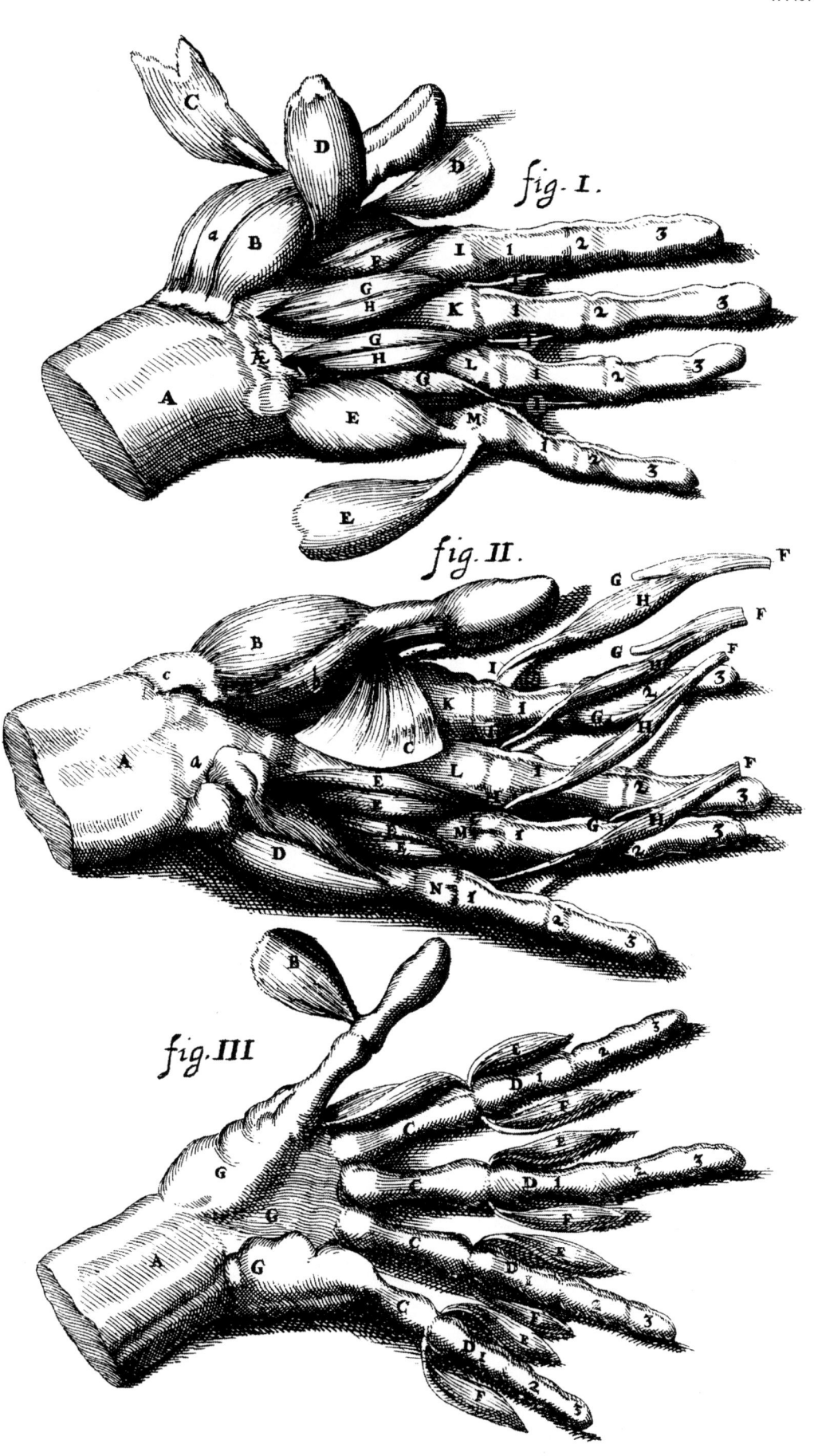

102. Muscles and tendons of the hand, tab 26, by Adriaan van de Spiegel, illustrated by Giulio Casseri and Odoardo Fialetti, 1631

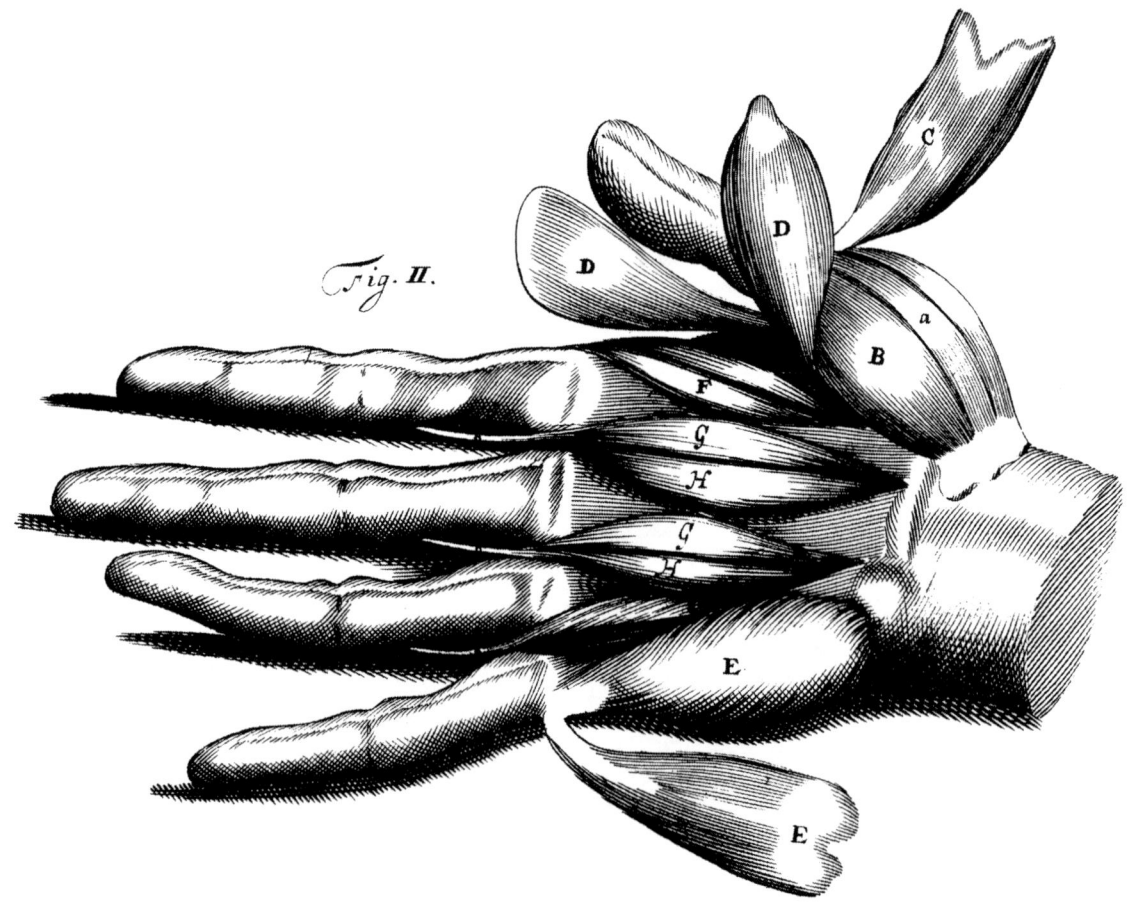

103. Muscles of the hand tab 21 fig 1, 2 by John Browne 1642–ca. 1700

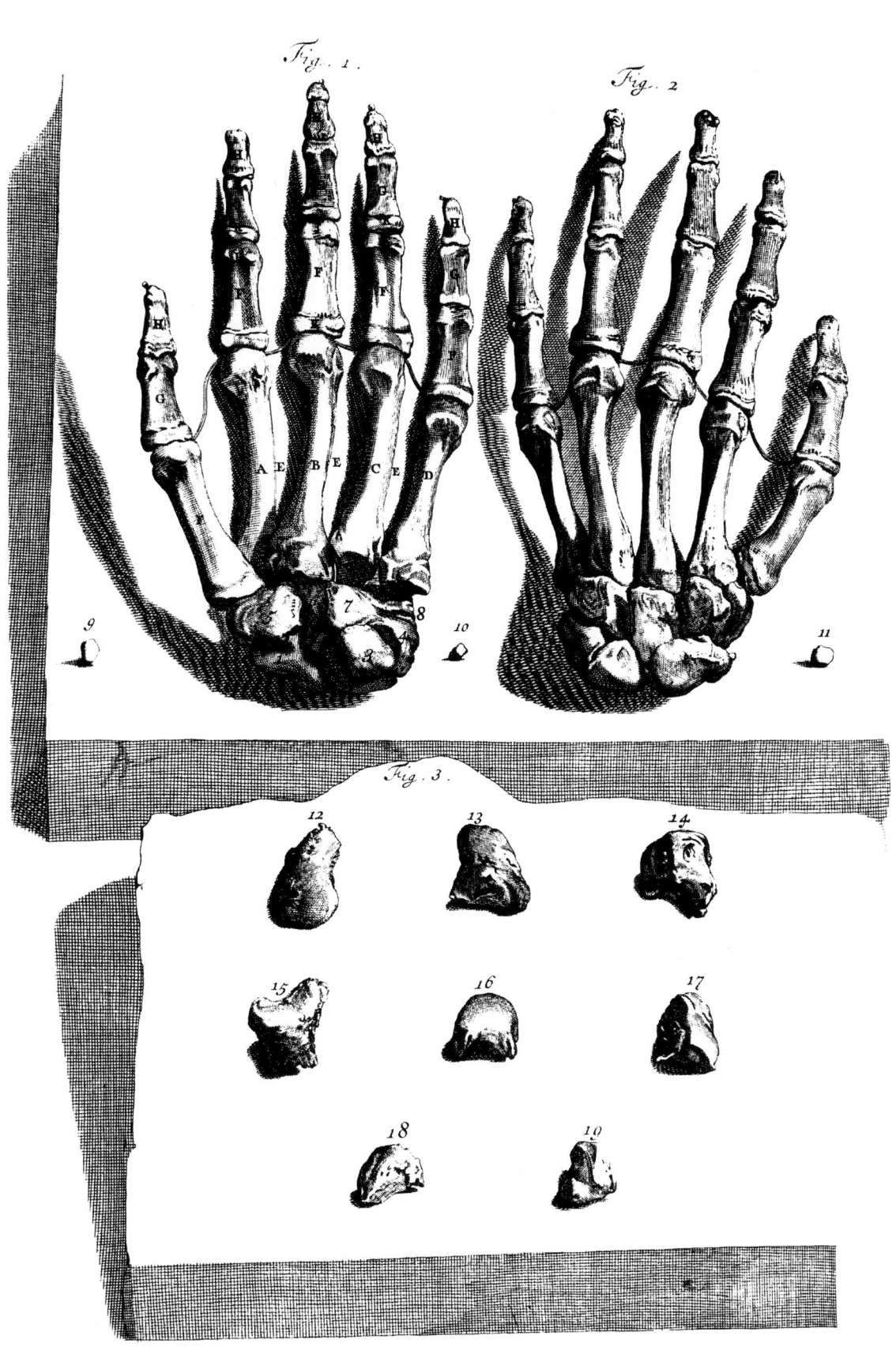

104. Bones of the hand, tab 97, by Govard Bidloo,1649–1713

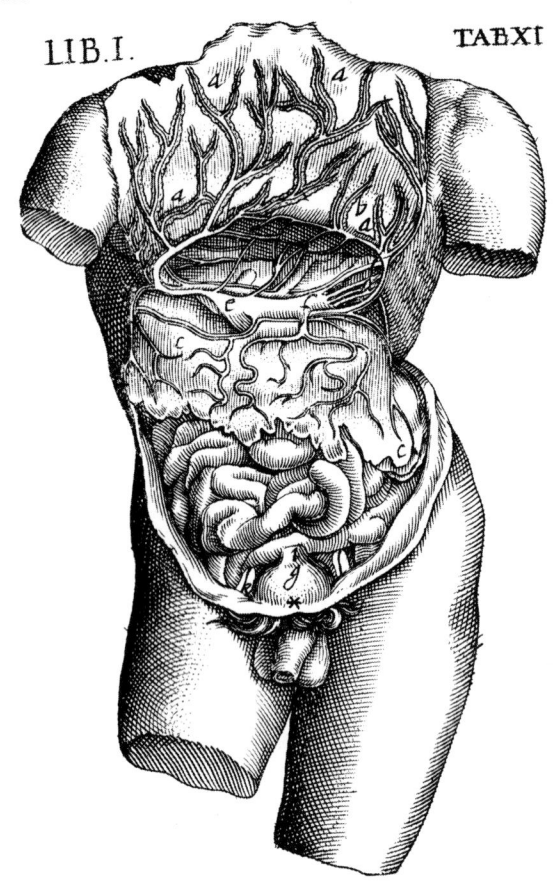

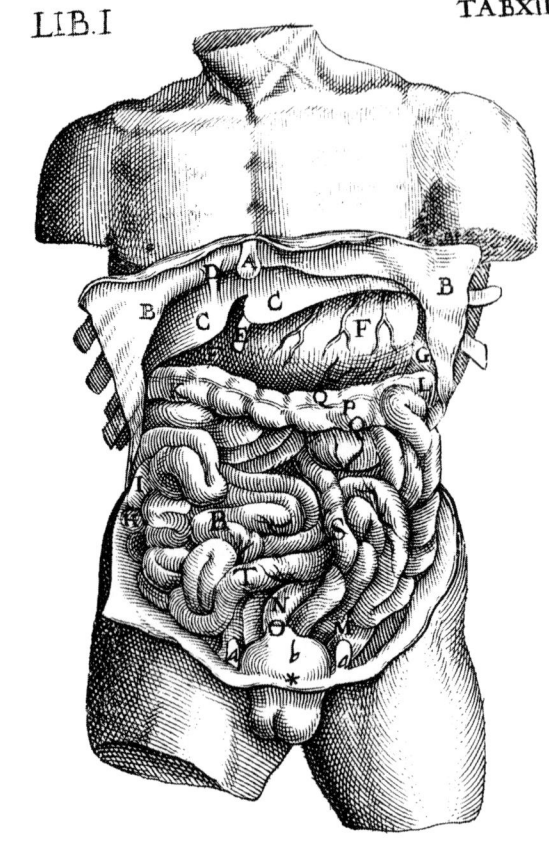

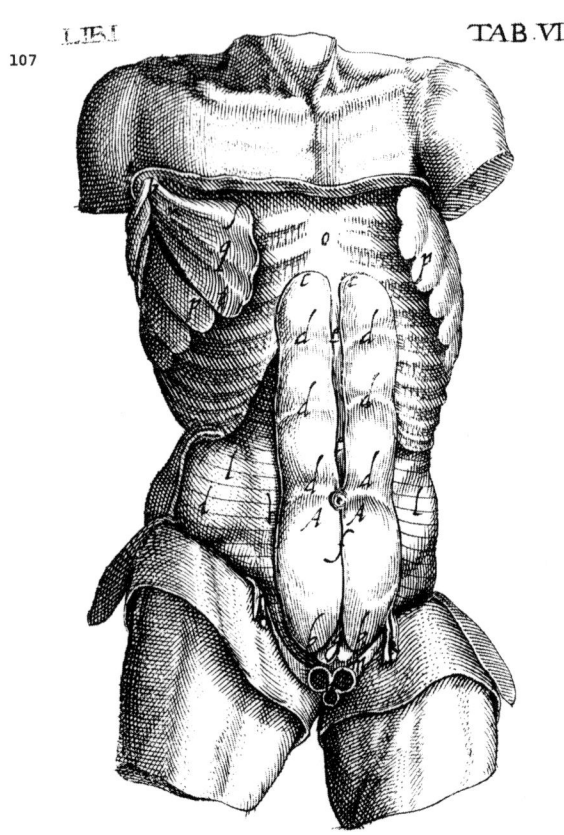

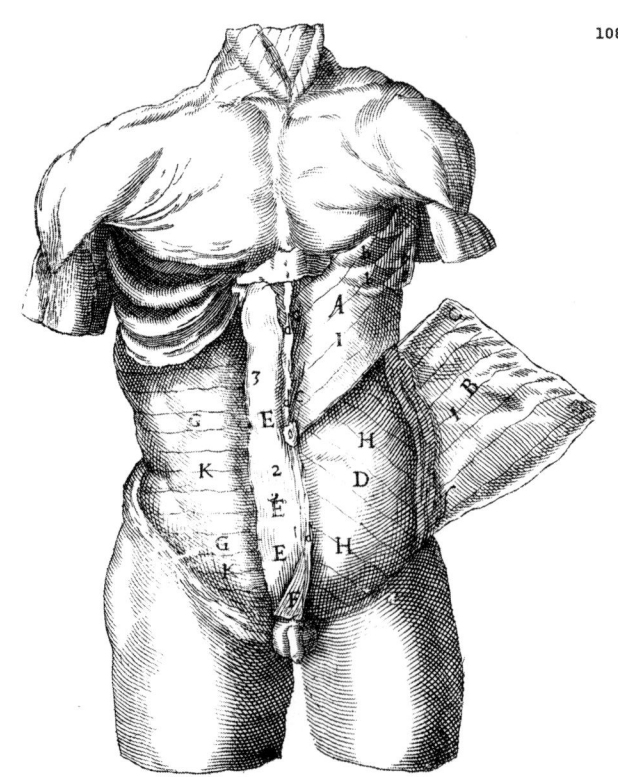

105. Abdominal organs tab 11 by Kaspar Bauhin, 1560–1624

106. Abdominal organs tab 12 by Kaspar Bauhin, 1560–1624

107. Abdominal muscles tab 7 by Kaspar Bauhin, 1560–1624

108. Abdominal muscles tab 6 by Kaspar Bauhin, 1560–1624

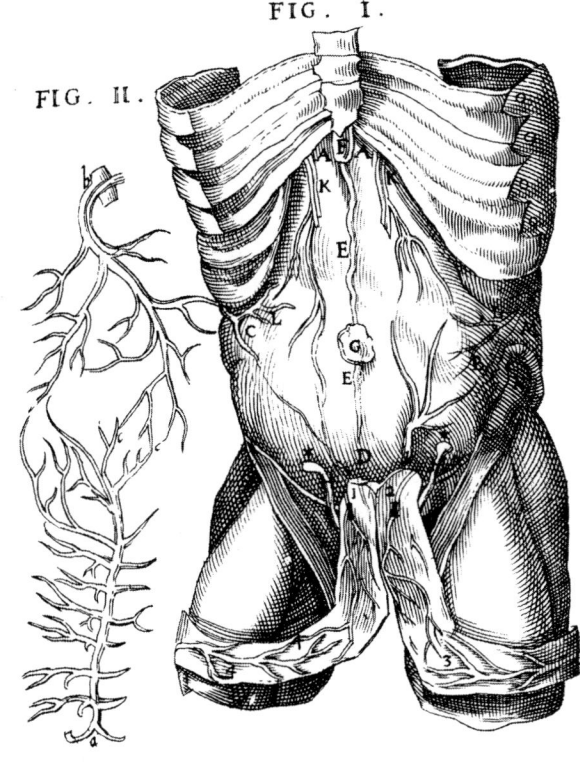
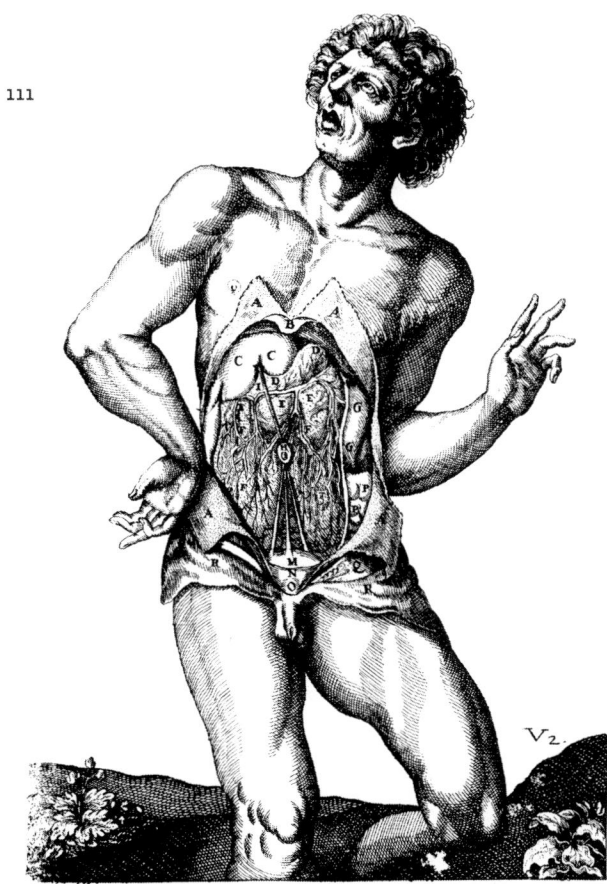
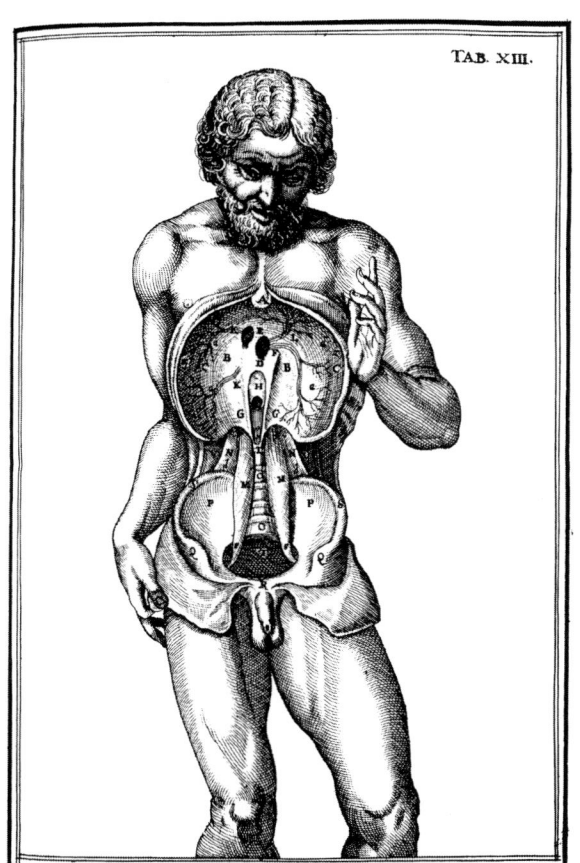

109. Abdomen, peritoneum tab 9 by Kaspar Bauhin, 1560–1624

110. Abdominal wall, epigastric blood vessels by Kaspar Bauhin, 1560–1624

111. Dissection of the abdomen, tab 3, lib 8, by Adriaan van de Spiegel, illustrated by Giulio Casseri and Odoardo Fialetti, 1631

112. Abdomen, peritoneal cavity by Adriaan van de Spiegel, illustrated by Giulio Casseri and Odoardo Fialetti, 1631

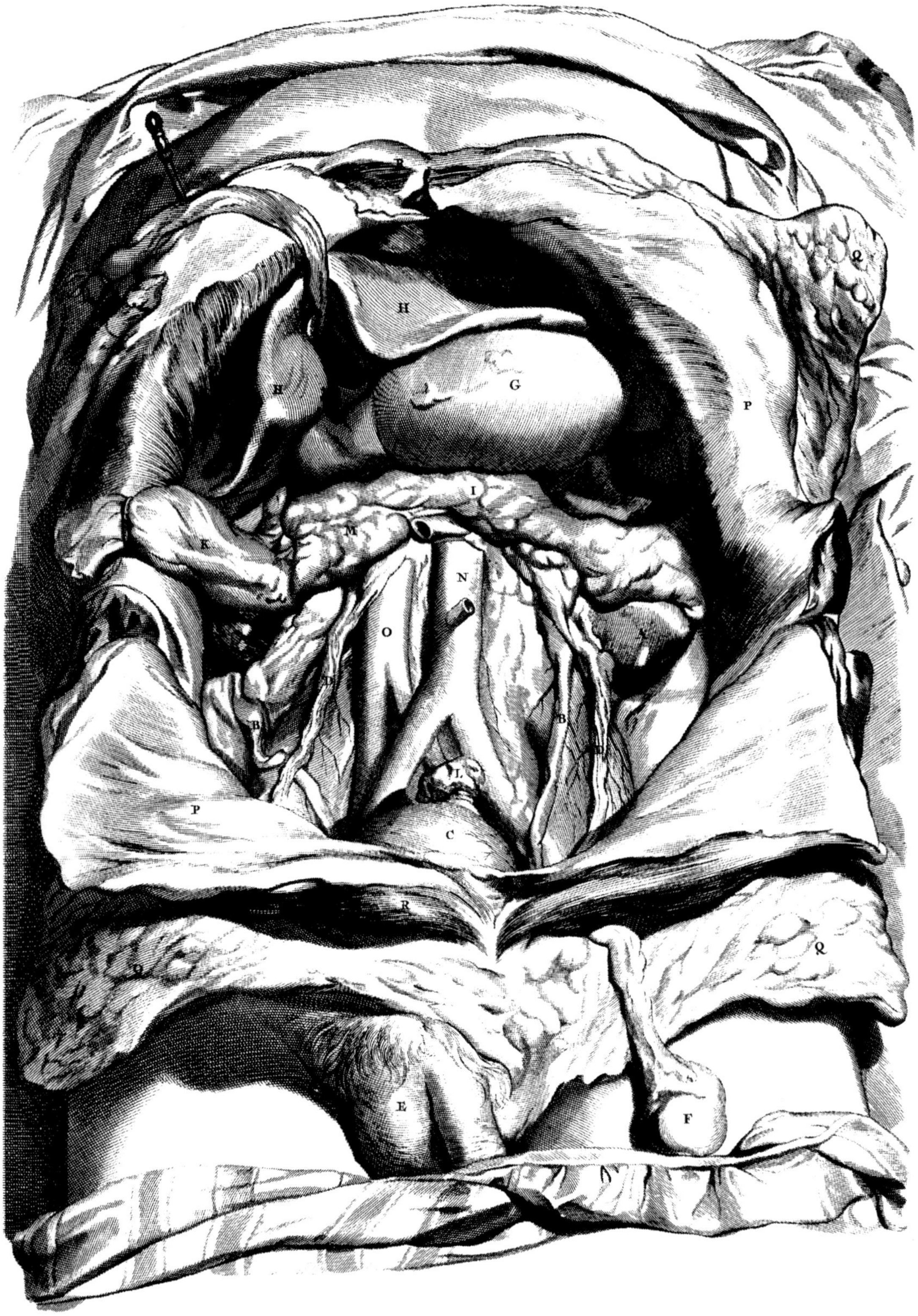

113. Abdominal organs by Govard Bidloo, 1649–1713

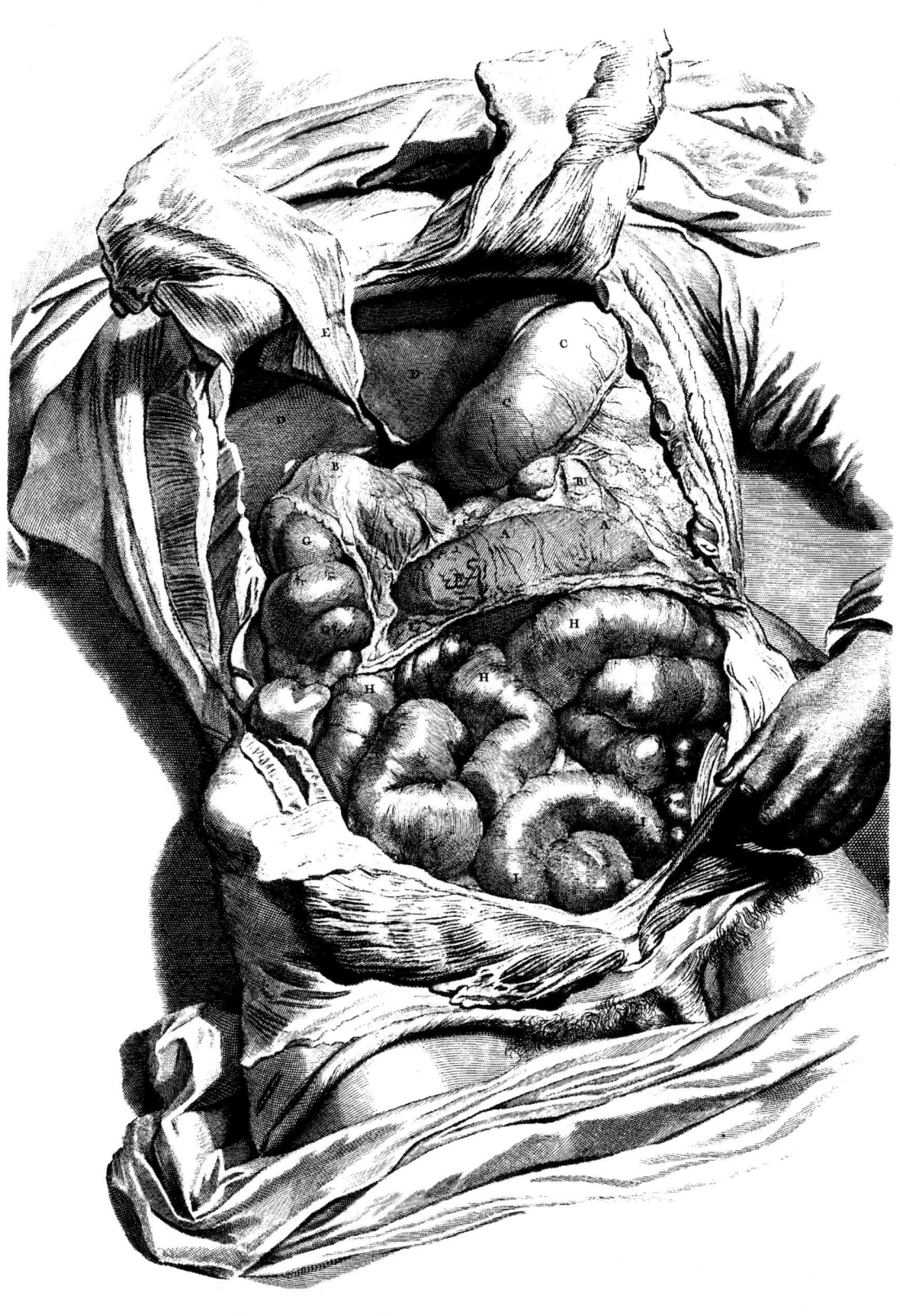

114. Abdominal organs T33 by Govard Bidloo, 1649–1713

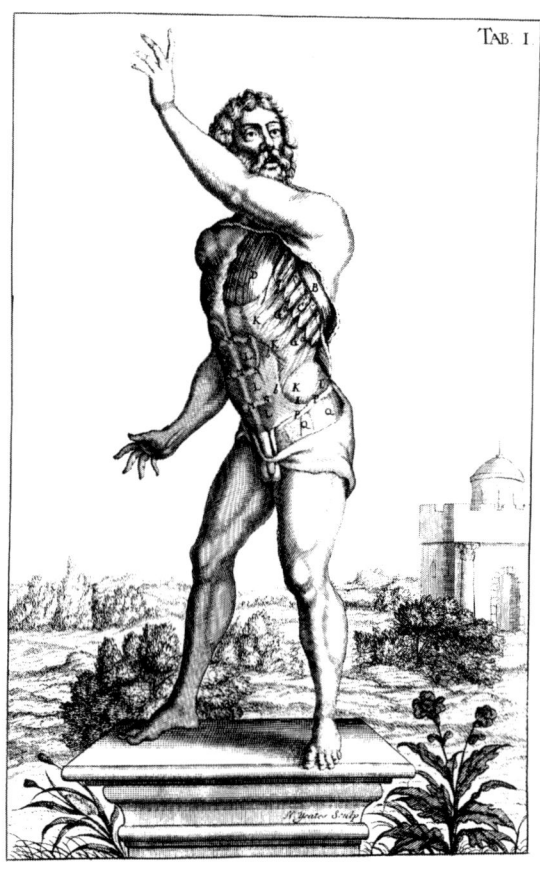

115. Muscles of the abdomen, tab 1, by John Browne 1642–ca. 1700

116. Muscles of the abdomen, tab 2, by John Browne 1642–ca. 1700

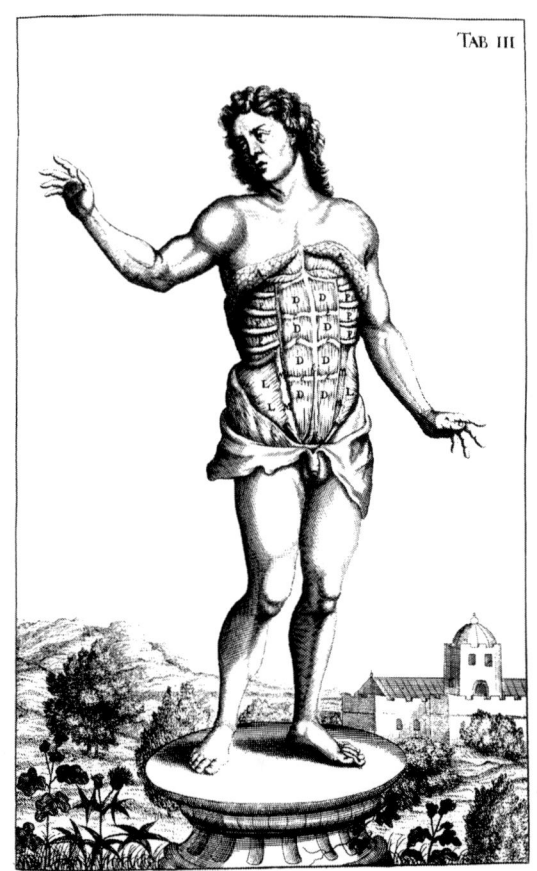

117. Muscles of the abdomen, tab 3, by John Browne 1642–ca. 1700

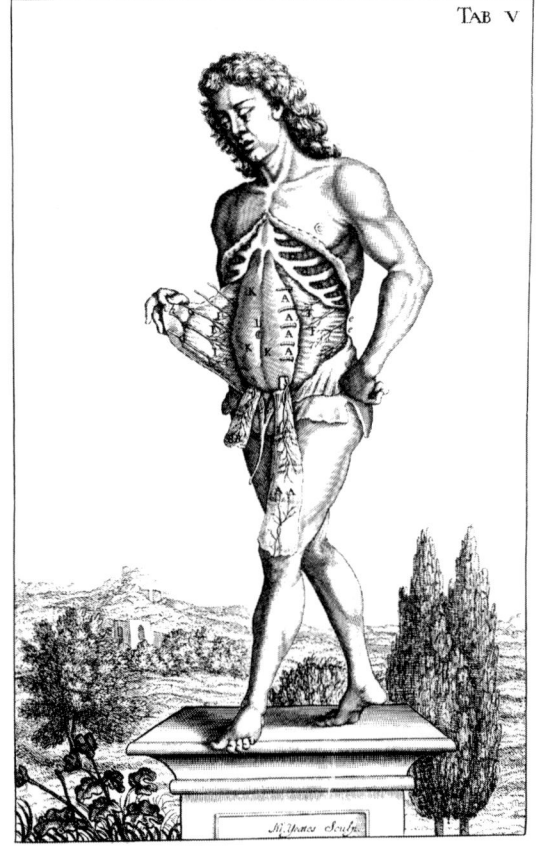

118. Muscles of the abdomen, tab 5, by John Browne 1642–ca. 1700

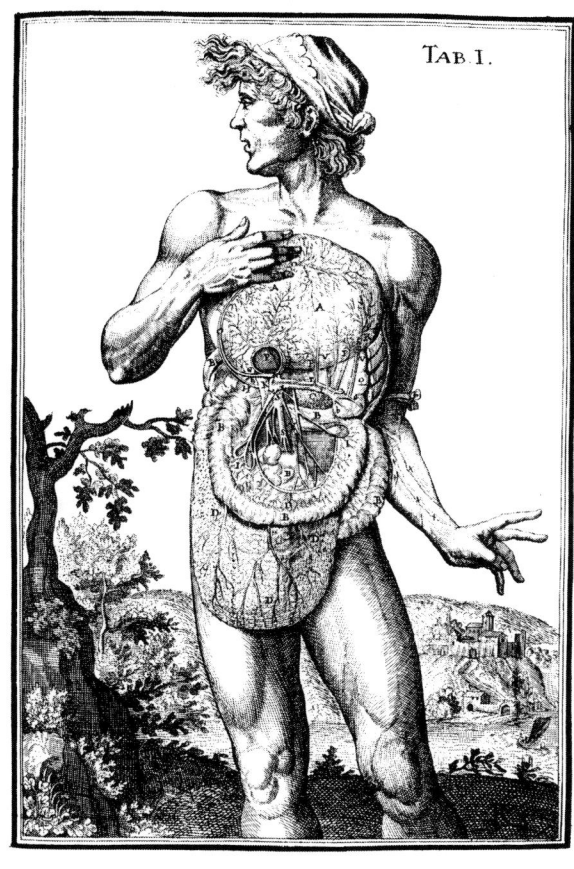

119. Dissection of the abdomen, tab 1, by Adriaan van de Spiegel, illustrated by Giulio Casseri and Odoardo Fialetti, 1631

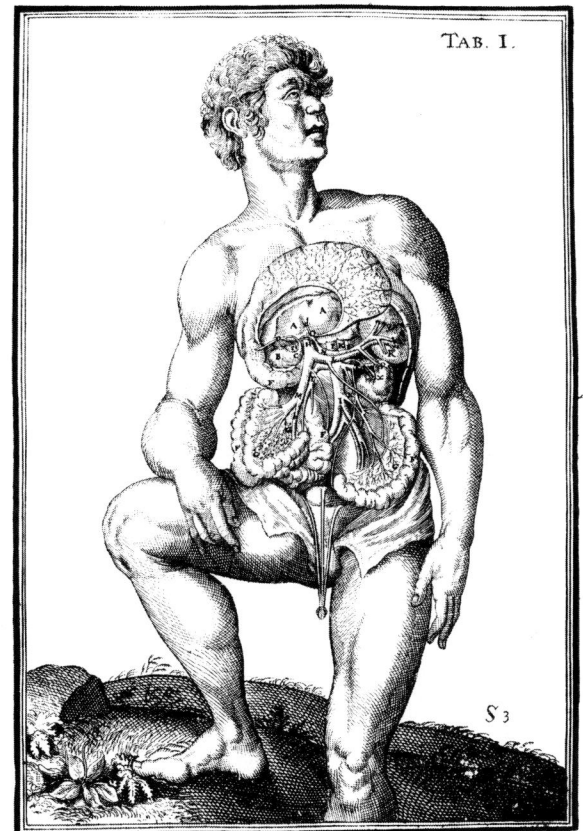

120. Dissection of the abdomen, tab 3, by Adriaan van de Spiegel, illustrated by Giulio Casseri and Odoardo Fialetti, 1631

121. Dissection of the abdomen, tab 6, by Adriaan van de Spiegel, illustrated by Giulio Casseri and Odoardo Fialetti, 1631

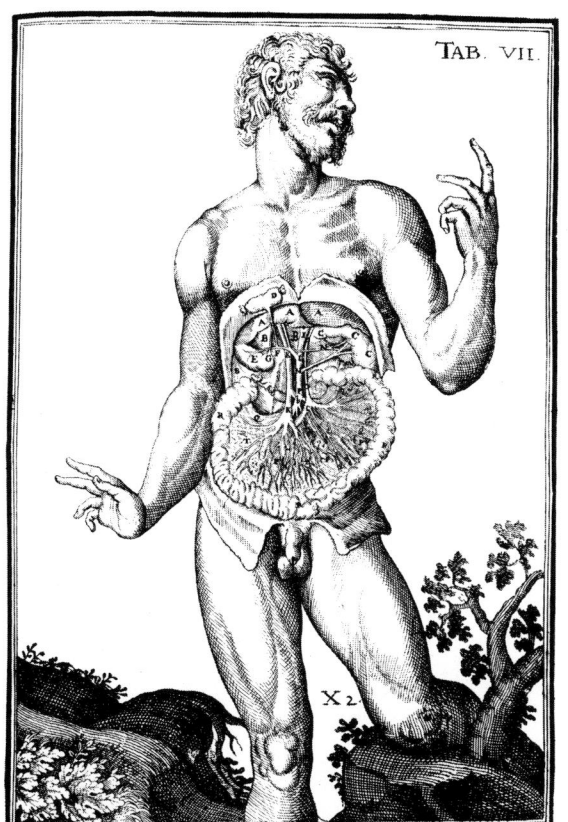

122. Dissection of the abdomen, tab 7, by Adriaan van de Spiegel, illustrated by Giulio Casseri and Odoardo Fialetti, 1631

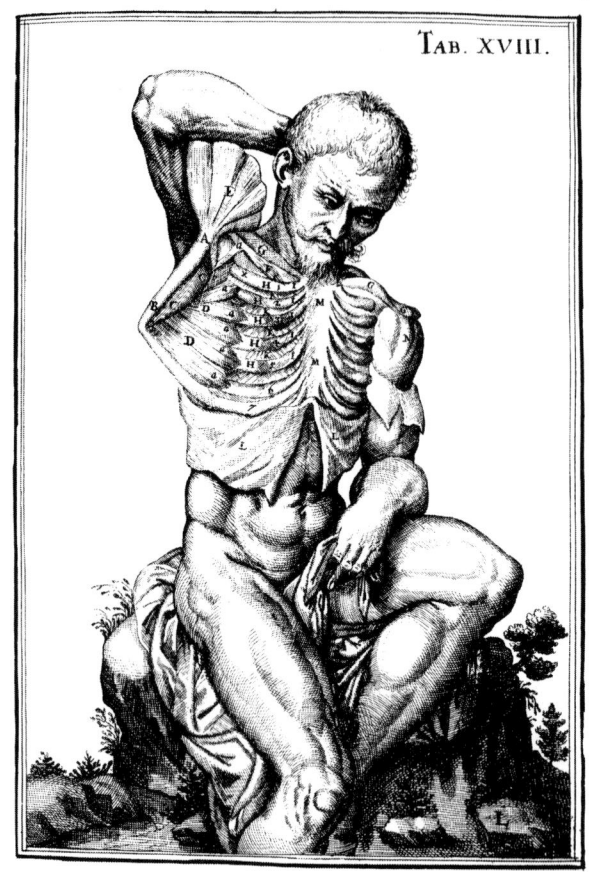

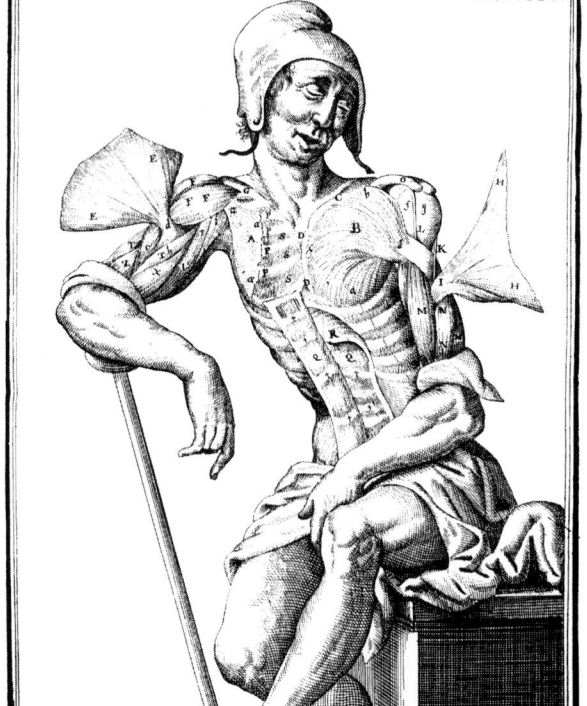

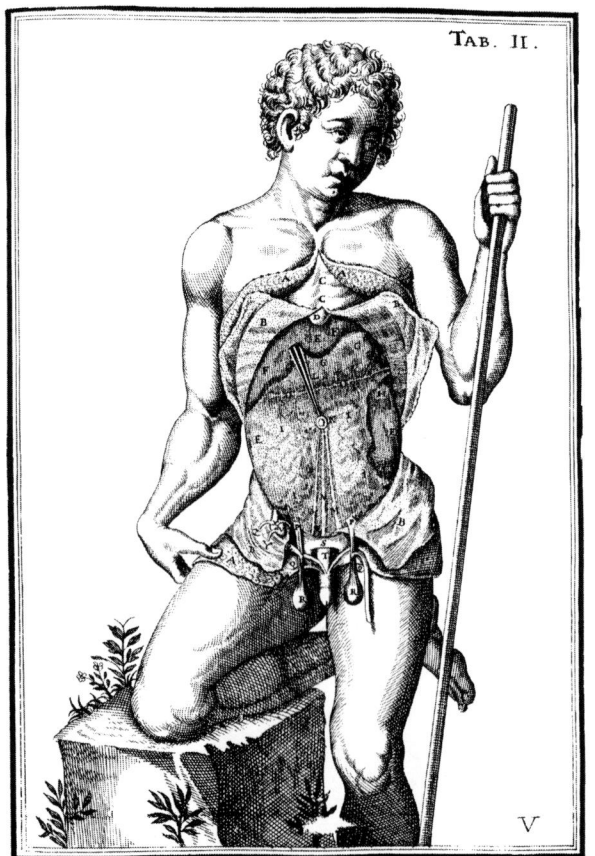

123. Muscles of the abdomen by Adriaan van de Spiegel, illustrated by Giulio Casseri and Odoardo Fialetti, engraved by Francesco Valesio, 1631

124. Muscles of the thorax and shoulder by Adriaan van de Spiegel, illustrated by Giulio Casseri and Odoardo Fialetti, 1631

125. Muscles of the thorax, abdomen and arm, tab 17, by Adriaan van de Spiegel, illustrated by Giulio Casseri and Odoardo Fialetti, 1631

126. Abdominal wall and peritoneum, tab 2, by Adriaan van de Spiegel, illustrated by Giulio Casseri and Odoardo Fialetti, 1631

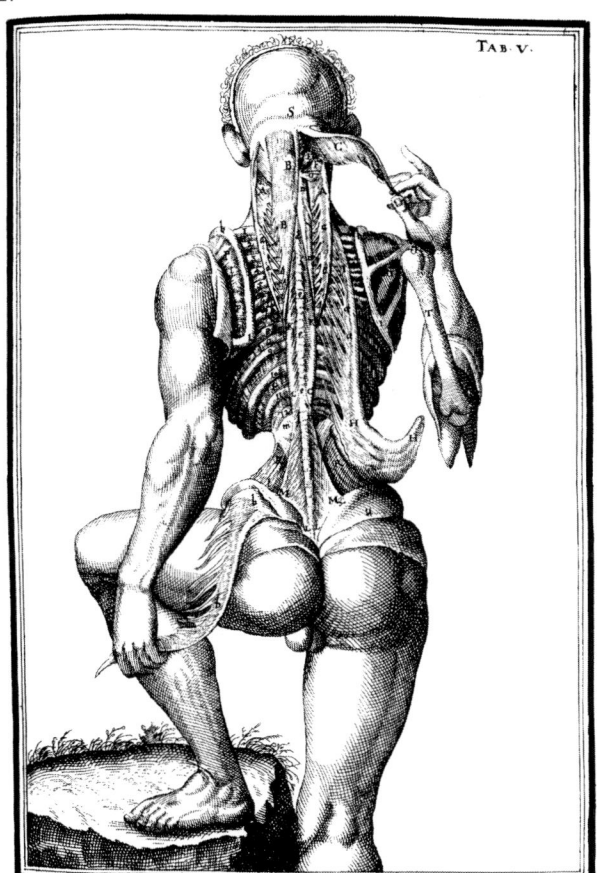

127. Back muscles, neck muscles, bones of the arm by Adriaan van de Spiegel, illustrated by Giulio Casseri and Odoardo Fialetti, 1631

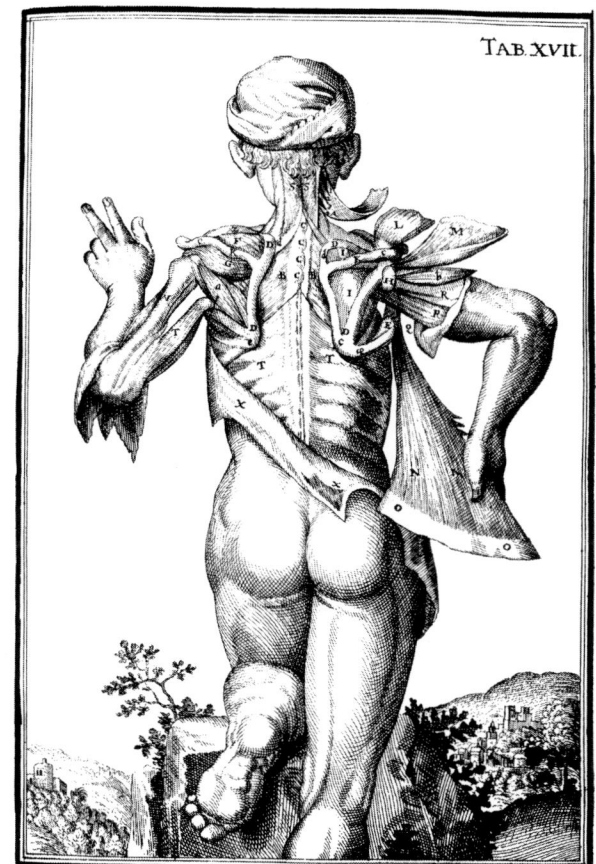

128. Back muscles, neck muscles, and shoulder muscles, tab 16, by Adriaan van de Spiegel, illustrated by Giulio Casseri, 1631

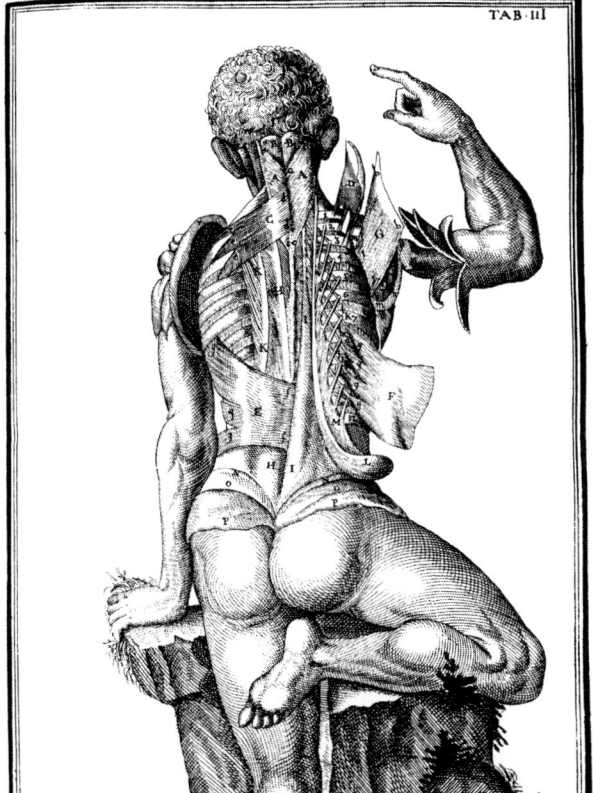

129. Back muscles, neck muscles, and rotator cuff muscles by Adriaan van de Spiegel, illustrated by Giulio Casseri, 1631

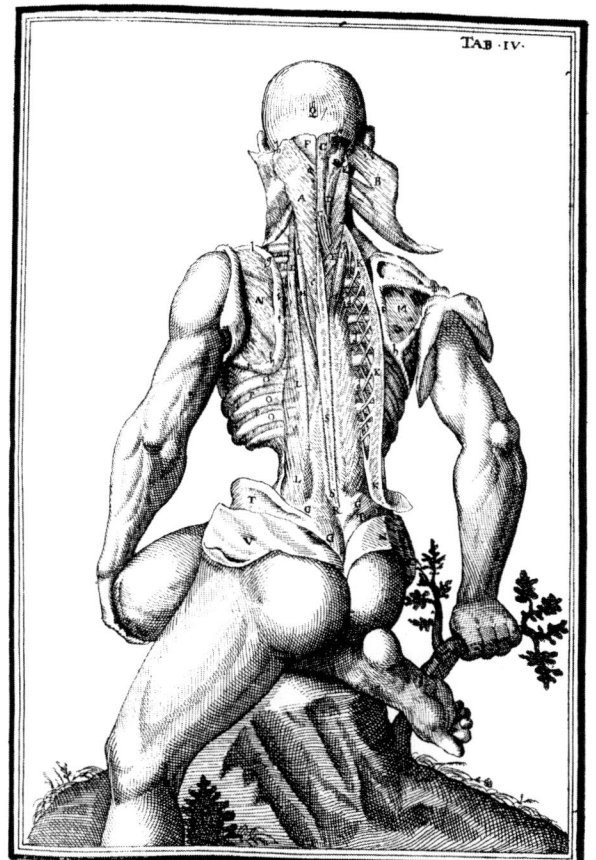

130. Back muscles, neck muscles, ribs and scapula by Adriaan van de Spiegel, illustrated by Giulio Casseri, 1631

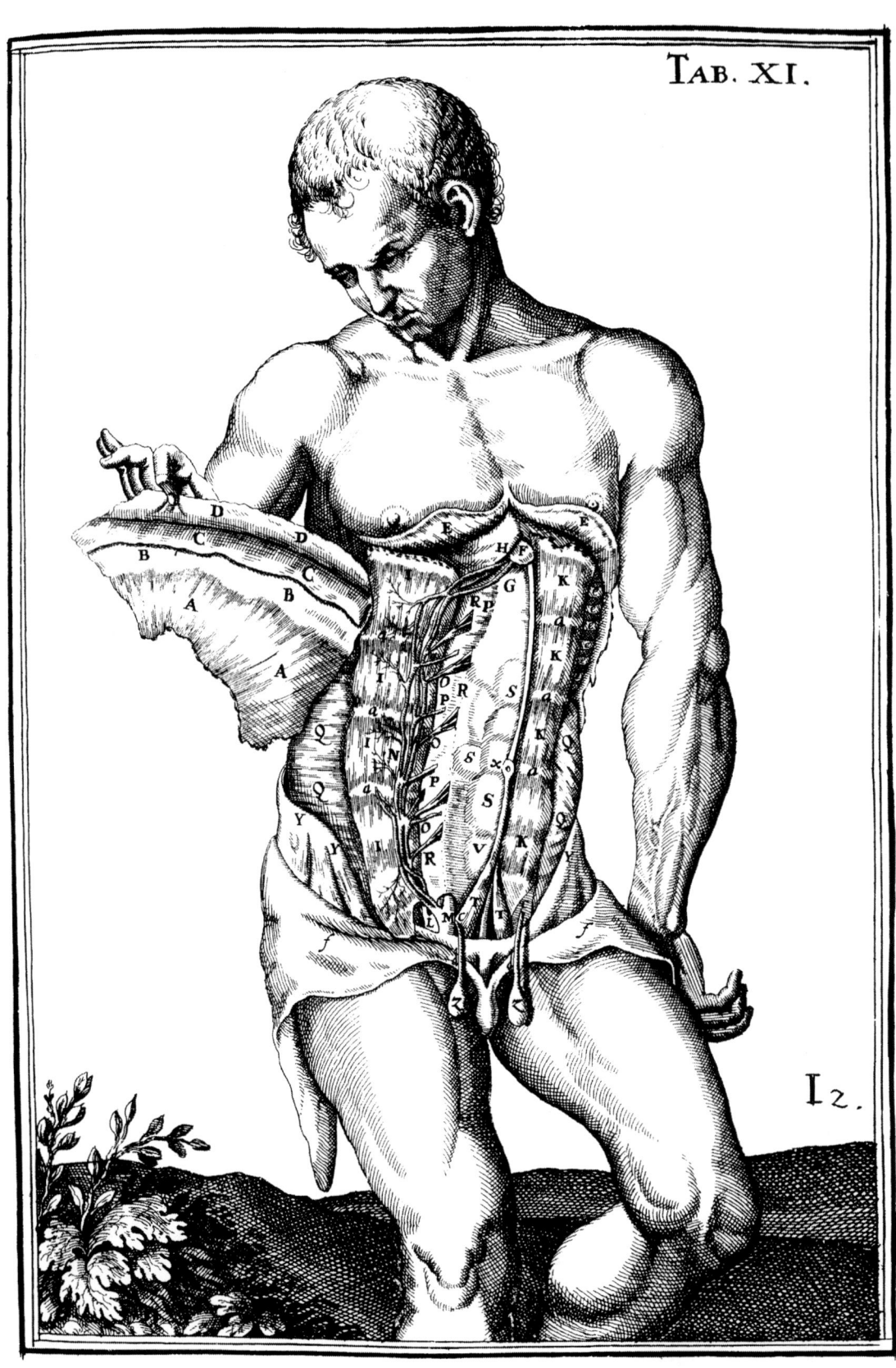

131. Muscles and superficial blood vessels of the abdominal wall by Adriaan van de Spiegel, illustrated by Giulio Casseri, 1631.

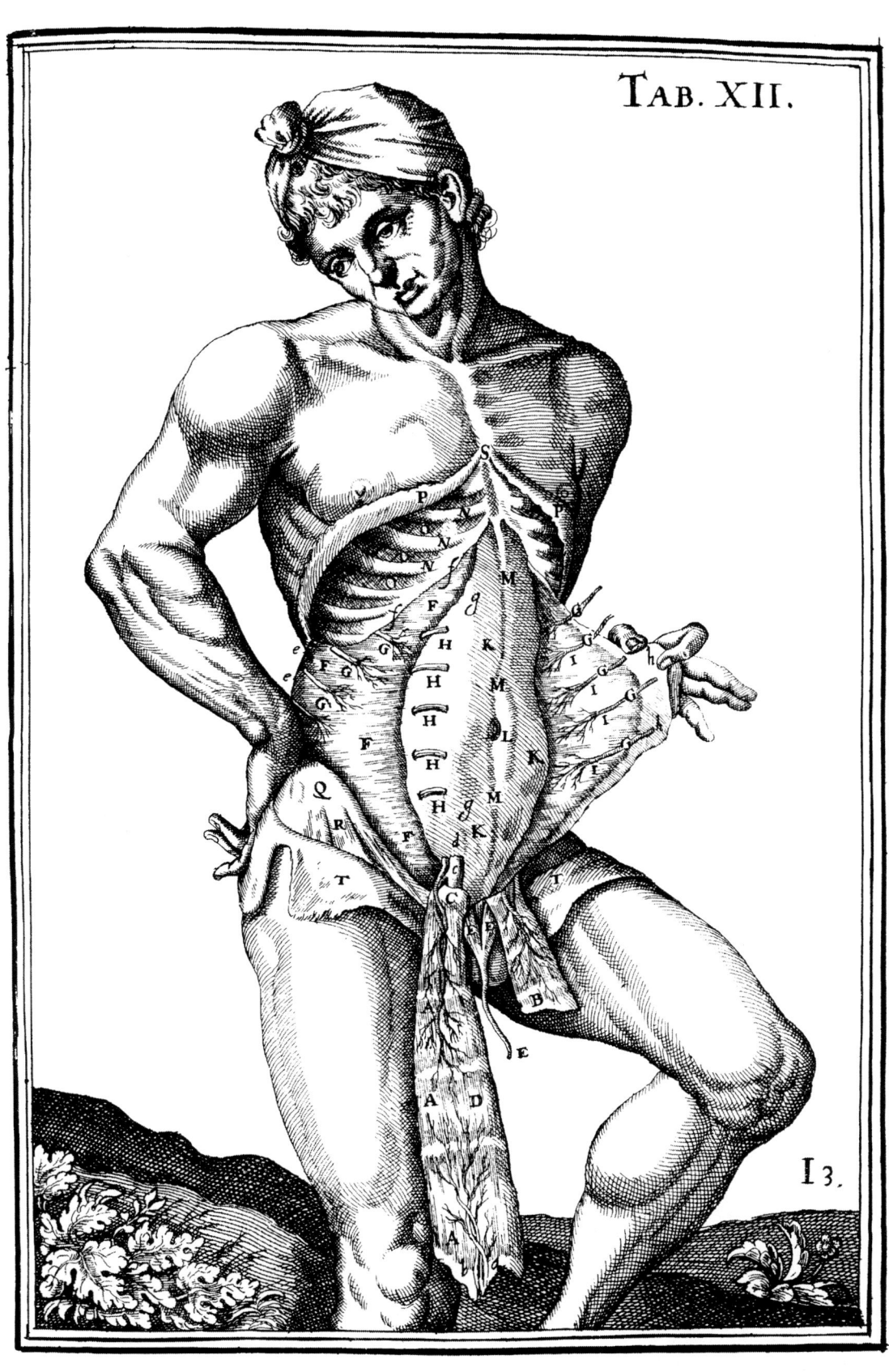

132. Muscles and blood vessels of the abdominal wall by Adriaan van de Spiegel, illustrated by Giulio Casseri and Odoardo Fialetti, 1631

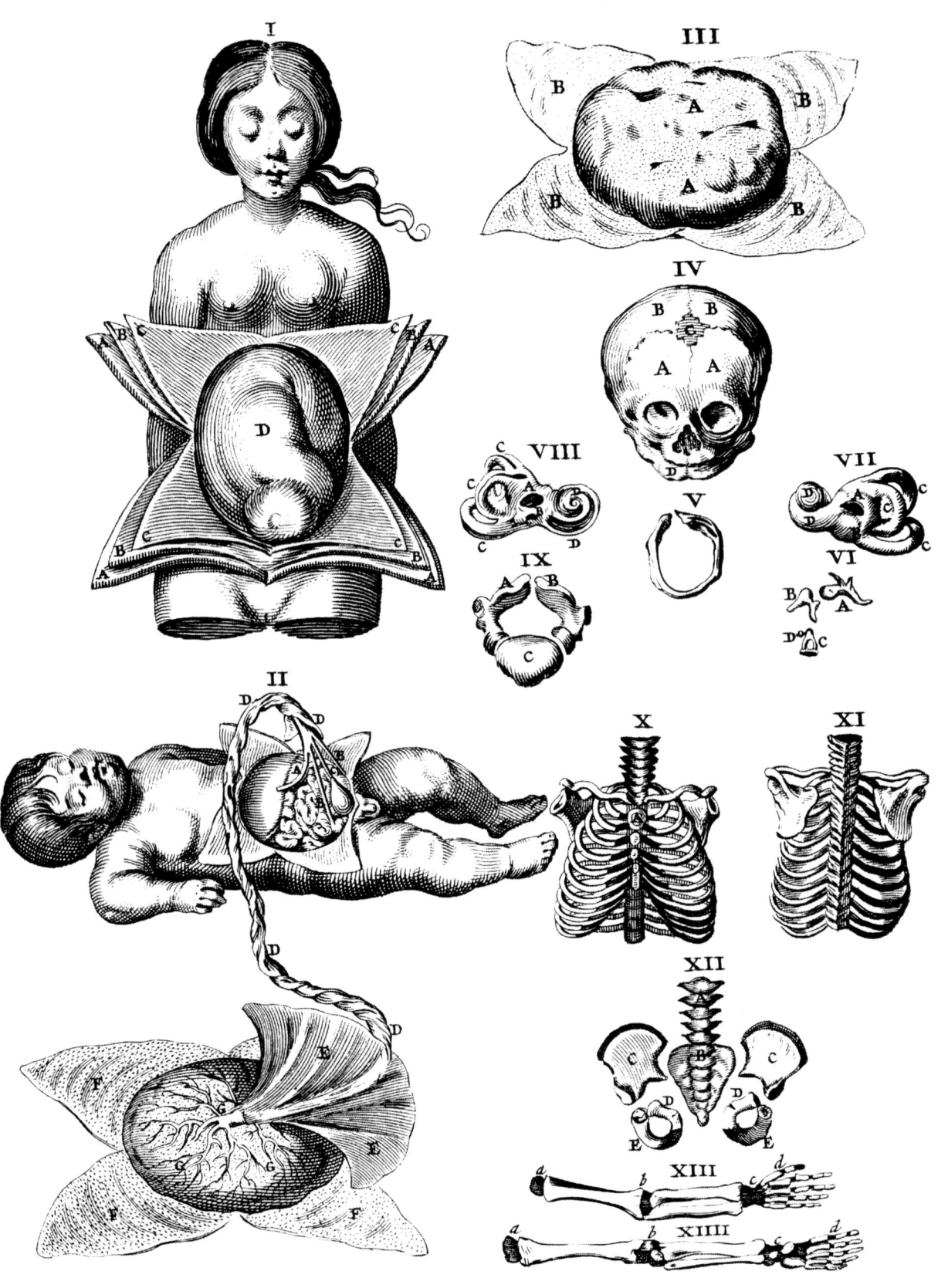

133. Pregnancy, female genitalia, fetus and fetal skeleton by Jean Riolan, 1649

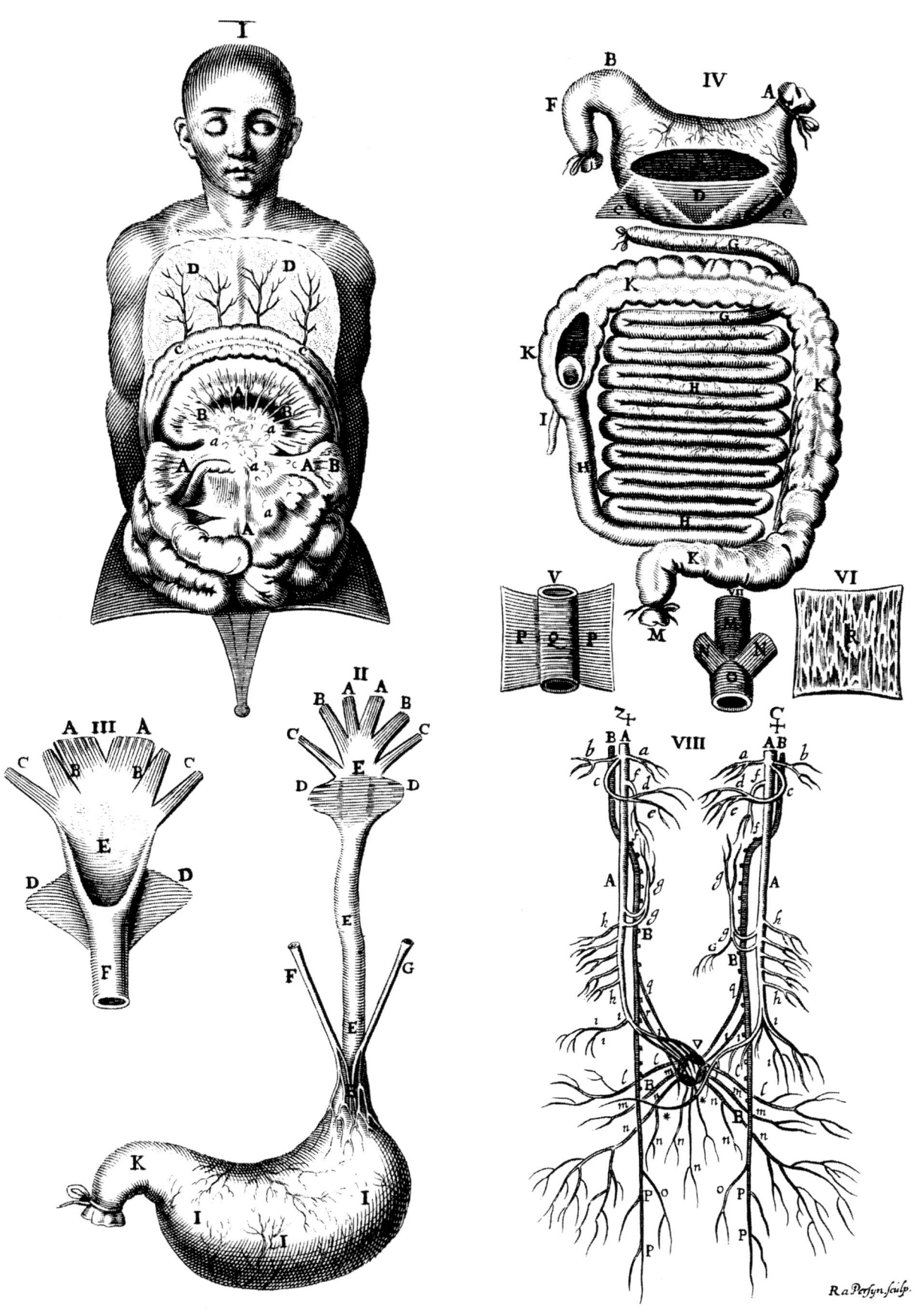

134. Abdominal organs, vagus nerve and sympathetic nerves by Jean Riolan, 1649

135. Muscles of the legs and pelvis, by John Browne 1642–ca. 1700

136. Muscles of the buttocks and thighs, tab 28,
by John Browne 1642–ca. 1700

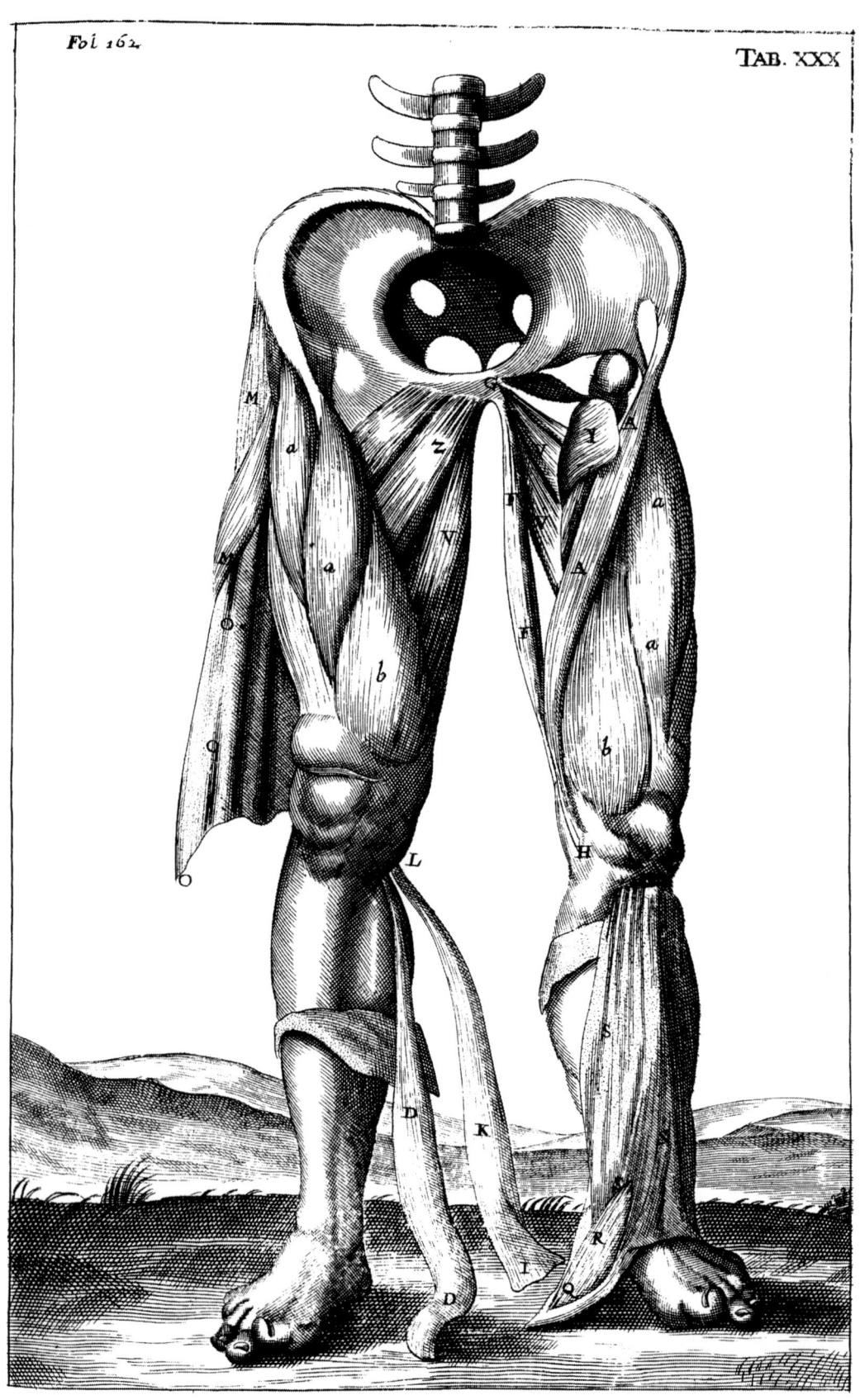

137. Muscles of the buttocks and thighs, tab 30, by John Browne 1642–ca. 1700

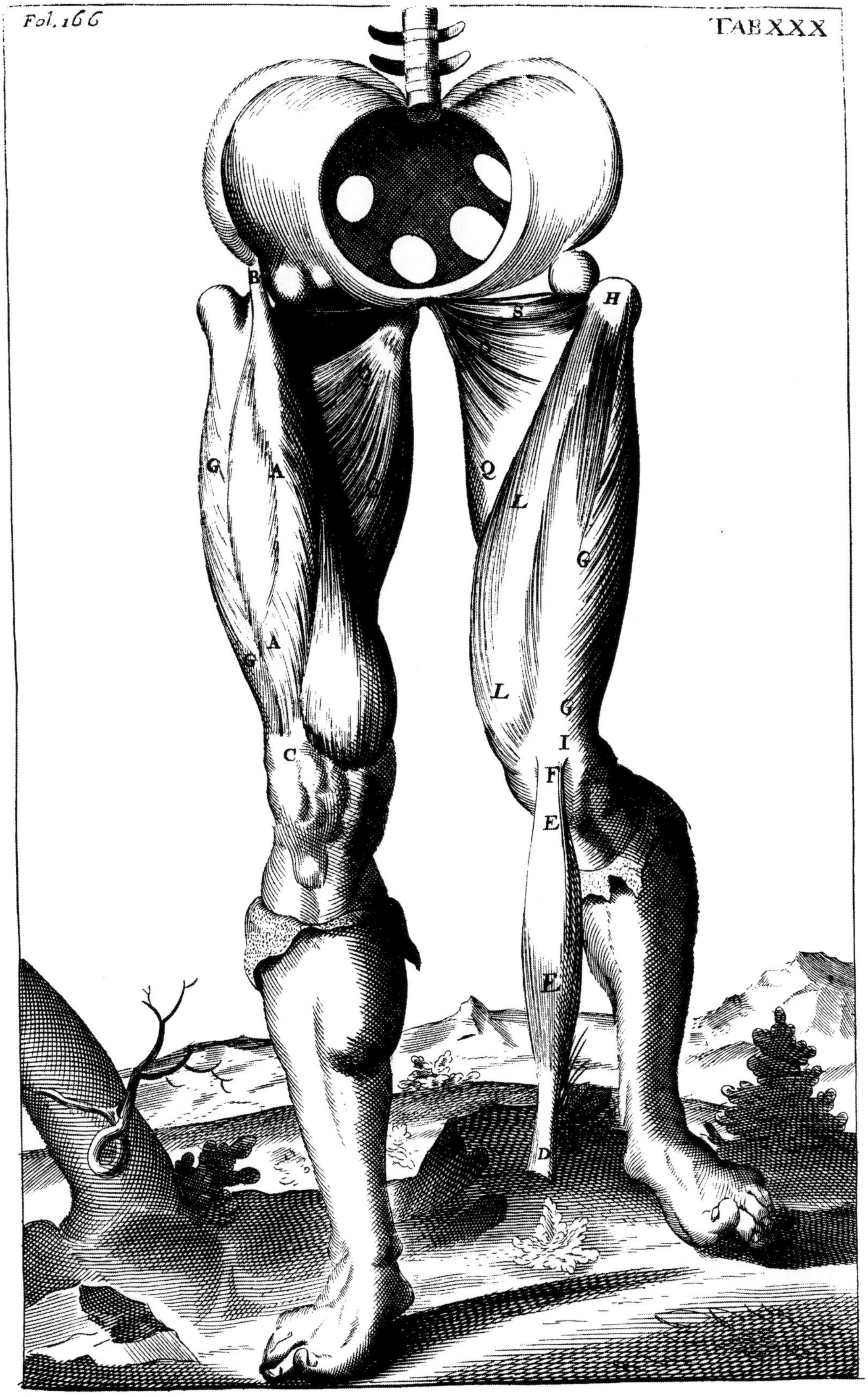

138. Muscles of the buttocks and thighs, tab 31,
by John Browne 1642–ca. 1700

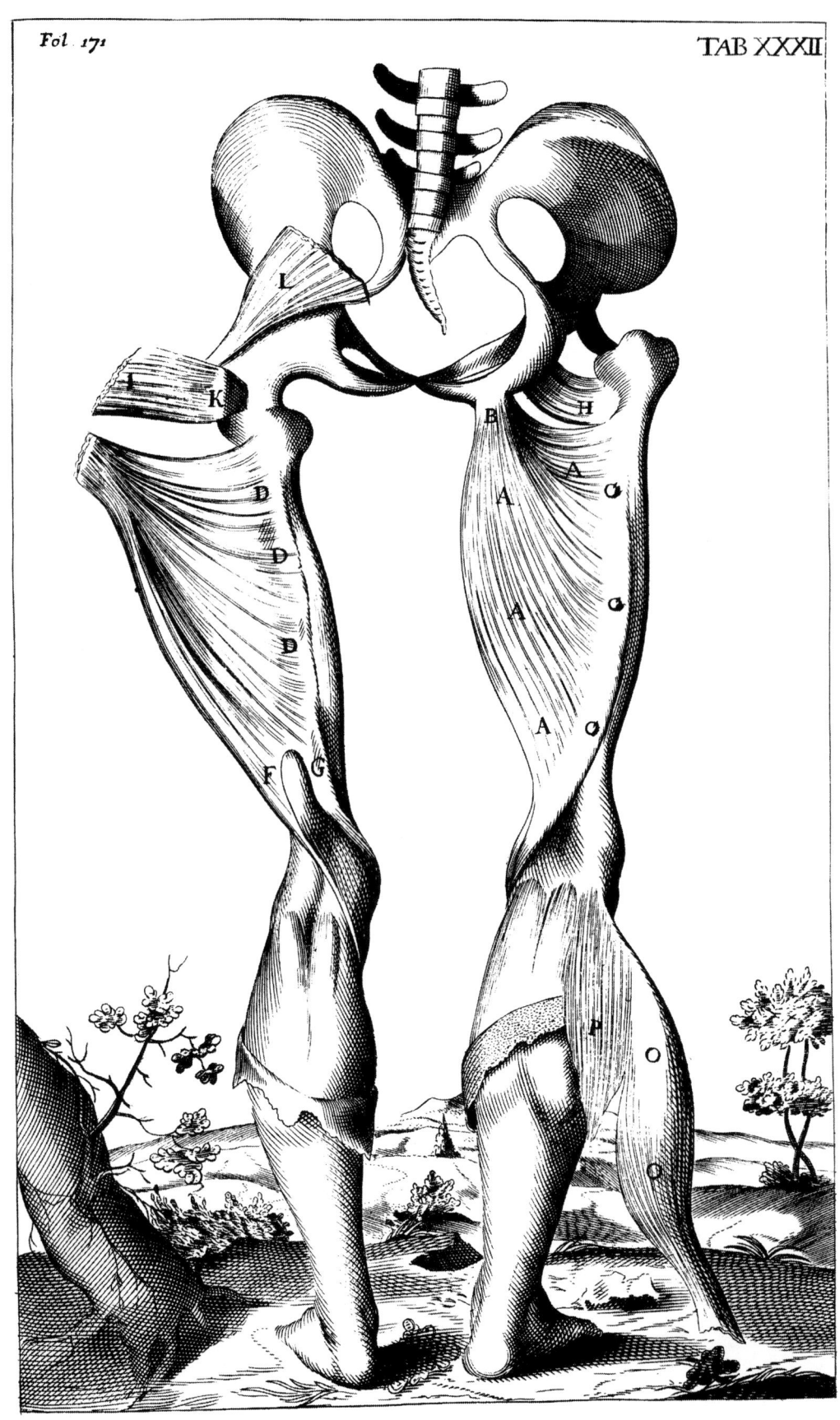

139. Muscles of the lower legs by John Browne
1642–ca. 1700

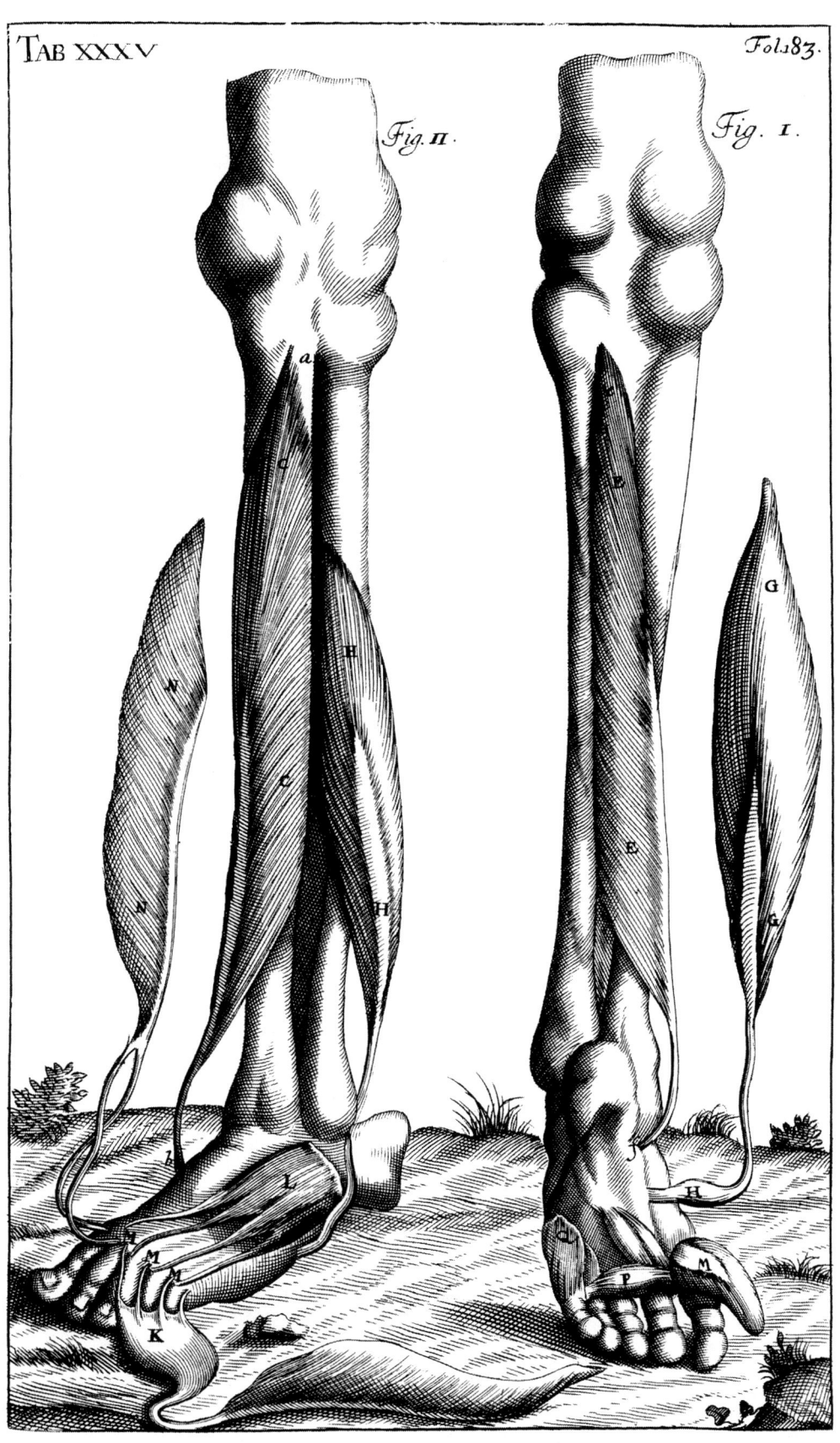

140. Bones and muscles of the leg and foot, tab 35 fig 1,2 by John Browne 1642–ca. 1700

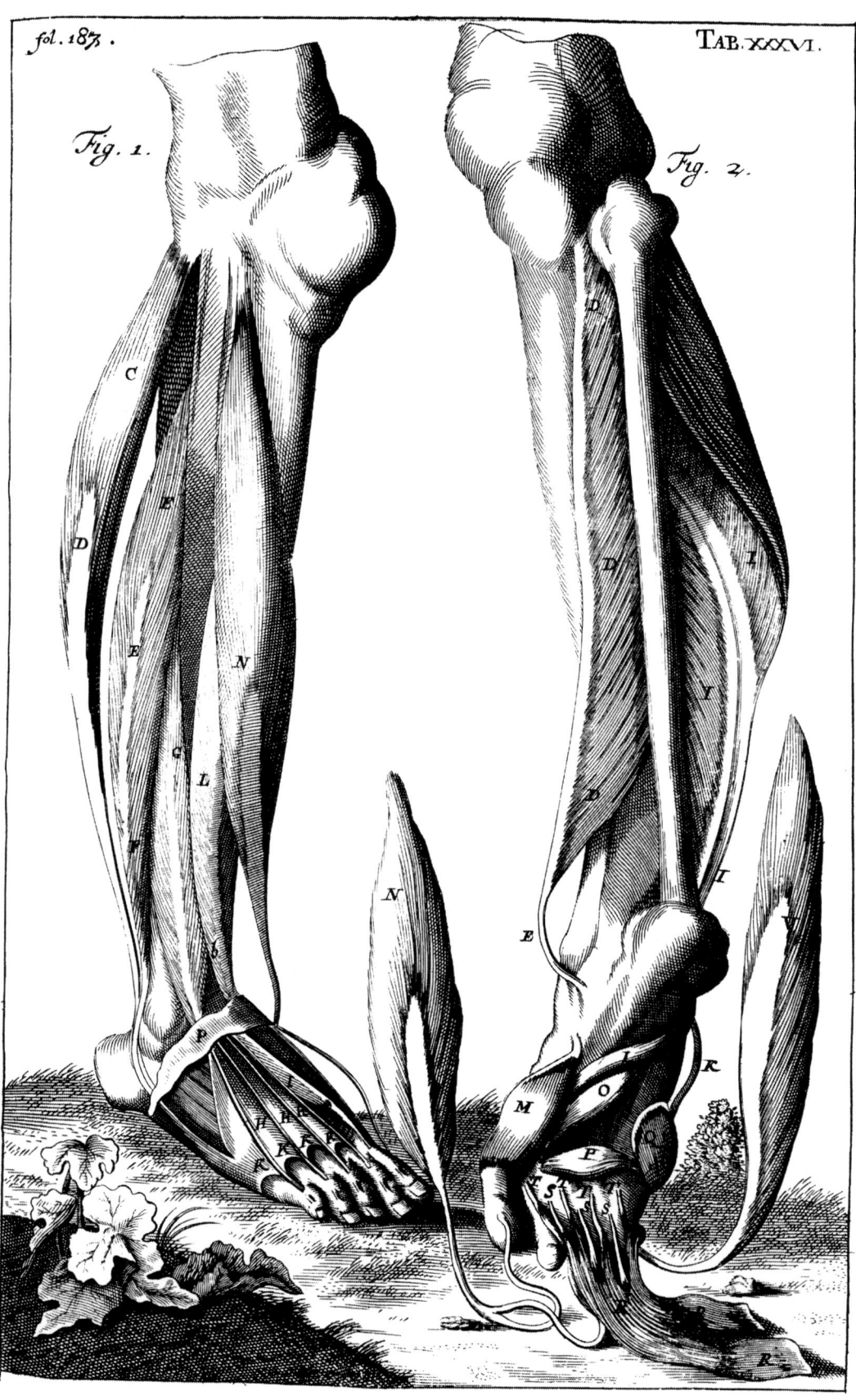

141. Bones and muscles of the leg and foot, tab 36, by John Browne 1642–ca. 1700

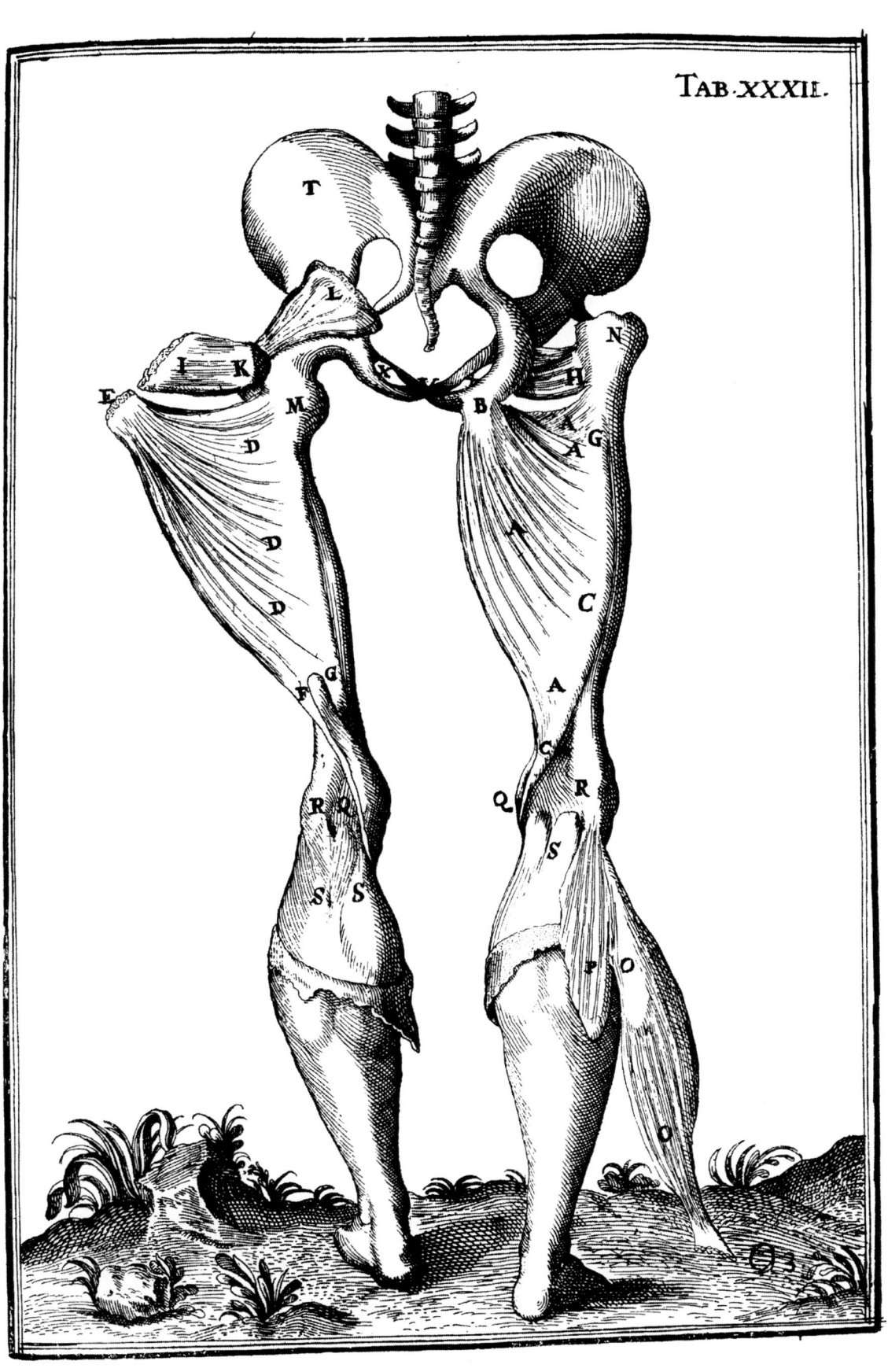

142. Pelvis, muscles of the thigh, tab 32, by Adriaan van de Spiegel, illustrated by Giulio Casseri and Odoardo Fialetti, 1631

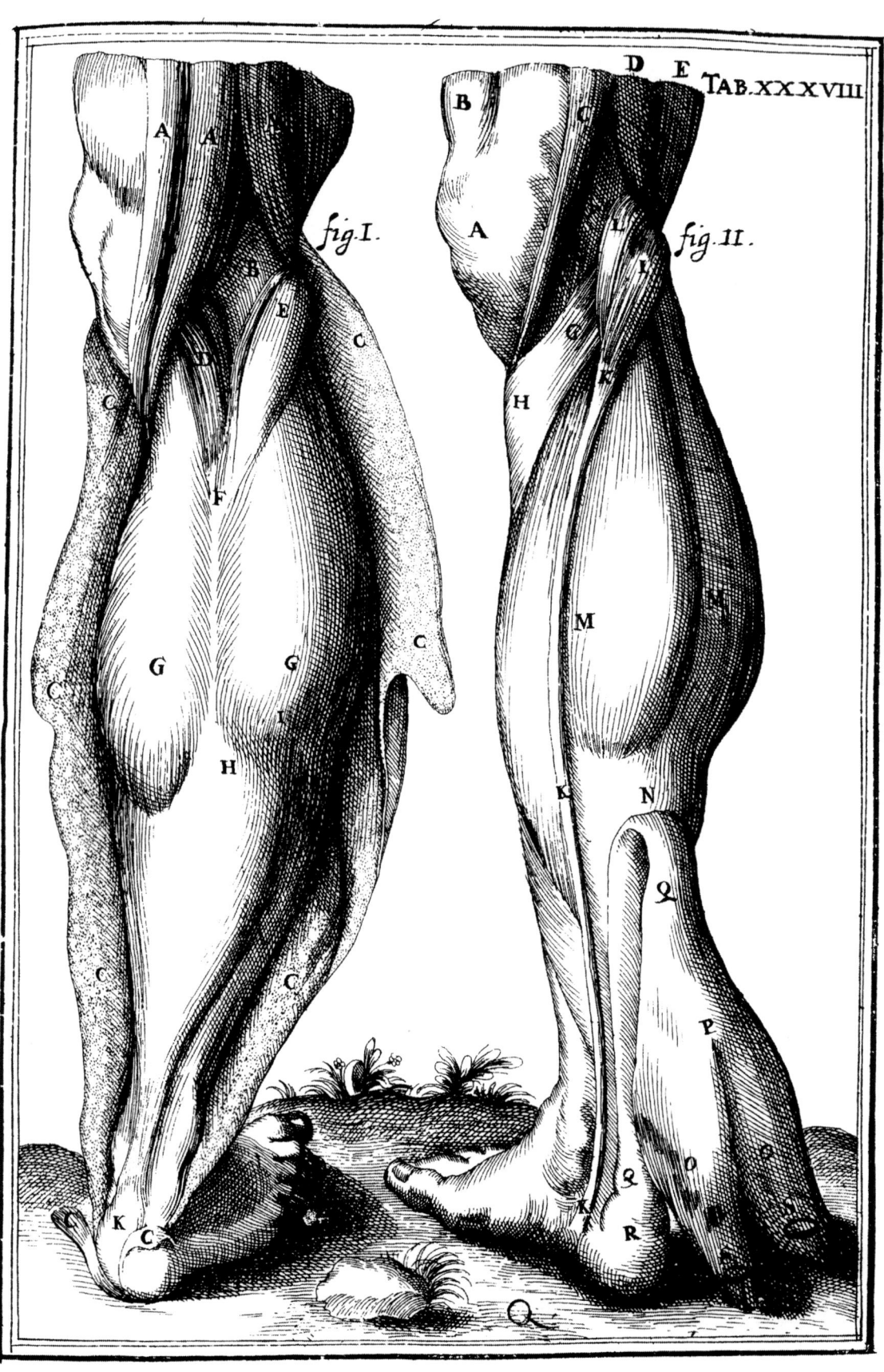

143. Muscles of the lower leg, tab 38, by Adriaan van de Spiegel, illustrated by Giulio Casseri and Odoardo Fialetti, 1631

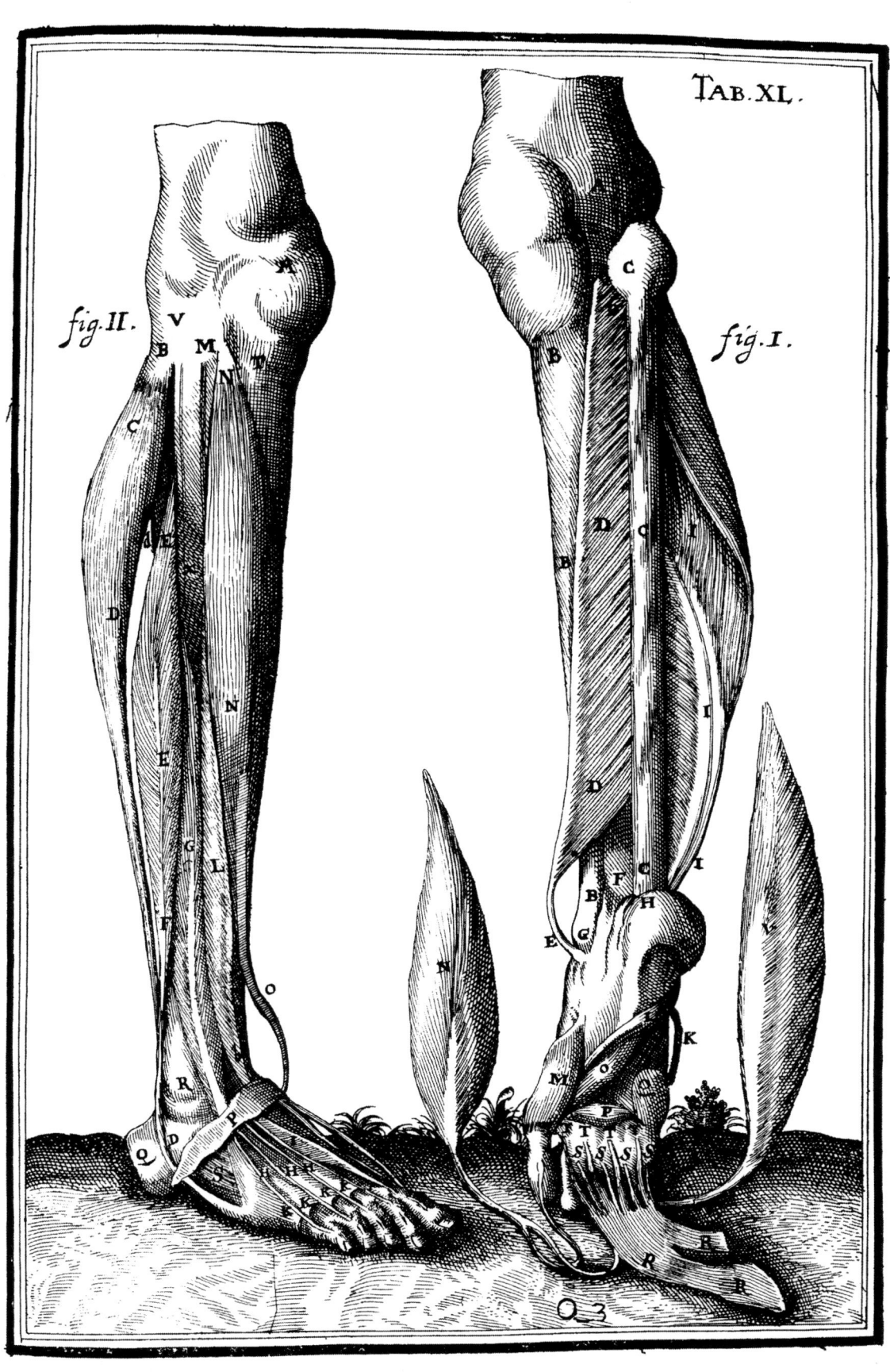

144. Muscles of the lower leg, tab 40, by Adriaan van de Spiegel, illustrated by Giulio Casseri and Odoardo Fialetti, 1631

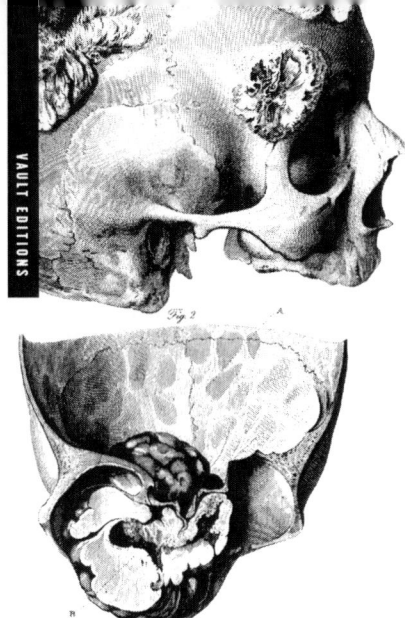

LEARN MORE

At Vault Editions, our mission is to create the world's most comprehensive collection of image archives for the practical use of artists and designers. If you have enjoyed this book, you can discover more of our titles at vaulteditions.com

REVIEW THIS BOOK

As a family-owned and operated independent publisher, reviews are essential to the success of our business. Please leave an honest review of this book wherever you purchased it.

JOIN OUR COMMUNITY

Are you the creative and curious type? If so, you will love our community on Instagram. Every day, we share bizarre and beautiful artwork ranging from 17th and 18th-century natural history and scientific illustrations to mythical beasts, ornamental designs, anatomical drawings and more; join our community of 280K+ people today by searching @vault_editions on Instagram.

STEP ONE

Enter the following web address on a desktop or laptop computer in your web browser.

vaulteditions.com/pages/maa

STEP TWO

Enter the following password to access the download page:

maap6382838sxda

STEP THREE

Follow the prompts to access your high-resolution files.

CONTACT

For technical support please email: info@vaulteditions.com

Copyright © 2024
Vault Editions Ltd

Made in United States
North Haven, CT
30 April 2025